pedigree points:
dogs

pedigree points:
dogs

A handbook of what judges look for in
over 100 of the most popular breeds

JANICE GARDNER

Consultant Editor: BRIAN LEONARD

INTERPET PUBLISHING

THIS EDITION PRODUCED FOR
INTERPET PUBLISHING

Interpet House
Vincent Lane
Dorking
Surrey RH4 3YX

ISBN 1-84286-066-6

QUAR.PEDI

Conceived, designed, and produced by:
Quarto Publishing plc
The Old Brewery
6 Blundell Street
London N7 9BH

Project editor Nadia Naqib
Art editor Sheila Volpe
Picture research Anna Carr, Penny Cobb
Assistant art director Penny Cobb
Text editors Maggie O'Hanlon, Pat Farrington
Indexer Susan Boobis
Art director Moira Clinch
Publisher Piers Spence

Manufactured by Universal Graphics PTE, Ltd

Printed by Leefung-Asco Printers Ltd, China

9 8 7 6 5 4 3 2 1

1

SPORTING GROUP

2

HOUND GROUP

3

WORKING GROUP

CONTENTS

4

TERRIER GROUP

5

TOY GROUP

6

NON SPORTING GROUP

7

HERDING GROUP

INTRODUCTION

This book provides sufficient details on a wide range of dog breeds to enable the reader to understand the process by which a dog show judge determines which dogs are of insufficient exhibition quality, which dogs are better, and which dog is best. The process of analyzing all the points of an individual dog involves the use of eyes and hands, and then mentally comparing that dog to the ideal for its breed (the standard). All this requires a deep understanding of the breed's correct structure and how that structure enabled the dog to fulfill the purpose for which it was historically intended. Development of the skill and knowledge needed to make this analysis takes many years of experience and study. Such an understanding cannot be provided in one book, but enough information is provided here to enable you to understand what the judge is doing and why.

A careful reading of this book will also help you to choose a typical, sound dog for yourself. An understanding of the history and behavior of each breed should also help you to make the right choice of the dog you will own and enjoy for many years.

THE BREEDS OF DOGS

ABOVE One of the oldest distinct sight hound breeds, the Saluki has a highly developed hunting instinct.

HOW DID THE DIFFERENT BREEDS DEVELOP?

Humans have purposely bred certain animals since the development of agriculture thousands of years ago. Then, and now, their goal was to set and enhance certain qualities, first by practical understanding and later genetically. Selective breeding was also employed to benefit animals by increasing their longevity, soundness, resistance to disease, or intelligence. On that unknown day long ago when a human decided which animal should be given the opportunity to mate with another, the age of purposeful breeding began.

Guarding breeds (Mastiff types) were developed and bred in China between 2,000 and 3,000 years ago. Sight hounds such as the Greyhound, Borzoi, Saluki, and Afghan Hound have been distinct for even longer. The Spitz breeds were distinguished probably more than 2,000 years ago in what are now the northern reaches of the former Soviet Union.

In the mid to late 1800s the purposeful development of distinct dog breeds took off, and many of our current breeds came into being or were refined and bred since that time. In some cases breeds have been crossed to make a dog better suited to a new job (Bullmastiff). In a few instances breeds were refined to fit the then-current ideals of beauty (Afghan Hound, Saint Bernard) or because a dog was needed that would be better suited to a specific job (Airedale Terrier). When these refinements or changes could be accomplished without sacrificing the breed's typical character, functionality, or soundness, clear improvements resulted. The new dog was usually healthier, sounder (both benefits to the dog), and better able to perform a task (a benefit to the owner). In some cases (Bulldog, some Toy breeds), breeders of the new versions accepted a certain degree of unsoundness as a fair return for other desired qualities.

NATIONAL REGISTRIES OF DOG BREEDS

A total of 51 countries have registries for dog breeds. Most registries concern themselves, broadly speaking, with the classification and registration of dogs, the adoption and enforcement of uniform rules to regulate dog shows and most importantly, with the setting of the breed standards by which pure-bred dogs must be judged.

ABOVE The Saint Bernard is believed to be descended from Asian Mastiff-type dogs that came to Switzerland with the Romans.

The largest registry is in India and the smallest is probably in Guernsey, in the Channel Islands off the coast of France. By far the greatest number of dogs is registered by the American Kennel Club (AKC) in the United States (U.S.). The United Kennel Club, a large, privately owned registry in the U.S., focuses primarily on various coon hounds and other hunting breeds. The AKC currently recognizes over 150 breeds of dog and the breeds are organized into seven groups: Sporting, Hound, Working, Terrier, Toy, Non-Sporting, and Herding. The (British) Kennel Club (KC) was established in 1873, making it the oldest kennel club in the world. The KC currently recognizes 197 breeds. These are organized into two broad categories of Sporting and Non-Sporting. These subdivide further: Sporting breeds are divided

RIGHT Historically bred to fight bulls and other animals, today's Bulldog lacks the savage tendencies of its predecessors

RIGHT The Airedale Terrier was bred originally to hunt river otters but over time became a versatile hunting dog, able to hunt foxes, badgers, and small game in Yorkshire, England.

ABOVE The Chihuahua is the smallest dog breed in the world. It is quite likely that this dog came to North America from Malta.

into the Hound, Gundog, and Terrier groups, and Non-Sporting breeds are divided into the Utility, Working, Pastoral, and Toy groups. The Canadian Kennel Club (CKC) was founded in 1888 and currently recognizes 166 breeds of dog. These are organized into seven groups (Sporting, Hound, Working, Terrier, Toy, Non-Sporting, and Herding). The Australian National Kennel Council (ANKC), which is an umbrella organization that incorporates Australia's eight canine organizations, currently recognizes 180 breeds of dog, classed into seven groups: Toy, Terrier, Gundog, Hound, Working, Utility, and Non-Sporting.

Many of the European, Central American, and South American national registries support the Féderation Cynologique Internationale (FCI) shows. The FCI is a Belgium-based organization created in 1911 to promote and protect the science and breeding of pure-bred dogs across the world. It recognizes only one governing organization in each country. It is not a registry; its purpose is to coordinate dog shows in member countries, to record show results, and to regulate individuals who judge at FCI shows. It therefore does not set breed standards. With some notable exceptions, the FCI adopts the standard of a breed's country of origin. For example the FCI recognizes the KC breed standard for the English Springer Spaniel, the ANKC standard for the Australian Cattle Dog, the Verband fur das Deutsche Hundewesen (German national registry of dog breeds) standard for the Dachshund, and the AKC standard for the Boston Terrier. The FCI currently recognizes 346 different dog breeds. The FCI-recognized breeds are divided into ten main groups. Canada, the U.S., United Kingdom (U.K.), and Australia are among the registries that are not members of the FCI.

WHY THESE BREEDS?

The 105 breeds included in this book were selected on the basis of their popularity (the number of dogs registered in a year) in the U.S., Canada, the U.K., Europe, and

RIGHT The German Shepherd Dog was bred with a view to the creation of the ultimate dog for herding and guarding flocks. Today, it is used almost world-wide by police departments.

Australia and their importance as a foundation for other breeds.

A breed standard is a written description of what a dog should look like and a standard can stretch to hundreds of words. Standards are written using words and terminology that are not exact in meaning. Experts can debate the correct interpretation of a standard for hours. This ambiguity leads, in turn, to disagreement among judges at dog shows. Most breed standards vary slightly from country to country as dogs always reflect the society in which they are bred and the outlook on a standard in each country can change from time to time. If the changes become too great, a new breed arrives on the scene. A good example of this is the standard for the Cocker Spaniel, which eventually divided into two standards—the American and English versions.

The descriptions of each dog in this book, which are all based on the standard for each breed, as accepted by the AKC, are paraphrased to make them more accessible to the novice. The intention is not to help the reader become a dog show judge, but rather to help him or her understand the difference between the breeds and to understand and enjoy the judging at dog shows. Any significant departures from the AKC standard with respect to the KC, CKC, ANKC, and FCI standards are highlighted. Similarly, the dog breeds in this book are organized according to the seven groups of the AKC.

LEFT The English Springer Spaniel's name derives from the use of this type of Spaniel to startle birds into the air so that they spring upward.

WHY CHOOSE A PURE-BRED DOG?

For at least a hundred years anyone wishing to own a dog has had a huge variety of breeds from which to choose. Because of the ready availability of pure-bred dogs it is possible to find one that will suit any legitimate need or lifestyle.

One advantage of a pure-bred over a cross-bred (a dog with parents of two different breeds), or a mongrel (of unknown genetic heritage), is that there should be no real surprises. It is possible to predict, with fair accuracy, the ultimate size and appearance of the dog, the amount of coat care and exercise that it will require, what health issues may arise, its response to training, and its general personality.

It is this predictability that should make it easy for anyone to select a puppy or adult dog that will enhance their life, and that they will come to love and value. Problems arise when a prospective owner makes a choice based primarily on a puppy's appearance (fluffy

RIGHT Long removed from its days as a herding dog, the Collie is now primarily an affectionate pet.

puppies usually grow into dogs needing a great deal of coat care). Misleading images may be fostered by the media (for example, by the film "101 Dalmatians," or dogs like "Lassie" the Collie which appear on television.

For this reason it is hoped that readers of this book will give full consideration to the history, temperament, and training needs of the breeds they are interested in and not simply be influenced by the way they are portrayed in any spotlight.

DOG SHOWS

ORIGINS

The original purpose of competitive dog shows was to allow breeders to compare their dogs with those of other breeders. Dog shows also gave fanciers the opportunity to find outstanding dogs for purchase or to breed to their own dogs to incorporate additional desirable genes into a breeding program. Of course, then as now, competition gave dog enthusiasts the chance to acquire the bragging rights attendant on winning—"My dog is better than your dog."

These purposes are still in force, though in varying degrees, among individual exhibitors. At early shows in the U.S., almost all dogs were owned and shown by their breeders; today more than half are shown by professional handlers.

RIGHT A Bloodhound is handled at a dog show. Although not popular as a pet, the Bloodhound has proved invaluable as a search-and-rescue dog.

A hundred years ago (until the changes in society attendant on the end of World War II) almost all show dogs were bred and owned by relatively few, wealthy and/or titled individuals. Breeding and showing "blooded show stock" was a hobby limited to society's upper echelon. By about 1950, owning a pure-bred dog had become part of the American dream, along with a family automobile and a house in the suburbs. A similar situation was found in the U.K. and Europe. In 1900, a quality pure-bred dog cost a year's worth of a laborer's wages. Today, the cost is about a week's wages.

ABOVE The Pointer was developed as a far-ranging hunter and has the stamina to work steadily for many hours.

EARNING A TITLE

Dog shows are held throughout the world. Titles can be earned in conformation classes (comparison of a dog to the breed's standard for structure and movement), in Obedience or Agility (where a dog is scored on its performance of specific exercises), or in Field Trials and Hunting or Working Tests (where a dog performs hunting and/or retrieving in a simulated hunt setting). Titles are also available in Earthdog Trials (where small terriers and Dachshunds pursue caged rats in simulated, smallish man-made tunnels) and Herding Trials (where sheep and cattle herding breeds display their skill in handling livestock).

While there are similarities between countries, there are also important differences. The AKC licences roughly 1,500 all-breed shows and the same number of specialities (limited to one breed) each year where points can be earned toward a Championship.

To earn an AKC Championship a dog must accumulate 15 points, earned at a minimum of three shows and under a minimum of three different judges. The 15 points must include at least two "majors" (wins of 3, 4, or 5 points). Points earned are based on the number of dogs defeated in the same sex in its breed, with the maximum available at one show being 5 points. Puppies must be a minimum of six months old to compete.

An outstandingly good, and outstandingly lucky, dog might finish its championship in three shows; the norm is probably 10–12 shows.

Points are awarded to the male judged best in the classes for its sex and awarded Winners dog; points are also awarded for Winners bitch. These two then compete with any champions entered in the Best of Breed class; this is normally the only time that class dogs (non-champions) must compete with Champions and it has no negative effect on the points already won for Winners in either sex.

The main difference between this system and that used in the U.K. is that, at KC championship shows, class dogs compete with Champions for Challenge Certificates (CCs). The KC Championship title requires a dog to win three CCs, won under three different judges. A maximum of one CC in each sex can be won at any one show. The KC approves only about 30 all-breed shows each year, plus anything up to 10 specialities for CCs and not all of them offer CCs in each breed. It sometimes happens that one dog being shown very successfully can prevent others of its breed of the same sex from completing their title for a year or more. The ANKC follows a system broadly similar to that of the KC. The CKC Championship requires the accumulation of 10 points, won from three different judges. The dog must be registered by the CKC before the title will be conferred, but CKC registration is not necessary in order to compete. A maximum of 5 points can be won at any one show, and points are given for Group placements, in addition to those won in the breed, up to 5 points. The CKC licenses about 100 shows each year.

To become an International (FCI) Champion a dog must win four Certificates of Aptitude for International Beauty (CACIBs) from four different judges at FCI shows, after the age of 15 months. Generally, the last CACIB must be won at least 12 months after the first one, and at least one of the awarding judges must be from a continent different from that of the other three judges

THE BIG DOG SHOWS

The best-known, but certainly not the largest, American dog show is the Westminster Kennel Club show, which is held every February in Madison Square Garden, New York City. Entries are limited to 2,500 dogs over two days, and each dog entered must be a Champion. The show is the centerpiece of a week of educational seminars, lectures, parties, and award dinners. For many Americans, watching "the Garden" on television is the closest they will ever get to attending a dog show, and the televised version is enormously popular.

RIGHT The Boxer is a good example of a dog breed whose ears are cropped in some parts of the world and not in others.

Crufts dog show, now held in the National Exhibition Centre in Birmingham, England, in early March, is currently the world's largest dog show. Entries average 21,000 dogs, over four days, and the crowds of spectators from around the world fill this huge venue to bursting. Vendors on site offer an astonishing variety of things to buy— everything from high-quality dog art and collectibles to grooming aprons, food, books, and clothing for humans. The Crufts committee provides a steady stream of dog experts to advise prospective and current dog owners on behavioral, nutritional or management problems. It also offers demonstrations and competitions in Dog Agility, Obedience (including "free form"), herding, and field work. The World show, sponsored by the FCI, is held in a different country each year. At this show only, the title "World Champion" for the year can be awarded to the winners of each Best of Breed and Best of Opposite Sex. Recent World shows have been held in Mexico City, Mexico, in Dortmund , Germany and in Amsterdam, The Netherlands.

RIGHT The Australian Cattle Dog was developed in Australia from crosses between the native Dingo and Highland Collies.

SURGERIES: COSMETIC OR BENEFICIAL?

The ongoing debate about the issue of elective surgeries for dogs has resulted in a ban on tail docking and ear cropping in the U.K. and parts of Europe. Both are still allowed in the U.S., Canada and some other countries, but animal rights organizations are campaigning to ban both cropping and docking in the U.S., too.

The animal rights community's campaigns against cropping and docking are based on their contention that both practices are frivolous, painful, and unnecessary, and therefore cruel. Unfortunately their arguments are based more on emotional appeals than on provable fact, which leads many to believe that proposed bans on cropping and docking have more to do with

the promotion of a specific political agenda than with a real concern about the welfare of animals.

Professional animal groomers and experienced breeders cite centuries of medical and animal management history to support the benefits (to the animal) of cropping and docking procedures.

The full-length tail of an adult dog is at risk of injury in the normal course of events. Tails wagging against hard surfaces, or caught in doorways, are subject to abrasions or cuts. Dogs that work (herd, track, trail, hunt, retrieve, or even hike) are at risk of tail injuries. Ultimately, about half the injured dogs must have their tail surgically removed. Whereas docking the tail of a four-day old puppy causes no lasting pain or discomfort because of the immaturity of the puppy's nervous system, and the speed with which the tiny cut heals, the same surgery on an adult dog requires general anesthesia, heals very slowly, and is prone to infection. A case could be made that docking the tail of young puppies lessens the risk of later injury.

Dogs that have drop ears are susceptible to inner-ear infections unless their owners are assiduous about keeping the ear interior clean and dry at all times. Bacteria thrive in the moist, dark inner ear; ear infections are very painful and can cause deafness. Ears that are heavily haired are at even greater risk of infection.

Ears are normally cropped when the puppy is a few weeks old. The surgery, performed by a licensed veterinarian, requires general anesthesia; during the healing process, ears are taped upright to assist healing and to hold their shape. Upright and cropped ears have good air circulation, which dries the inner ear and limits bacterial growth. Both cropping and docking are elective surgeries, as are spaying, castration, dewclaw removal (dogs) and de-clawing of cats. Spay and castration surgery are invasive procedures, and especially when performed on very young puppies and kittens, are accompanied by a risk to life.

Each of these medical procedures serves a purpose; they eliminate unwanted pregnancies (spay and castration); reduce risk of injury or infection (crop, dock, dewclaw removal) or prevent injuries to humans or their property (de-clawing). Those who are concerned about animal welfare (which includes animal care, safety, health, well-being and comfort) are supportive of procedures that provide a benefit to the animals. It is unfortunate that any medical procedure with a proven value to animals and their owners should become the focus of a political agenda.

HOW TO USE THIS BOOK

This book provides breed standards for 105 dog breeds. The entry for each breed is composed of introductory text, a photograph of the breed, descriptions from the breed standards for the main body parts, and a side panel detailing the breed's broader desired characteristics.

Abbreviations used:
AKC American Kennel Club
KC (British) Kennel Club
ANKC Australian National Kennel Council
FCI Féderation Cynologique Internationale
CKC Canadian Kennel Club

NAME The breed's name is provided at the head of each entry.

REGISTRY RECOGNITION Each entry names those dog registries that officially recognize the breed being shown (see panel, left, for abbreviations).

SIDE PANEL Other aspects of the breed's desired characteristics are detailed on the colored side panel. These include general appearance, size, and temperament. The "Characteristics" category outlines the breed's distinguishing features.

Recognized → AKC, ANKC, CKC, FCI, KC

CHOW CHOW

INTRODUCTION The introductory text for each entry provides an outline of the breed's history and origins.

Due to a lack of early written history of dogs, the age of this Chinese breed can only be estimated. The Tartars who invaded China in the tenth century B.C. are known to have brought with them great packs of large, lionlike dogs with black tongues. Some theories suggest that the Chow Chow is a descendant of the Tibetan Mastiff and the Samoyed. Others claim that it was the first of the Spitz breeds, and therefore probably a predecessor of the Samoyed. Whatever its source, the Chow served as a herder, home guard, and sporting dog in its early years. As both a pointer and a retriever of birds and other game, it often lived in vast kennel compounds, being cared for by royal servants. When the tradition of imperial hunts ceased, so did these kennels. Importation of the Chow Chow into the U.K. did not begin in any numbers until about 1880.

The Chow is adorable as a puppy, but will grow into a very strong-willed dog. It is said that it will die for you, but not obey you.

HEAD AND SKULL
Large in proportion to size of dog. Typical scowl caused by face wrinkles and shape and placement of ears and eyes. Excessive loose skin not desired. Topskull broad and flat. Toplines of muzzle and skull approximately parallel. Moderate stop.
NOSE Broad and black.

EYES AND EARS
EYES Moderately sized, deep and wide apart, set obliquely. COLOR Dark brown, with black rims. SHAPE Almond.

EARS Small, moderately thick, triangular; slightly rounded tips. Carried stiffly erect with slight forward tilt. Placed wide apart.

BODY AND TOPLINE
Topline straight, strong and level. Body strongly muscled, deep. Body, back and croup must all be short. Chest broad, deep and muscular.

NECK
Strong, full, and nicely arched.

TAIL
Set high and carried close to back.

MOUTH AND JAWS
MUZZLE Short compared to topskull, but never less than a third of head length. Broad, width and depth being equal.
LIPS Edges black. A solid black mouth is ideal.
BITE Scissor.

PHOTOGRAPH Each entry features a full-color photograph of the breed. For double-page entries, close-ups of some body parts and different coat colors are also pictured.

FOREQUARTERS
SHOULDERS Strong, tips of blades moderately close together.
FORELEGS Length of upper arm never less than shoulderblade. Elbows well-back, close to chest. Heavily boned. Widely spaced around broad chest.
PASTERNS Short and upright. Wrists should not knuckle-over.
DEWCLAWS May be removed.

FEET
Round and catlike.
PADS Thick.

HINDQUARTERS
Broad, powerful, well-muscled in hips and thighs, heavy boned. Widely spaced from a broad pelvis.
HINDLEGS Stifles have little angulation. Hocks well-let-down, almost straight.
DEWCLAWS May be removed.

→ **GENERAL APPEARANCE**
The Chow Chow is a powerful, sturdy, square, Arctic-type dog, medium in size, with strong muscles, heavy bone, high tail-set and a heavy, square head.

→ **CHARACTERISTICS**
The profuse double coat, heavy head with wrinkles, and stilted rear gait are typical.

→ **TEMPERAMENT**
The Chow Chow is keenly intelligent, independent, and reserved with strangers. Displays of aggression or timidity are unacceptable. The deep-set eyes reduce its peripheral vision, so the dog should be approached from within its visual range.

→ **GAIT/MOVEMENT**
Movement is sound, agile, quick, and powerful. The rear gait is short and stilted because of the straight rear assembly. There is no roll through the midsection, and the front and rear must be in equilibrium.

→ **COAT**
There are two types of coat; rough and smooth. Both are double coated.
ROUGH—outercoat abundant, straight, offstanding, and rather coarse. Undercoat soft and wooly. Profuse ruff around the head and neck, generally more so in males than females.
SMOOTH—hard, dense, smooth outercoat. Definite undercoat. No ruff or feathering on legs or tail.

→ **COLOR**
Allowed colors are red, black, blue, cinnamon, and cream.

→ **SIZE**
HEIGHT (average adult)
17–20in (42.5–50cm)
Square in profile.
KC/FCI/ANKC Males 19–22in (47.5–55cm); Females 18–20in (45–50cm)

→ **DISQUALIFICATIONS**
■ Drop ears or ears
■ Nose spotted or distinctly other than black, except in blue Chows
■ Top surface or edges of tongue pink or red, or with one or more spots of red or pink

125

NON-SPORTING

GROUP The name of the group into which the breed is classified is provided on the side of each entry. This book follows the classification of the American Kennel Club (AKC).

SIZE The ideal height and weight ranges for each breed are provided, where they are part of the breed standard. Height is always measured at withers unless stated otherwise.

DISQUALIFICATIONS The disqualifications provided in this book are those recognized by the AKC alone. Variations with regard to the CKC, ANKC, and FCI standards are not listed. The KC does not list disqualifications as part of its breed standards.

STANDARDS FOR BODY PARTS The most up-to-date ideal standards for each of the dog's main body parts are provided in summary form. The standards follow those recognized by the AKC. If the standard of the KC, CKC, ANKC, or FCI departs significantly from the standard provided, this is highlighted for the reader, and the nature of the variation outlined. The same applies to information provided on the colored side panel.

BRITTANY

The Brittany is an all-purpose bird dog, retrieving like a spaniel and working game like a setter. The breed has been admired for over four centuries in Europe. In the 1800s, a popular pastime for English gentry was woodcock-hunting in France. Most brought their own dogs, and inevitably some of these pointers and setters bred with native spaniels; the resulting puppies proved superior to their parents. The Brittany became very popular with French gentry, and also with poachers. The dog was unbeaten in its ability to find gamebirds, could both point and retrieve, and was very obedient. The breed's popularity continues to grow today because of its hunting ability. The Brittany has high energy, intelligence, and great affection for its family. It does not respond well to rough handling, but kindness reaps rewards during training and every day thereafter.

HEAD AND SKULL

Medium length, rounded on top, very slightly wedge shaped, with a well-defined but gently sloping stop. Occiput only apparent to the touch. Should never be "apple headed" and should never have an indented stop.

EYES AND EARS

EYES Well-protected by heavy brows. Prominent eyes should be heavily penalized. Skull well-chiseled under eyes so that lower lid does not form a pocket to catch seeds, dirt, and weed dust. COLOR Darker color preferred.

EARS Set above eye level. Short and triangular, reaching about half the length of muzzle, lying flat and close to head, slightly rounded tips. Well-covered with dense, but short hair. **KC** Vine-shaped.

MOUTH AND JAWS

MUZZLE About two-thirds the length of skull, tapering gradually to nostrils.

JAWS Overshot or undershot to be heavily penalized.

BITE True scissor.

NECK

Medium length, strong. Throatiness not a serious fault, no dewlaps.

BODY AND TOPLINE

Back straight and short, never sway, or roach backed. Height at shoulders slightly more than at rump. Chest deep, reaching to level of elbow. Ribs well-sprung and deep. Flanks rounded, fairly full. Slight tuck-up. Loins short.

TAIL

Tail-less to approximately 4 in (10cm) long (natural or docked). Set on high. **KC** Also undocked. **FCI** Lively tail movement when active.

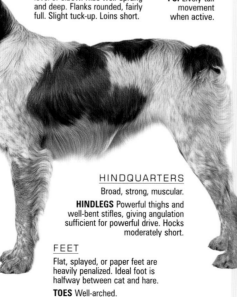

FOREQUARTERS

SHOULDERS Shoulder blades sloping and muscular, should not be too wide apart. Blade and upper arm should form nearly a 90-degree angle.

FORELEGS Not too wide apart. Elbows and feet turning neither in nor not.

PASTERNS Slightly sloping. Elbows at approximately equal distance from ground and withers.

DEWCLAWS All four may be removed.

HINDQUARTERS

Broad, strong, muscular.

HINDLEGS Powerful thighs and well-bent stifles, giving angulation sufficient for powerful drive. Hocks moderately short.

FEET

Flat, splayed, or paper feet are heavily penalized. Ideal foot is halfway between cat and hare.

TOES Well-arched.

PADS Thick.

→ GENERAL APPEARANCE

A compact, closely-knit dog of medium size. It is leggy, strong, vigorous, energetic, and quick of movement.

→ CHARACTERISTICS

This predominately white, square dog can be tail-less, or have the tail docked to approximately 4 in (10cm).

→ TEMPERAMENT

Happy and alert, neither mean nor shy.

→ GAIT/MOVEMENT

Clean movement, coming and going, is very important, but most important is the side gait, which is smooth, efficient, and ground covering. At a trot, the hindfoot should step into or beyond the print left by the forefoot.

→ COAT

The coat is sufficient to protect the dog, but not excessive. The hair should be dense, flat, or wavy, never curly, and the texture should be neither wiry nor silky. There should be some feathering on the forelegs and hindlegs, but too much is objectionable. Dogs with long or profuse feathering should be severely penalized. The skin is fine and fairly loose to reduce likelihood of punctures and tearing.

→ COLOR

The Brittany is primarily a white dog with orange or liver markings, in either clear or roan pattern. Some ticking is desirable, but washed-out colors not desired. Orange or liver is found in standard parti-color or piebald patterns. Tri-colors (liver and white with orange markings) are allowed but not preferred. Any black is a disqualification.

FCI/ANKC Allows white and black. A narrow blaze is desirable with any coat color.

→ SIZE

HEIGHT (from ground to highest point of shoulders)

17½–20½ in (43.75–51.25cm)

FCI/ANKC Males 48–51cm (19–20 in); females 47–50cm (18½–20 in).

WEIGHT

30–40 lb (13.6–18.2kg)

KC No weight specified.

→ DISQUALIFICATIONS

- Height below 17½ in (43.75cm) or above 20 in (51.25cm)
- Black nose
- Black in the coat

POINTER

The Pointer was probably the first dog used to stand or "point" game and was developed as a distinct breed much before any of the setters. Early Pointers were hard-headed dogs, unwilling to submit to control. In the early 1800s, they were crossed with setters to improve their disposition, making them more amenable to working with people. Since about 1650, the Pointer has been used by shooting men to indicate the presence and position of sitting game. A good, Pointer therefore needs superb scenting powers, speed over the ground, and steadiness on point.

The modern Pointer is an independent dog, but also gentle and eager to please. Developed as a far-ranging hunter, with the stamina to work steadily for hours, the Pointer is very energetic and may be too boisterous for children or even some adults.

GENERAL APPEARANCE
The Pointer looks like a dog bred for field sport with the look of compact power and agile grace. The head is noble and proudly carried, the muscular body bespeaks both staying power and dash. Every movement shows it to be a hard-driving hunting dog possessing stamina, courage, and the desire to go.

CHARACTERISTICS
A clean-limbed dog, the Pointer has a short coat and a nose "upturned" at the end. It is very active with great stamina.

TEMPERAMENT
Even temperament and alert good sense make the Pointer a congenial companion in the field or at home. It should be dignified and should never show timidity toward man or dog.

GAIT/MOVEMENT
Movement smooth, with a powerful hindquarter drive. The head is carried high, and the tail moves from side to side rhythmically with its pace. A balanced, strongly-built hunting dog, the Pointer is capable of top speed combined with great stamina. Hackney gait must be faulted.

COAT
The coat is short, dense, and smooth, with a sheen.

COLOR
Colors include liver, lemon, black, and orange, either solid-colored or in combination with white. A good Pointer cannot be a bad color.

SIZE
Balance and overall symmetry are more important than size.

HEIGHT

males	females
25–28 in	23–26 in
(62.5–70cm)	(57.5–65cm)

KC/FCI/ANKC Prefers slightly smaller males and slightly larger females.

WEIGHT

males	females
55–75 lb	45–65 lb
(25–34.1kg)	(20.5–29.5kg)

KC/FCI No weights specified.

EYES AND EARS
EYES Of ample size, rounded, and intense. COLOR Dark in contrast to color or markings, the darker the better.

EARS Set on at eye level. Should reach just below lower jaw, close to head, little or no folding. Somewhat pointed at the tip, soft and thin in leather.

HEAD AND SKULL
Skull, approximately as wide as length of muzzle, giving an impression of length rather than width. Slight furrow between eyes. Cheeks cleanly chiseled. Pronounced stop.

NOSE Black or brown in darker dogs; lighter or flesh colored in lighter colored dogs. Nostrils well-developed; wide open.

BODY AND TOPLINE
Back strong and solid, slight rise from croup to top of shoulders. Loins of moderate length, powerful, slightly arched. Croup falling only slightly. Tuck-up apparent, not exaggerated.

TAIL
Heavier at root, tapering to a fine point. Length no greater than to hock. Carried without curl, and no more than 20 degrees above the line of the back; never carried between legs.

MOUTH AND JAWS
MUZZLE Good length from stop forward, nose is slightly higher at tip than muzzle at stop. Should be deep without pendulous flews.

JAWS Ending square and level.

BITE Even or scissor. **KC/FCI** Scissor only.

NECK
Long, dry, muscular, slightly arched.

FOREQUARTERS
Chest deep rather than wide. Breastbone bold, not prominent. Ribs well-sprung, descending to elbow.

FORELEGS Elbows well-let-down, directly under withers. Straight and with oval bone. Knee joint never to knuckle over.

PASTERNS Of moderate length, perceptibly finer in bone than leg, and slightly slanting.

DEWCLAWS May be removed.

HINDQUARTERS
HINDLEGS Muscular and powerful. Thighs long, well-developed. Stifles well-bent. Hocks clean. Decided angulation is the mark oF power and endurance.

FEET
Oval.

TOES Long, closely-set, arched.

PADS Well padded and deep.

GERMAN SHORTHAIRED POINTER

The development of this breed reads like a recipe for creating a dog that fits exactly defined needs. The old German Pointer became established in the Black Forest area of south-western Germany in the late eighteenth century. It was a slowish pointing bird dog that would also trail by scent. Over time, attempts were made to infuse it with other breeds, including the English Pointer, which contributed the desired elegant working style, but it was averse to working in water and lacked aggression toward predators. Before the turn of the nineteenth century the goal of producing a versatile hunting dog that was intelligent, obedient, and had a sound temperament had been met. A pointing bird dog, night trailer, and duck dog which retrieves on land or water, this breed is an excellent pet for anyone desiring a versatile hunting dog, and an intelligent and devoted companion.

GENERAL APPEARANCE
An aristocratic, well balanced, symmetrical, medium-sized dog, whose conformation indicates power, endurance, and agility, with a look of intelligence and animation. The ideal is a dog well balanced in all points.

CHARACTERISTICS
Medium-size, balanced hunting dog; liver or liver and white color; docked tail.

TEMPERAMENT
Friendly, intelligent, and willing to please. It possesses a keen enthusiasm for work, with no indication of nervousness or flightiness.

GAIT/MOVEMENT
Has a smooth and lithe gait in which the hindquarters drive smoothly and with great power. The forelegs show great reach.

COAT
The hair is short and thick, and feels tough to the touch. It is somewhat longer on the underside of the tail and back edges of the haunches. The hair on the ears and head is softer, thinner, and shorter.

COLOR
Solid liver or a combination of liver and white, such as liver and white-ticked, liver-patched and white-ticked, or liver roan.
KC Allows black and white.

SIZE
HEIGHT

males	females
23–25 in (57.5–62.5cm)	21–21 in (52.5–57.5cm)

FCI/ANKC Males 24–26 in (62–66cm); females 23–25 in (58–63cm).

WEIGHT

males	females
55–70 lb (25–31.8kg)	45–60 lb (20.5–27.3kg)

DISQUALIFICATIONS
- China or wall eyes
- Flesh-colored nose
- Extreme overshot or undershot jaw
- A dog with any area of black, red, orange, lemon or tan, or solid white

HEAD AND SKULL
Skull reasonably broad, slightly rounded on top. Occipital bone not conspicuous. No discernible stop.
NOSE Brown, the larger the better, with nostrils well open and broad.

EYES AND EARS
EYES Medium-sized, neither protruding nor sunken. COLOR Dark brown. SHAPE Almond.
EARS Broad and set fairly high, lying flat and close to head. Placement just above eye level.

BODY AND TOPLINE
Chest deeper than broad, reaching to elbows. Ribs sprung. Back short, strong, and straight, with slight rise from root of tail to withers. Loins strong, of moderate length, slightly arched. Hips, broad. Body either square or slightly longer than tall.

NECK
Nape muscular. Moderate throatiness permitted.

TAIL
Docked, leaving approximately 40 percent of its length, and set high.
KC/ANKC Customarily docked. Undocked: not reaching below the hocks and similar to Pointer.

MOUTH AND JAWS
MUZZLE Length equal to that of skull.
JAWS Powerful.
TEETH Strong; molars intermesh.
BITE True scissor.

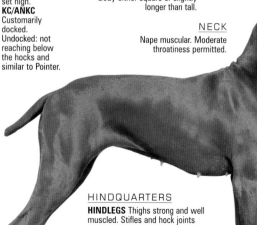

HINDQUARTERS
HINDLEGS Thighs strong and well muscled. Stifles and hock joints well angulated and strong.

FEET
Compact, round- to spoon- shaped.
TOES Sufficiently arched and heavily nailed.
PADS Strong, hard, and thick.
DEWCLAWS May be removed.

FOREQUARTERS
SHOULDERS Shoulder blades lie flat and well laid-back with a 45 degree angle.
FORELEGS Upper arm long. Legs straight, muscled, Toes turn neither in nor out.
PASTERNS Strong, short, and nearly vertical with a slight spring.

GERMAN WIREHAIRED POINTER

The German Wirehaired Pointer is not just a wiry version of the German Shorthaired Pointer. The two breeds share many attributes, but each is quite distinct. Whereas British breeders of hunting dogs tended over time to produce breeds with specialized skills, the Germans had little patience with one-purpose dogs, preferring rugged dogs that could work any type of small game, on any terrain. This GWP is a relatively young breed. Developed between the mid-1800s and 1920, it was as quick and effective in the field as the Shorthaired Pointer, though its nose was not as good. It was claimed to be superior in forest and water, and at hunting game. Its original temperament was meant to match the toughness of its coat, but it is now a much more aimiable companion that would suit an outdoor-loving adult, who wants an intelligent, all-weather friend with great energy.

GENERAL APPEARANCE

A well muscled, medium-sized dog. Balanced in size and sturdily built, it is typically Pointer in character and style, and is an energetic, intelligent, and determined hunter.

CHARACTERISTICS

The weather-resistant, wirelike coat and facial furnishings are the breed's distinguishing characteristics.

GAIT/MOVEMENT

Movement should be free and smooth, with good reach in the forequarters and good driving power in the hindquarters. The topline should remain firm when in motion.

COAT

The functional wiry coat is weather-resistant and somewhat water-repellent. The undercoat is dense enough in winter to insulate against the cold, but so thin in summer as to be almost invisible. The distinctive outercoat is straight, harsh, wiry, and flat-lying, and is 1–2in (2.5–5cm) long (**KC** Not longer than 1½ in [3.75cm]). The hair on the lower legs, feet, skull, and ears is of softer texture and shorter. The tail is devoid of feather. The eyebrows are of strong, straight hair, and the beard and whiskers are of medium length. In a puppy, the coat may be shorter than in an adult, but it must have the correct texture.

COLOR

The hair is liver and white, or solid liver. The head is liver, sometimes with a white blaze. The ears are also liver.

KC Includes black and white.

FCI/ANKC Uses the word brown rather than liver.

SIZE

The body is a little longer than its height (10:9). Correct size and proportion is essential to high performance.

HEIGHT

males	females
24–26 in (60–65cm)	22 in (minimum) (55cm) (minimum)

FCI/ANKC Males up to 27 in (68cm); females up to 26 in (64cm).

WEIGHT

KC Males 55–75 lb (25–34kg); females 45–64 lb (20.5–29kg).

HEAD AND SKULL

Head moderately long. Skull broad. Occipital bone not prominent. Stop medium.

NOSE Dark brown, with wide-open nostrils.

BODY AND TOPLINE

Chest deep and capacious, sprung ribs. Tuck-up apparent. Back short and strong. Loins taut and slender. Hips broad with croup nicely rounded. Topline shows perceptible slope down from withers to croup.

EYES AND EARS

EYES Medium sized, overhung with medium-length eyebrows. COLOR Brown. SHAPE Oval.

EARS Rounded but not too broad, hanging close to head.

TAIL

Set high. Docked to approximately two-fifths of its original length. **KC/FCI/ANKC** Customarily docked. Undocked: may be carried slightly saber.

NECK

Medium length, slightly arched, and devoid of dewlap.

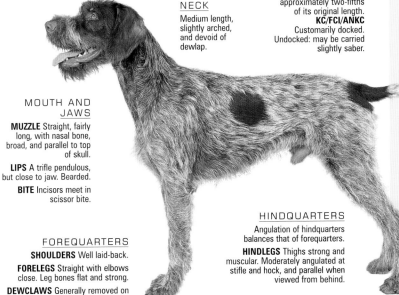

MOUTH AND JAWS

MUZZLE Straight, fairly long, with nasal bone, broad, and parallel to top of skull.

LIPS A trifle pendulous, but close to jaw. Bearded.

BITE Incisors meet in scissor bite.

HINDQUARTERS

Angulation of hindquarters balances that of forequarters.

HINDLEGS Thighs strong and muscular. Moderately angulated at stifle and hock, and parallel when viewed from behind.

FEET

Round in outline.

TOES Close, high arched, and webbed.

PADS Thick and hard.

NAILS Strong and quite heavy.

FOREQUARTERS

SHOULDERS Well laid-back.

FORELEGS Straight with elbows close. Leg bones flat and strong.

DEWCLAWS Generally removed on all four feet.

Recognized → AKC, ANKC, CKC, FCI, KC

CHESAPEAKE BAY RETRIEVER

The history of the Chesapeake Bay Retriever, unlike that of almost all other breeds, is very precisely known. It began very dramatically in 1807 when an American ship rescued the crew from an English brigantine off the coast of Maryland. The entire crew was saved, along with two Newfoundland puppies. Both puppies were eventually trained to retrieve ducks—at which they proved eminently talented. From these two puppies, which were mated to a variety of area retrievers, came the Chesapeake Bay Retriever, or Chessy. Early Chessies had much longer coats than modern dogs, but although the coat has since diminished, the desire to brave nature in order to retrieve ducks certainly has not. The modern Chessy is bright and happy, with an affectionate nature. It is certainly the hardiest of the retrievers and probably the most difficult for a novice to train.

→ GENERAL APPEARANCE

A strong, active, balanced, and powerfully built duck retriever, on land or water. It is medium in height and fairly heavy.

→ CHARACTERISTICS

Light, yellowish or amber eyes, hindquarters as high as or a trifle higher than the shoulders, and a distinctive double coat that may wave on shoulders, neck, back, and loins.

→ GAIT/MOVEMENT

Gait should be smooth, free, and effortless, giving the appearance of great power and strength. There should be good reach in the front and plenty of drive in the rear, with good flexion of stifle and hock joints. The elbows should be held close to the body.

→ COAT

The coat should be thick and short, nowhere over 1½ in (3.75cm) long, and with a dense, fine, wooly undercoat. Hair on the shoulders, neck, back, and loins has a tendency to wave. Moderate feathering on the rear of the hindquarters and on the tail is permissible. Texture is very important because the Chesapeake is used for hunting in all weather conditions, often working in ice and snow. Oil in the outercoat and the wooly undercoat protects the skin and aids quick drying. The coat should resist water in the same way as a duck feather's.

→ COLOR

Color should be as close as possible to that of its working environment. Any color of brown, sedge, or deadgrass is acceptable. A white spot on breast, belly, toes, or back of the feet (immediately above the large pad) is permissible, but the smaller the spot the better.

→ SIZE

HEIGHT

males	females
23–26 in (57.5–65cm)	21–24 in (52.5–60cm)

Height should be slightly less than body length.

WEIGHT

males	females
65–80 lb (29.5–36.4kg)	55–70 lb (25–31.8kg)

→ DISQUALIFICATIONS

- Specimens lacking in breed characteristics
- Teeth overshot or undershot
- Dewclaws on hind legs
- Coat curly, or with a tendency to curl all over the body
- Feathering over 1¾ in (4.4cm) long on the tail or legs
- Black color
- White on any part of the body except breast, belly, toes, or back of feet

EYES AND EARS

EYES Medium large, very clear, and wide apart. COLOR Yellowish or amber.

EARS Small, set well up on head, hanging loosely; of medium leather.

HEAD AND SKULL

Intelligent expression. Skull broad and round; medium stop.

NOSE Medium short.

BODY AND TOPLINE

Chest strong, deep, and wide. Rib cage barrel-round and deep. Back should be short, well coupled, and powerful. Body of medium length, flanks well tucked-up. Depth extends at least to elbow. Equal distances from shoulder to elbow and elbow to ground.

MOUTH AND JAWS

MUZZLE Approximately same length as skull.

LIPS Thin, not pendulous.

JAWS Of sufficient length and strength to carry large waterfowl with an easy, tender hold.

BITE Scissor preferred, but level acceptable.

NECK

Medium length with a strong, muscular appearance.

TAIL

Medium in length, and medium heavy at base. Straight or slightly curved.

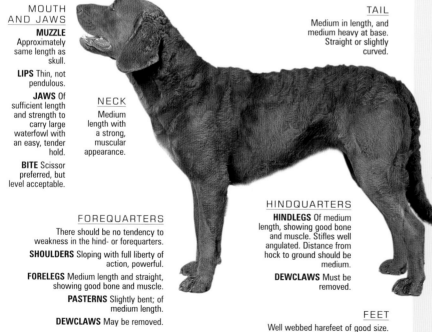

FOREQUARTERS

There should be no tendency to weakness in the hind- or forequarters.

SHOULDERS Sloping with full liberty of action, powerful.

FORELEGS Medium length and straight, showing good bone and muscle.

PASTERNS Slightly bent; of medium length.

DEWCLAWS May be removed.

HINDQUARTERS

HINDLEGS Of medium length, showing good bone and muscle. Stifles well angulated. Distance from hock to ground should be medium.

DEWCLAWS Must be removed.

FEET

Well webbed harefeet of good size.

TOES well rounded and close.

FLAT-COATED RETRIEVER

Dogs used by cod fishermen off Newfoundland formed the basis of this breed, as they did the Labrador Retriever and the Newfoundland. These dogs were highly valued for their ability to retrieve fish that had escaped from the nets, and items that had been dropped from the small fishing boats. Of indeterminate type and varying size, they were excellent swimmers and willing retrievers.

In the late 1800s, this breed was stabilized to form the Flat-coated Retriever that we know today. A tireless worker in the field, the modern Flat-coat is equally useful in rough cover or cold water. Very active outdoors, and needing regular hard exercise and swimming, the dog is also happy and content to spend quiet time indoors with its family.

HEAD AND SKULL

Head is long and lean. The fairly flat skull is of moderate breadth, and flat, clean cheeks appear to be "cast in one piece." Stop is barely discernible. Brows slightly raised and mobile. Occiput not accentuated, the skull forming a gentle curve.

NOSE Large, open nostrils.

EYES AND EARS

EYES Medium-sized, set wide apart. COLOR Dark brown or hazel. SHAPE Almond.

EARS Relatively small, lying close to head and thickly feathered. Not low-set.

BODY AND TOPLINE

Chest deep, reaching to elbow. Forechest prominent and well developed. Rib cage deep, showing good length and only moderately broad. Loins strong, well muscled, and long. Rump moderately broad and well muscled. Topline strong and level.

NECK

Strong and slightly arched for retrieving strength. Moderately long and free from throatiness. Hair on neck untrimmed.

TAIL

Fairly straight and well set-on, with bone reaching approximately to hock joint.

MOUTH AND JAWS

MUZZLE Long, strong, deep. Nearly equal in length and breadth to skull.

JAWS Long and strong.

LIPS Fairly tight and dry to minimize the retention of feathers.

TEETH Broken teeth not to count against the dog.

BITE Scissor preferred, level acceptable. **KC/FCI** Level not acceptable.

FOREQUARTERS

SHOULDERS Long, well laid-back, upper arm of approximately equal length. Musculature wiry. Elbows close to body and set well back under withers.

FORELEGS Straight and strong, with medium bone.

PASTERNS Slightly sloping, strong.

DEWCLAWS Removal optional.

HINDQUARTERS

HINDLEGS Powerful, angulation in balance with front assembly. Upper thighs well muscled. Good turn of stifle. Second thighs as long as upper thigh. Hock joint strong and well let-down.

DEWCLAWS None.

FEET

Oval or round, medium-sized and tight.

TOES well arched.

PADS Thick.

GENERAL APPEARANCE

A versatile family companion and hunting retriever, traditionally described as showing "power without lumber and raciness without weediness." It shows a proud carriage, responsive attitude, waving tail, and overall look of functional strength, quality, style, and symmetry.

CHARACTERISTICS

The distinctive feature of this breed is the silhouette, featuring the unique "one-piece" head. This utilitarian retriever is well balanced, strong, but elegant.

TEMPERAMENT

The Flat-coat is primarily a family companion and hunting retriever. It loves to hunt and can readily adapt to changing circumstances on a variety of upland game and waterfowl. As a companion, it is sensible, alert, and highly intelligent—a light-hearted and adaptable friend. Typically it retains these qualities well into old age.

GAIT/MOVEMRNT

Its movement appears balanced, free flowing, and well coordinated. Fore- and hindlegs reach well forward and extend well back, achieving long clean strides. The topline is level in motion.

COAT

The coat is of moderate length, density, and fullness, with a high luster. Ideally, it is straight and flat-lying. Slight waviness is permitted. It must provide protection and insulation from all types of weather, water, and ground cover. A mane of longer, heavier coat on the neck, extending over the withers and shoulders, is considered typical, especially in the male dog.

COLOR

Color is solid black or solid liver.

SIZE

HEIGHT

males	females
23–24½ in (57.5–61.25cm)	22–23½ in (55–58.75cm)

WEIGHT

Dogs should be shown in lean, hard condition, free of excess weight.

KC/FCI/ANKC Males 60–80 lb (27–36kg); females 55–70 lb (25-32kg)

DISQUALIFICATIONS

- Yellow, cream, or any color other than black or liver

GOLDEN RETRIEVER

The Golden Retriever was developed to retrieve, and while many excel at field trials and hunting, most never get a chance to work, spending their entire lives as delightful house pets. Most Golden Retrievers are chosen for personality rather than hunting ability.

Some breeds develop in a specific region, often as a joint effort of many people with a common need. A few breeds owe their existence to the dedicated work of one individual, and such is the case with the Golden Retriever. Lord Tweedmouth, whose home was located in Inverness-shire, in the Scottish Highlands, was responsible for developing a breed that could work in heavy cover, swim strongly, and retrieve from cold water. These abilities, the dog's attractive shape and color, plus its enthusiastic, happy nature helped to ensure the Golden's enormous worldwide popularity. Lord

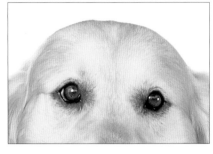

HEAD AND SKULL

Skull broad, slightly arched laterally and longitudinally, without prominence of frontal bones (forehead) or occipital bones. Stop well defined but not abrupt. Foreface deep and wide, nearly as long as skull.

NOSE Black or brownish black, though fading to a lighter shade in cold weather not serious.
KC/FCI/ANKC Preferably black.

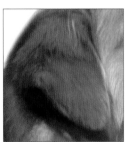

EYES AND EARS

EYES Friendly and intelligent, medium large, with close-fitting eye rims. Set well apart and reasonably deep in sockets. COLOR Dark brown preferred; medium brown accepted. Dark eye rims. **KC/FCI/ANKC** Only dark brown.

EARS Rather short, with front edge attached well behind and just above eye and falling close to cheek. When pulled forward, tip should just cover eye.

NECK

Medium long, merging gradually into well laid-back shoulders. No throatiness.

MOUTH AND JAWS

MUZZLE Straight in profile, blending smoothly and strongly into the skull. In profile or from above, slightly deeper and wider at stop than tip. No heaviness in flews. Removal of whiskers permitted but not preferred.

TEETH Full dentition.

BITE Scissor.

FOREQUARTERS

Muscular, well coordinated with hindquarters, and capable of free movement.

SHOULDERS Shoulder blades long and well laid-back, with upper tips fairly close together at withers. Upper arms appear about same length as shoulder blades, setting elbows beneath withers.

FORELEGS Legs straight with good bone, but not coarse.

PASTERNS Short and strong, sloping slightly.

DEWCLAWS May be removed, but are usually left on.

FEET

Medium-sized, round, compact, and well knuckled. Excess hair may be trimmed to show size and contour.
PADS Thick.

Tweedmouth began with a yellow Wavy-coated Retriever, which he bred to a Tweed Water Spaniel. From 1868 until 1890, he line-bred to this original combination, with the occasional introduction of other breeds. Early pictures show how little changed the Golden now appears, compared to the earliest results of Lord Tweedmouth's project.

Until 1913 Golden Retrievers were registered with the KC as "Flat- or Wavy-coated Retrievers (Golden or Yellow)." In 1920 they became "Retrievers (Golden)." The first Golden Retriever was registered by the AKC in 1925.

The Golden Retriever needs constructive activity and more exercise than most pet Goldens get. Other than hunting, and obedience and retriever training, swimming and long walks in open areas help to keep the dog's mind and body exercised.

→ GENERAL APPEARANCE

A symmetrical, powerful, active dog, sound and and not clumsy or long in leg. It has a kindly expression.

→ CHARACTERISTICS

The lustrous golden coat is characteristic of this medium-sized dog.

→ TEMPERAMENT

Friendly, reliable, trustworthy, eager, and confident.

→ GAIT/MOVEMENT

When trotting, the gait is free, smooth, powerful, and well coordinated, showing good reach.

→ COAT

The coat is dense and water-repellent, with a good undercoat. The outercoat is firm and resilient, not coarse nor silky, lying close to body. The hair may be straight or wavy. There is a natural ruff, moderate feathering on the back of the forelegs and on the underbody, and heavier feathering on the front of the neck, back of the thighs, and the underside of the tail. The feet may be trimmed and stray hairs neatened, but the natural appearance of the coat or outline should not be altered by cutting or clipping.

→ COLOR

The color is a rich, lustrous gold of various shades, with no white except for a few white hairs on chest.

→ SIZE

Length from breastbone to point of buttocks should be slightly greater than height at withers in a ratio of 12:11.

HEIGHT

males	females
23–24 in (57.5–60cm)	21–22 in (53.75–56.25cm)

WEIGHT

males	females
65–75 lb (29.5–34.kg)	55–65 lb (25–29.5kg)

→ DISQUALIFICATIONS

- Deviation of more than 1 in (2.5cm) above or below standard height.
- Undershot or overshot bite.

BODY AND TOPLINE
Body well balanced, short-coupled, deep through the chest. Chest between forelegs at least as wide as a man's closed hand, with well developed forechest. Brisket extends to elbow. Ribs long and well sprung but not barrel-shaped, muscular, wide, and deep with very little tuck-up. Topline strong and level from withers to slightly sloping croup, whether standing or moving.

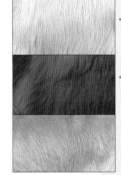

TAIL
Well set-on, thick and muscular at base, following natural line of the croup. Tailbones extend to, but not below, point of hock. Carried with merry action, level or with some moderate upward curve.
KC/FCI/ANKC Only level.

HINDQUARTERS
Broad and strongly muscled. Croup slopes slightly. Pelvic bone slopes at a slightly greater angle.
HINDLEGS Stifles well bent. Hocks well let-down, with short, strong rear pasterns.

↓ LABRADOR RETRIEVER

The Labrador Retriever does not come from Labrador. In fact, it would be more correctly named the St. John's Retriever because many came from the area around St. John in Newfoundland, Canada. No record exists of how the dog came to live and work with cod fishermen there, but it is thought to have originated in Devon, England, and to have been brought to North America by fishermen. The dog was appreciated for its utility and resourcefulness, and for its ability to track and retrieve the scarce game in Newfoundland. This vital role helped to prevent starvation for man and dog, especially when storms prevented fishing. Eventually the St. John's Newfoundland in Canada faded into history, largely because of the imposition of a high dog tax. Ironically, it was the dogs that had been reimported into

HEAD AND SKULL

Skull should be wide and well developed, but without exaggeration. Skull and foreface are on parallel planes and of approximately equal length. Stop moderate. Brow slightly pronounced. Head should be clean-cut and free of fleshy cheeks.
NOSE Wide, with well developed nostrils.

EYES AND EARS

EYES Medium-sized, set well apart, and neither protruding nor deep set. Eye rims self-colored.

EARS Hanging moderately close to head, set rather far back, and somewhat low on skull.

NECK

Should be long enough to allow dog to retrieve easily. Muscular, free from throatiness, and with a moderate arch.

MOUTH AND JAWS

LIPS Should not be squared off or pendulous, but should fall away in a curve toward the throat.

JAWS Powerful.

TEETH Strong.

BITE Scissor; level acceptable, but not desirable. **KC/FCI** Scissor only.

FOREQUARTERS

Muscular, well coordinated, and balanced with the hindquarters.

SHOULDERS Well laid-back, long and sloping, forming an angle with upper arm of approximately 90 degrees. Length of shoulder blade should equal length of upper arm.

FORELEGS Straight. Elbows should be directly under withers.

PASTERNS Strong, short, and with slight slope.

DEWCLAWS May be removed.

FEET

Strong and compact.

England in around 1800 that formed the basis of the breed as we know it. Crosses with other retrievers increased the breed's "bird sense," but fortunately the characteristics unique to the Labrador proved dominant and were not diffused.

Currently a small percentage of Labradors work as hunting and trial dogs, but most are beloved pets. Their size, equable temperament, and intelligence also suits them admirably for obedience and agility competition, as scent-tracking dogs for the police and customs department, and as assistance dogs for blind or handicapped people.

Sadly, as with the Golden Retriever, Labradors have also suffered the negative effects of popularity. Consequently, great care must be taken when purchasing a dog in order to avoid health, structural, or temperament problems.

Little grooming is required, other than to control seasonal shedding, but much exercise of mind and body is needed to avoid health or behavior problems.

BODY AND TOPLINE

Body should be short-coupled, with good spring of ribs tapering to a moderately wide chest. Chest breadth should not be too wide or too narrow for efficient movement and stamina. Underline almost straight, with little or no tuck-up. Loins short, wide, and strong. Topline level from withers to croup. Back strong.

TAIL

Very thick at base, gradually tapering toward tip, of medium length, and extending no longer than to hock. It should have no feathering and be covered all around with short, dense hair, giving the appearance of a rounded "otter" tail.

HINDQUARTERS

Broad and muscular.
HINDLEGS well developed from hip to hock. well turned stifles and strong, short hocks. Angulation of rear should balance that of front.
DEWCLAWS May be removed.

→ GENERAL APPEARANCE

The Labrador Retriever was bred primarily as a working gun dog, and structure and soundness are of great importance. It is a strongly built, medium-sized, short-coupled dog with a sound, athletic, well balanced conformation that enables it to function as a retrieving gun dog, and also gives it the temperament to be a family companion.

→ CHARACTERISTICS

The short, dense, and weather-resistant coat, and the "otter" tail are the distinguishing features of this dog.

→ TEMPERAMENT

This Labrador has a kindly, outgoing, tractable nature. It is eager to please and nonaggressive toward man or animals.

→ GAIT/MOVEMENT

Gait is free and effortless, with all parts in balance and with good power. The forelegs and shoulders should reach well forward. The hindlegs should provide adequate drive and power, with good follow-through.

→ COAT

The coat is a distinctive feature, being short, straight, and very dense. A soft, weather-resistant undercoat provides protection from water, cold, and all types of ground cover. A slight wave down the back is permitted.

→ COLOR

Black, yellow, or chocolate are the only permitted colors. A small white spot on chest is admissible.

→ SIZE

HEIGHT

males	females
22½–24½ in (56.25–61.25cm)	21½–23½ in (53.75–58.75cm)

WEIGHT (approximate desired)

males	females
65–80 lb (29.5–36.4kg)	55–70 lb (25–31.8kg)

→ DISQUALIFICATIONS

- Any deviation greater than ½ in (1.25cm) above or below height prescribed
- Thoroughly pink nose or nose lacking in pigment
- Eye rims without pigment
- Docking or otherwise altering the length or natural carriage of the tail
- Any other color or a combination of colors other than black, yellow, or chocolate, as described in the standard

ENGLISH SETTER

Prior to the introduction of firearms for hunting, various methods were employed to catch game birds. Traps and thrown nets were most common. However, the birds still had to be found. Dogs were trained to seek birds and then to crouch motionless near them until the hunter arrived and threw the net. This type of dog became known as a "setter," from the posture it adopted when it found the birds. Development of the English Setter as we know it today began around the 1800s. Today there are two different strains of the breed; the field dog, which is the smaller, carries less coat, and is more energetic, and the show type, which is larger, carries more coat, and is more laid back. English Setters of both types have kept their popularity because of their usefulness, beauty, and sweetness.

GENERAL APPEARANCE

The English Setter is an elegant, substantial, and symmetrical gun dog, with the ideal blend of strength, stamina, grace, and style. Males should be decidedly masculine without coarseness, and females decidedly feminine without overrefinement.

CHARACTERISTICS

An attractive, basically white, medium-sized dog, the English Setter has a flowing coat of straight hair with feathering on the legs, underbelly, chest, and tail. It is a sturdy and stylish hunting dog.

TEMPERAMENT

This dog is gentle, affectionate, and friendly, without shyness, fear, or viciousness.

GAIT/MOVEMENT

The English Setter moves effortlessly, demonstrating endurance while covering the ground efficiently. It has a long forward reach and a strong rear drive, with a lively tail and proud head carriage. The back is strong, firm, and free of roll.

COAT

The coat is flat, with no curl or wooliness. Feathering on the ears, chest, abdomen, underside of the thighs, back of all legs, and on the tail, should be of good length, but not so excessive that it obscures the dog's lines or affects its function as a sporting dog.

COLOR

The intermingling of darker hairs with the white ground color results in belton markings, which vary from clear, distinct flecking to roan shading; flecked all over is preferred. Colors are orange belton (white with orange markings), blue belton (white with black), tricolor (blue belton with tan on the muzzle, over the eyes, and on the legs), lemon belton, and liver belton.Head and ear patches are acceptable, but heavy patches of color on the body are undesirable.

SIZE

HEIGHT

males	females
25 in (62.5cm)	24 in (60cm)

EYES AND EARS

EYES Fairly large. Lids fit tight, haw is not exposed. COLOR Dark brown, the darker the better. Eyelids dark, fully pigmented. SHAPE Nearly round.

EARS Set well back and low, even with or below eye level. When relaxed carried close to head. Of moderate length, slightly rounded at ends. Moderately thin leather.

HEAD AND SKULL

Long and lean; well defined stop. Head planes (top of muzzle, top of skull, and bottom of lower jaw) are parallel. Skull oval, of medium width. Length of skull from occiput to stop equal to length of muzzle.

NOSE Black or dark brown.

BODY AND TOPLINE

Forechest well developed, point of sternum projecting slightly in front of point of shoulder/upper arm joint. Chest deep. Brisket reaches to elbow. Ribs long, well sprung. Back straight and strong. Loins strong, Tuck-up moderate. Croup nearly flat. Hip bones wide apart.

MOUTH AND JAWS

MUZZLE Long and square from the side, of good depth, with flews squared and fairly pendant.

BITE Close scissor preferred; even is acceptable. **KC/FCI** Scissor only.

NECK

Long and graceful, muscular and lean, arched at the crest.

FOREQUARTERS

SHOULDERS Fairly close at the top. Well laid-back. Upper arm equal in length to and forming a near right angle with shoulder blade.

FORELEGS Straight. Elbows turn neither in nor out. Arm flat and muscular. Bone substantial but not coarse.

PASTERNS Short, strong, and nearly round, with very slight slope.

DEWCLAWS May be removed.

FEET

Face directly forward.

TOES Closely set, strong, and well arched.

PADS Well developed and tough.

TAIL

Tapers to a fine point, reaches to the hock joint. Carried straight and level with back.

HINDQUARTERS

Pelvis equal in length to and forming a near right angle with upper thigh.

HINDLEGS Muscular thighs. Stifle well bent. Lower thigh only slightly longer than upper thigh. Hock joint well bent. Rear pasterns short, strong, nearly round, and perpendicular to ground.

GORDON SETTER

Black-and-tan setters are known to have existed in Scotland since at least 1620, but it was not until the fourth Duke of Gordon began to breed them in the late 1770s and early 1800s that they were consistently bred to type. Once called Gordon Castle Setters, they were greatly valued for their beauty, staying power, excellent nose, and devotion to family. Gordons were also considered easy to train and very reliable, with excellent bird sense, increasing hunters' esteem of these handsome dogs.

There is little distinction between show and field types of Gordons. Many bench champions are excellent field dogs, and field-trial winners acquit themselves well at shows. Maintenance of a Gordon can be mastered easily, with regular, vigorous exercise necessary for adults.

GENERAL APPEARANCE

A good-sized, sturdily built, well muscled dog. It is active, upstanding, and stylish. It suggests strength and stamina rather than extreme speed. Symmetry and quality are most essential. A dog well balanced in all points is preferable to one with both outstanding good qualities and defects.

CHARACTERISTICS

The Gordon is the largest and heaviest of the three setters, set apart by its black-and-tan coat, fairly large head, and sturdy bone.

TEMPERAMENT

Alert, fearless, willing, intelligent and capable, the Gordon is loyal and affectionate, but also strong-willed and determined. With sufficient exercise and work, the dog makes a very satisfactory companion for a loving master. It can be wary of intruders, but with its own family is gentle and very responsive.

GAIT/MOVEMENT

A bold, strong, driving, straight and smooth gait is desired, with no throwing in or out of feet. Good reach and drive are ideal, along with good follow-through. The head is carried up, and the tail "flags" constantly while the dog is in motion.

COAT

The coat is soft, straight, or slightly wavy, never curly, with long hairs on the ears, under the stomach and on the chest, back of the legs, and the tail. The feather which starts near the root of the tail grows shorter toward the end.

COLOR

The only permitted color is black with "tan" markings of rich chestnut or mahogany. The border between the two colors is clearly marked. A white spot on the chest is allowed, but the smaller the better.

SIZE

The dog measures approximately square.

HEIGHT

males	females
24–27 in (60–67.5cm)	23–26 in (57.5–65cm)

WEIGHT

males	females
55–80 lb (25–36.4kg)	45–70 lb (20.5–31.8kg)

DISQUALIFICATIONS

- Predominantly tan, red, or buff dogs lacking the typical pattern or markings

EYES AND EARS

EYES Fair size, neither too deep set nor too bulging, with tight lids. COLOR Dark brown. SHAPE Oval.

EARS Set low on head, approximately on line with eyes. Fairly large and thin, well folded, and carried close to head.

HEAD AND SKULL

Head deep rather than broad. Skull nicely rounded, broadest between the ears. Cheeks narrow. Clear stop at midpoint of skull.

NOSE Broad, black in color.

BODY AND TOPLINE

Body short from shoulder to hip. Chest deep, but forechest pronounced. Chest reaches to elbows. Ribs well sprung. Loin short, broad, and not arched. Croup nearly flat. Topline moderately sloping from withers to croup.

MOUTH AND JAWS

MUZZLE Fairly long. Flews not pendulous. Top of muzzle is parallel to the top line of skull.

TEETH Strong, white.

BITE Scissor preferred; level not a fault. **KC/FCI** Scissor only.

TAIL

Short (does not reach below hocks), thick at the root, and finishing in a fine point.

NECK

Long, lean, arched, with no throatiness.

FOREQUARTERS

SHOULDERS Well laid-back, with tops of shoulder blades close together. Angle of shoulder blade and upper arm is approximately 90 degrees.

FORELEGS Big-boned, straight, with elbows free.

PASTERNS Straight.

DEWCLAWS May be removed.

HINDQUARTERS

HINDLEGS From hip to hock long, flat, and muscular; from hock to heel, short and strong. Stifle and hock joints well bent.

DEWCLAWS May be removed.

FEET

Catlike. Feet turned neither in nor out

TOES Close-knit, well arched toes with plenty of hair between.

IRISH SETTER

The Irish Setter (called the Irish Red Setter by the FCI) was developed in Ireland, probably from a mix based on early Spaniels, plus an alleged infusion of a black, racy Pointer type from Iberia (whence came longer legs and increased speed, plus a darker color), a Bloodhound (intensified "nose"), and perhaps a small dash of Gordon Setter, English Setter, and Irish Water Spaniel. By the eighteenth century the Irish Red-and-White Setter was breeding reasonably true to type. In time the solid red Setter gained favor over the Red-and-White for the newly invented dog shows, and by the late 1800s the Irish Red Setter was achieving great success at shows. Slow to mature physically and mentally, the Irish Setter was developed to work hard all day and still needs regular exercise. It is tough enough to hunt in rough brush all day, yet gentle enough to be a charming family companion.

GENERAL APPEARANCE
The correctly built Irish Setter exhibits balance. Each part flows and fits into a pleasing whole. The dog is substantial, yet elegant in build.

CHARACTERISTICS
An active, aristocratic gun dog, with a rich red coat and substantial yet elegant build. In the field it is a swift-moving hunter. At home it is a sweet-natured, trainable companion.

TEMPERAMENT
Has a "rollicking" personality. An outgoing, stable temperament is the essence of the breed. Shyness, hostility, or timidity are uncharacteristic.

GAIT/MOVEMENT
At the trot the gait is big, very lively, graceful, and efficient. At an extended trot the head reaches slightly forward. There is good reach in the forelegs, but not a Hackney gait, and great power and drive in the rear.

COAT
The hair is short and fine on the head and forelegs, but on all other parts it is of moderate length and flat. Feathering is long and silky on the ears, back of forelegs and thighs. The fringe on the tail is moderately long and tapering. All coat and feathering should be straight and free from any curl or wave. The top third of the ears and the throat, nearly to the breastbone, should be trimmed. Feet should be trimmed only to show the natural outline.

KC Does not mention trimming.

COLOR
Mahogany or rich chestnut red, with no black. A small amount of white on the chest, throat, or toes, or a narrow center streak on the skull should not be penalized.

SIZE
The dog is slightly longer than tall. Males should appear masculine without coarseness and females feminine without being slight of bone.

HEIGHT

	males	females
	27in (67.5cm)	25in (62.5cm) (62.5cm)

WEIGHT

males	females
70 lb (31.8kg)	60 lb (27.3kg)

FCI Males 23–26½ in (58–67cm); females 21½–24½ in (55–62cm).

HEAD AND SKULL
Head lean, length at least double width between ears. Delicate chiseling along muzzle, below eyes, and on cheeks. Skull oval from front, slightly domed in profile. Distinct stop midway between tip of nose and well defined occiput.

EYES AND EARS
EYES Medium-sized, placed rather well apart, neither deep set nor bulging. COLOR Dark to medium brown. SHAPE Somewhat almond shaped. **KC/ANKC** Preferably unshelled almond shape.

EARS Set well back and low, not above level of eye. Leather thin, hanging in a neat fold close to head and nearly long enough to reach tip of nose.

NECK
Moderately long, strong but not thick, and slightly arched. Free from throatiness.

BODY AND TOPLINE
Body sufficiently long to permit straight, free stride. Chest deep and moderately wide, reaching to elbows, with moderate forechest. Ribs well sprung. Loins firm, muscular, and moderately long.

TAIL
Set-on nearly level with croup, strong at root, and tapering to a fine point.

MOUTH AND JAWS
MUZZLE Moderately deep.

JAWS Underline of jaw almost parallel with top line of muzzle.

BITE Scissor preferred, or even. **KC** Scissor only.

FEET
Rather small, very firm, toes arched and close.

FOREQUARTERS
SHOULDERS Shoulder blades long, wide, sloping well back, fairly close at withers. Upper arm and shoulder blades approximately same length. Elbow in line with withers and moves freely.

↓ COCKER SPANIEL

This breed is known as the Cocker Spaniel in the U.S., but the rest of the world calls it the American Cocker Spaniel. Progenitors of all the spaniels were known in the thirteenth century. Eventually the many types of spaniels devolved into land and water retrievers. The water spaniels are the forerunners of many modern gun dog breeds. Cockers came from the dogs who specialized in land retrieving. Over time these dogs were crossed with other spaniels, and even with toy spaniels. By 1830 an English Spaniel had been developed—a major step toward the later American and English varieties of Cockers. The smallest breed in the Sporting Group, the Cocker earned its name from its proficiency at finding and retrieving woodcock. Intelligent and easy to train—many do well in obedience competiton—the breed is potentially an excellent family companion.

HEAD AND SKULL

Skull rounded but not exaggerated. Eyebrows clearly defined with pronounced stop. Well chiseled beneath eyes; well developed nostrils.

NOSE Black in black, black-and-tan, and black-and-whites; brown, liver or black (the darker the better) in other colors. Color of nose harmonizes with color of eye rims.

BODY AND TOPLINE

Chest deep, reaching to elbows, not too wide. Ribs deep and well sprung. Back strong. Topline sloping slightly toward muscular, rounded quarters.

TAIL

Docked. Never carried straight up. Tail action merry when dog is in motion. **KC** Customarily docked. Undocked: carried level and merry. Tapering from root to tailset and feather in proportion to rest of the dog's coat.

NECK

Muscular, free from throatiness. Arches slightly toward head.

EYES AND EARS

EYES Round and full, looking directly forward, dark brown, the darker the better. Slightly almond in shape. **KC** Includes black.

EARS Lobular, long, of fine leather, well feathered, and placed no higher than lower part of eye.

MOUTH AND JAWS

MUZZLE Broad and deep, with square, even jaws. Distance from stop to tip of nose is half the distance from the stop to base of skull.

LIPS Upper lip full.

TEETH Strong.

BITE Scissor.

FOREQUARTERS

SHOULDERS Well laid-back, forming an angle with upper arm of approximately 90 degrees, allowing for good front reach. Elbows below highest point of shoulders.

FORELEGS Straight, strongly boned, and muscular.

PASTERNS Short and strong.

DEWCLAWS May be removed.

HINDQUARTERS

Hips wide.

HINDLEGS Strongly boned, muscular, with moderate angulation at stifle.

DEWCLAWS May be removed.

FEET

Compact, large, round and firm, turning neither in nor out.

→ GENERAL APPEARANCE

The Cocker Spaniel has a sturdy, compact body and a cleanly chiseled, refined head. It is capable of great speed and endurance. It must be free and merry, sound and well balanced.

→ CHARACTERISTICS

A chiseled head with a pronounced stop, and full feathering.

→ TEMPERAMENT

Equable with no suggestion of timidity.

→ GAIT/MOVEMENT

Balance between front and rear assemblies is crucial for sound movement, allowing a strong, driving rear and unrestricted front reach. Gait is coordinated, smooth, and ground covering. Excessive animation should not be mistaken for proper gait.

→ COAT

Short and fine on the head and of medium length on the body, with enough undercoat to give protection. Ears, chest, abdomen, and legs are well feathered, but not enough to obscure the dog's lines and movement, or to affect its function as a sporting dog. Texture is most important—the coat is silky, flat, or slightly wavy. Trimming should appear as natural as possible.

→ COLOR

There are three color categories. Black includes solid jet black, and black with tan points. Any Solid Color Other Than Black (ASCOB) ranges from lightest cream to darkest red, and includes brown, and brown with tan points. Parti-Color is two or more solid, well broken colors, one of which must be white.

→ SIZE

The body is very slightly longer than tall.

HEIGHT (adult)

males	females
15 in (37.5cm)	14 in (35cm)

→ DISQUALIFICATIONS

- Deviation of ½ in (1.25in) above the stated height for an adult
- Any color or combination of colors other than specified in standard
- Black dogs with white markings, except on chest and throat
- ASCOB with white markings, except on chest and throat
- Parti-color—primary color 90 percent or more
- Tan markings in excess of 10 percent
- Absence of tan markings in black or ASCOB dogs in any of the locations specified

ENGLISH COCKER SPANIEL

Before the seventeenth century all the smaller retrieving gun dogs were lumped together as "spaniels." Earlier, in the thirteenth and fourteenth centuries, spaniels were found in many parts of the world, and were adept at increasing the hunter's supply of game. These dogs were essentially the same everywhere, but terrain and local game varied sufficiently for hunters to prefer one size or type over another, leading to the establishment of localized "breeds." This led to the various breeds that exist today. In essence, the larger spaniels became Springers and the smaller ones, Cockers. With time, the weight limits were dropped so that differentiation came to take place only by type.

Everywhere but in the U.S. the English Cocker was, and is, far more popular than its American cousin. It is still considered among the best hunters of the small spaniels, though it is unusual now for the same dog to function in the field and the show ring and be a pet. It is intelligent and easy

HEAD AND SKULL

Strong, yet free from coarseness, softly contoured, with no sharp angles. As a whole, parts combine to produce the typical expression. Skull arched and slightly flattened when seen from side and front. Brow not appreciably higher than back of skull. From above, sides of skull are in roughly parallel planes to those of muzzle. Stop definite but moderate, and slightly grooved.

NOSE Black, except in livers and parti-colors, when it may be brown; in reds and parti-colors it may be brown, but black is preferred. Nostrils wide.

EYES AND EARS

EYES Medium-sized and set wide apart. Lids tight. Haws inconspicuous and may be pigmented or not. COLOR Dark brown, except in livers and liver parti-colors, where hazel is permitted—the darker the hazel the better. SHAPE Full and slightly oval.

EARS Set low, lying close to head. Leather fine, extending to nose, well covered with long, silky, straight, or slightly wavy hair.

MOUTH AND JAWS

MUZZLE Equal in length to skull and well cushioned. Only slightly narrower than skull and cleanly chiseled under eyes.

LIPS Square, but not pendulous or showing prominent flews.

JAWS Strong, capable of carrying game.

BITE Scissor; level allowed though not preferred.

NECK

Graceful and muscular, arching toward head and blending cleanly, without throatiness, into sloping shoulder. Of moderate length and in balance with length and height of dog.

FOREQUARTERS

Moderate angulation, with sloping shoulders and upper arm of approximately equal length. Angulation should be sufficient for elbow to rest under shoulder point when dog is still.

FEET

Proportionate in size to legs, firm, round, and catlike.

TOES Arched and tight.

PADS Thick.

to train, doing well in obedience competition, and it makes a well behaved family pet.

It has a range of fourteen acceptable colors, is slightly higher on leg than the American Cocker, and has a more moderate head and generally much less coat. It is often more energetic than the American Cocker and so needs more exercise, but still less than other sporting breeds.

The English Cocker requires a complete brushing at least twice a week, and because of the long heavy drop ears, a careful ear-cleaning weekly. The hair on its head and the top third of its ears needs trimming at intervals of about six to nine weeks. Hair on feet and under the tail must be scissored at the same time.

In temperament the English Cocker resembles a slightly quieter, more sensible version of the American Cocker. This dog is happiest in the center of family activities. It can adapt to almost any situation, from quiet apartment living to playing with small children.

GENERAL APPEARANCE

An active, merry sporting dog, standing well up at the withers and compactly built. Alive with energy, its enthusiasm in the field and its active tail indicate how much it enjoys hunting.

CHARACTERISTICS

The head is especially characteristic. It is a dog of balance, standing or moving, without exaggeration in any part.

TEMPERAMENT

Merry and affectionate, of equable disposition, neither sluggish nor hyperactive, the English Cocker is a willing worker and a faithful, engaging companion.

GAIT/MOVEMENT

Capable of hunting in dense cover and upland terrain. Its gait is characterized more by drive and power than by speed. It has extension in the front and rear appropriate to its angulation. In the ring it carries its head proudly and keeps much the same topline standing and moving. It moves without crabbing or rolling.

COAT

The hair on the head is short and fine. That on the body is of medium length, flat or slightly wavy, and silky in texture. The English Cocker is well feathered, but not so profusely as to interfere with field work. Trimming is permitted to remove overabundant hair and to enhance the dog's true lines.

COLOR

Color is various. Parti-colors are either clearly marked, ticked or roan, the white appearing in combination with black, liver or shades of red. Solid colors are black, liver, or shades of red. White feet on a solid are undesirable, though a little white on the throat is acceptable. Tan markings, clearly defined and of a rich shade, may appear in conjunction with black, liver, and parti-color combinations of those colors. Black-and-tans and liver-and-tans are considered solid colors.

SIZE

Height at withers is slightly greater than distance from withers to set-on of tail.

HEIGHT

males	females
16–17 in (40–42.5cm)	15–16 in (37.5–40cm)

WEIGHTS (desirable)

males	females
28–34 lb (12.7–15.5kg)	26–32 lb (11.8–14.5kg)

KC/FCI Prefer slightly smaller sizes.

BODY AND TOPLINE

Body compact, giving the impression of strength without heaviness. Chest deep; prosternum projecting moderately beyond shoulder points. Brisket reaches to elbows and slopes gradually to a moderate tuck-up. Ribs well sprung; tapering back ribs of good length extend well back. Back short and strong. Loins short, broad, and very slightly arched. Croup slopes slightly. Topline sloping very slightly to a gently rounded croup.

TAIL

Docked. Should be carried horizontally and is in constant motion while dog is in action. If dog is excited, may be carried somewhat higher, but not cocked up. **KC/FCI/ANKC** Customarily docked. Undocked: carried in same line and merry. Tapering from root to tail and feather in proportion to the rest of the dog's coat.

HINDQUARTERS

Angulation moderate, in balance with forequarters. Hips relatively broad and well rounded.

HINDLEGS Upper thighs broad, thick, and muscular. Second thighs well muscled and approximately equal in length to the upper. Stifle strong, well bent. Hock to pad short.

↓ ENGLISH SPRINGER SPANIEL

All spaniels share an early history. In 1800 the Boughey family of Aqualate in Shropshire, England, developed a distinct strain of land spaniels and continued to breed Springers until the 1930s. The Norfolk family also deeply invested in breeding Springers during that time and met with good success. Boughey and Norfolk dogs are behind the pedigrees of many current English Springers.

In general, however, spaniels varied widely in size and type both in the U.K. and in the U.S., depending on the location and game they hunted (see English Cocker Spaniel). One litter could, and often did, contain dogs that could be called Springers and others that could be called Cockers, at a time when the primary difference was weight. In an effort to resolve any confusion, the American Spaniel Club was formed in 1880. When the American standard was written in 1927 it was aimed at supporting the Springer's natural abilities as a gun dog. The English Springer's name derives from the use of this type of Spaniel to startle birds into the air so that they spring upward.

HEAD AND SKULL

Skull of medium length and fairly broad, flat on top, and slightly rounded at the sides and back. Occiput inconspicuous. Head shows a combination of strength and refinement. Size in balance with rest of dog. Head approximately same length as neck. Stop moderate and must not be pronounced. Eyebrows well developed. Cheeks flat, with chiseling under the eyes.

NOSE Fully pigmented, liver or black in color, depending on coat color. Nostrils well opened.

BODY AND TOPLINE

Body short-coupled, strong, and compact. Chest deep, reaching to elbows, with well developed forechest. Ribs fairly long, well sprung. Underline stays level with elbows to a slight upcurve at the flank. Back straight, strong, and essentially level. Loins strong, short, and slightly arched. Hips nicely rounded. Croup sloping gently to the tail set. Topline from withers to tail firm and slopes very gently.

HINDQUARTERS

The English Springer should be in hard, muscular condition, with well developed hips and thighs.

HINDLEGS Thighs broad and muscular. Stifle joints strong. Angulation should match that of forequarters. Hock joints somewhat rounded. Pasterns short (about one-third the distance from hip joint to foot) and strong.

DEWCLAWS Usually removed.

TAIL

Carried horizontally or slightly elevated. Displays a characteristic lively, merry action when dog is on game.

KC/FCI/ANKC Customarily docked. Undocked: in balance with rest of dog.

FEET

Round or slightly oval. Forefeet compact and of medium size. Hindfeet smaller and more compact.

PADS Thick.

TOES Well arched, well feathered between toes.

→ GENERAL APPEARANCE

A well proportioned dog, free from exaggeration. Its appearance suggests power and endurance. It is endowed with style, symmetry, balance, and enthusiasm, and is every inch a sporting dog of distinct spaniel character.

→ CHARACTERISTICS

This medium-sized sporting dog is built to cover ground with agility and reasonable speed. It has a compact body and a docked tail. The dog's pendulous ears and soft, gentle expression make it an unmistakable member of the spaniel family.

→ TEMPERAMENT

Typically friendly and eager to please, the English Springer is quick to learn and willing to obey. It is tractable in the field, at shows, and in the home.

→ GAIT/MOVEMENT

The gait of a correctly-built English Springer results from good reach in front and strong drive from the rear. It has a ground-covering stride and carries a firm back, with no tendency to dip, roach, or roll from side to side.

→ COAT

The outercoat is of medium length, flat or wavy. The undercoat is short, soft, and dense. In combination, they help protect the dog from weather, water, and brush. Ears, chest, legs, and belly have feathering of moderate length. The head, front of forelegs, and below the hock joints on the hindlegs have short, fine hair. The coat may be trimmed to enhance the dog's functional appearance.

→ COLOR

The following combinations of colors are equally acceptable—black or liver with white markings, or predominantly white with black or liver markings; blue or liver roan; tricolor. Any white portion of the coat may be flecked with ticking.

→ SIZE

Length of body is slightly greater than height.

HEIGHT

males	females
20 in (50cm)	19 in (47.5cm)

WEIGHT

males	females
50 lb (22.7kg)	40 lb (18.2kg)

KC/FCI/ANKC No weights specified; height for both males and females approximately 20 in (51cm).

The English Springer Spaniel Field Trial Association, parent club of the breed in the U.S., was formed in 1924 and has held field trials steadily ever since. Springers have a loyal following among hunters who desire a dog that hunts fast, ranges far out, and both flushes and retrieves game.

The English Springer is happy, energetic, and quick to learn. Bred to range far and fast while hunting, this dog needs regular exercise and work. Long supervised runs and walks on leash, along with the mental stimulation of obedience or agility training, will keep the dog content and avoid behavior problems resulting from boredom.

EYES AND EARS

EYES Medium-sized, set rather well apart and fairly deep in sockets. Lids tight, with little or no haw showing. COLOR Iris harmonizes with color of dog—dark hazel in liver-and-white dogs, and black or deep brown in black-and-white dogs. Eye rims fully pigmented and matching coat in color. SHAPE Oval.

EARS Long and fairly wide, hanging close to cheeks, with no tendency to stand up or out. Leather thin and approximately long enough to reach nose tip. On level with eye and not too far back on head.

NECK

Moderately long, muscular, clean, and slightly arched at the crest.

MOUTH AND JAWS

MUZZLE Approximately same length and half the width of skull. Topline of skull and muzzle lie in approximately parallel planes. Nasal bone straight, not concave or convex.

TEETH Strong, clean, and good-sized.

BITE Scissor.

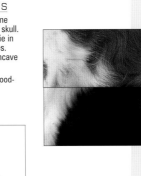

FOREQUARTERS

SHOULDERS Shoulder blades flat and tips are close together. Ideally shoulders and upper arm are of approximately equal length, forming an angle of nearly 90 degrees; this places forelegs directly beneath tips of shoulder blades.

FORELEGS Elbows close to body, and forelegs straight with strong bone that is slightly flattened.

PASTERNS Strong, short, slightly sloping.

DEWCLAWS Usually removed.

VIZSLA

The name Vizsla comes from a Hungarian word meaning "alert and obedient" and perfectly describes this lean, muscular, self-colored dog. Called the Hungarian Vizsla in the U.K., this breed developed on the plains of Hungary, probably by the Magyar tribes more than a thousand years ago. The Vizsla gained favor with medieval nobles and warlords, who controlled its ownership and breeding, thus assuring the purity of the breed. A true pointer, but with additional talents, the Vizsla was adept at hunting in marshy areas; it is a good swimmer and retriever; and equally strong at tracking ground game. It is especially good at hunting hare and deer. Still very popular in their native Hungary, Vizslas are gentle and affectionate while retaining their boldness and love of hunting. Some Vizslas are shy, some almost hyperactive, but if well trained and adequately exercised, they can prove a comfortable house pet and companion, especially suited to a person who enjoys outdoor activity.

EYES AND EARS

EYES Medium in size. Surrounding tissue covers the whites. COLOR Iris must blend with color of coat.

EARS Thin, silky, and proportionately long, with rounded ends, set fairly low and hanging close to cheeks.

HEAD AND SKULL

Head lean and muscular. Skull moderately wide between ears, with median line down the forehead. Stop moderate.

NOSE Brown.

TAIL

Set just below level of croup, thicker at root, and docked one-third off. Carried at or near the horizontal. **KC** Customarily docked. Undocked: slightly curved, tapering, reaching hocks.

BODY AND TOPLINE

Body, strong. Back, short. Topline slightly rounded to set-on of the tail. Chest moderately broad and deep, reaching to elbows. Ribs well sprung. Underline shows a slight tuck-up beneath loins.

NECK

Strong, smooth and muscular, moderately long, arched, and devoid of dewlap.

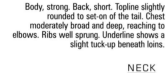

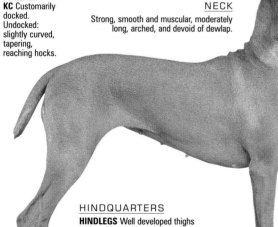

MOUTH AND JAWS

MUZZLE Foreface of equal length or slightly shorter than skull. Square and deep.

LIPS Cover jaws completely. Neither loose nor pendulous.

TEETH well developed, white.

JAWS Strong.

BITE Scissor.

HINDQUARTERS

HINDLEGS Well developed thighs with moderately angulated stifles and hocks.

DEWCLAWS Should be removed.

FEET

Catlike, round, and compact.

TOES Close.

NAILS Brown and short.

PADS Thick and tough.

GENERAL APPEARANCE

A medium-sized, short-coated hunting dog, the Vizsla is robust but rather lightly built.

CHARACTERISTICS

The Vizsla's solid golden-rust color is distinctive. Its bearing is athletic and aristocratic; tail is docked.

TEMPERAMENT

This natural hunter has a good nose and above-average ability to take training. Lively and gentle, it is demonstrably affectionate and sensitive, though fearless and with a well developed protective instinct.

GAIT/MOVEMENT

The gait is far-reaching, light-footed, graceful, and smooth.

COAT

The coat is short, smooth, dense, and close-lying, with no wooly undercoat.

COLOR

Color is a solid golden rust in different shadings. White on the forechest, preferably as small as possible, and on toes, is permissible.

SIZE

HEIGHT

males	females
22–24 in (55–60cm)	21–23 in (52.5–57.5cm)

WEIGHT

Not specified.

KC 44–66 lb (20–30kg)

DISQUALIFICATIONS

- Completely black nose
- Solid white extending above the toes or white anywhere else other than on the forechest
- White extending onto the shoulders or neck
- A distinctly long coat
- Deviation of more than 1½ in (3.75cm) above or below the stated height limits at the highest point over the shoulder blades

FOREQUARTERS

Front and rear angulation balanced.

SHOULDERS Shoulder blades proportionately long and wide, sloping moderately back and fairly close at top.

FORELEGS Muscular, with elbows close.

DEWCLAWS Should be removed.

WEIMARANER

Whereas British sportsmen-hunters tended to prefer specialist dogs, Europeans tended to breed dogs that were generalists. The Weimaraner was developed in the nineteenth century by nobles in the court of the German city-state of Weimar. The sportsmen who developed the breed sought a dog capable of success against the large game then hunted in Germany. The dog needed to be courageous and intelligent, but also fast, agile, and with a scent ability sufficient to find and track the game. Later, when such game became depleted in the countryside, the German Weimaraner Club took control of the breed, setting stringent standards for breeding. The Weimaraner was trained on upland game and as a water retriever, and proved excellent at both. Today this breed is valued as a personal gun dog more than as field trial competitor, although it takes to obedience training with great delight. It does best with a firm, fair trainer.

GENERAL APPEARANCE

A medium-sized dog, with fine, aristocratic features. A picture of grace, speed, stamina, alertness, and balance. The dog's conformation must indicate an ability to work with great speed and endurance in the field.

CHARACTERISTICS

The solid gray color, docked tail, and athletic outline distinguish this breed.

TEMPERAMENT

The Weimaraner should be friendly, fearless, alert, and obedient.

GAIT/MOVEMENT

Gait should be effortless and indicate smooth coordination. The topline should remain strong and level.

COAT

The coat is short, smooth, and sleek.

COLOR

The color is a solid, distinctive gray, varying from mouse-gray to silver-gray and usually blending to lighter shades on the head and ears. A small white mark on the chest is permitted, but not on any other portion of the body, unless it is the result of injury.

SIZE

HEIGHT

males	females
25–27 in	23–25 in
(62.5–67.5cm)	(57.5–62.5cm)

DISQUALIFICATONS

- Deviation of more than 1in (2.5cm) above or below standard height
- A distinctly long coat
- A distinctly blue or black coat

HEAD AND SKULL

Head moderately long and aristocratic; moderate stop; slight median line extending back over forehead. Prominent occipital bone. Length from tip of nose to stop is equal to that from stop to occipital bone. Skin drawn tight.
NOSE Gray.

EYES AND EARS

EYES Set well apart. COLOR Shades of light amber, gray, or blue-gray. When dilated under excitement, may appear almost black.

EARS Long and lobular, slightly folded, set high.

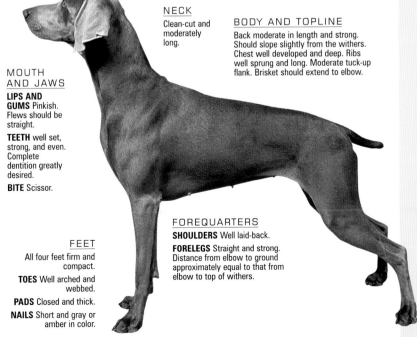

NECK

Clean-cut and moderately long.

BODY AND TOPLINE

Back moderate in length and strong. Should slope slightly from the withers. Chest well developed and deep. Ribs well sprung and long. Moderate tuck-up flank. Brisket should extend to elbow.

MOUTH AND JAWS

LIPS AND GUMS Pinkish. Flews should be straight.

TEETH well set, strong, and even. Complete dentition greatly desired.

BITE Scissor.

FEET

All four feet firm and compact.

TOES Well arched and webbed.

PADS Closed and thick.

NAILS Short and gray or amber in color.

FOREQUARTERS

SHOULDERS Well laid-back.

FORELEGS Straight and strong. Distance from elbow to ground approximately equal to that from elbow to top of withers.

TAIL

Docked. At maturity should measure about 6 in (15cm) and carried so as to express confidence. **KC** Also undocked. Tapering and down to hocks. **FCI/ANKC** Only undocked.

HINDQUARTERS

HINDLEGS well angulated stifles and straight hocks. Muscles well developed.

DEWCLAWS Should be removed from all four feet.

AFGHAN HOUND

The Afghan Hound came to the Western world from the general area of modern-day Afghanistan, where kings had kept kennels of hunting hounds for centuries. Afghans were also commonly bred by tribesmen, who used their hunting skills to provide meat for their families. Local terrain, ranging from barren desert to high mountains, plus extremes of weather and the variety of game available, led to versatility among the dogs. Afghans exhibit good speed when coursing, but with the added advantage of being sure-footed and nimble on very rough terrain. They still retain the ability to jump and turn with amazing dexterity.

Terrier-like, they also dug up and dispatched marmots, whose flesh and pelts were highly valued. Some worked to find and flush out birds for the falcons, like early Pointers in England. This hunting was done independently, with no direct

HEAD AND SKULL

Head of good length, showing much refinement. Skull evenly balanced with foreface. Occipital bone very prominent. Little or no stop. Bony structure falls away beneath eyes, allowing a totally clear outlook.

NECK
Of good length, strong and arched.

EYES AND EARS

EYES Never full or bulgy. COLOR Dark. SHAPE Almond (almost triangular).

EARS Long, approximately level with outer corners of eyes. Leathers reach nearly to end of nose.

MOUTH AND JAWS

MUZZLE Slight prominence of nasal bone gives a slightly Roman appearance.

JAWS Long and punishing. Underjaw shows great strength.

BITE Level (teeth from upper and lower jaw meet evenly, neither overshot nor undershot). The desired level bite is very difficult to breed. A scissor bite is even more punishing and can more easily be bred than a level bite. Scissor bite should not be penalized. **KC/FCI** Scissor bite only.

FOREQUARTERS

SHOULDERS Plenty of angulation so that legs are well set under the dog. Too much straightness of shoulder causes pasterns to break down, a serious fault.

FORELEGS Straight and strong, with great length between elbow and pastern. Elbows held in.

PASTERNS Long and straight.

FEET

Feet turning neither in nor out. Large in both width and length and covered with long, thick, finely textured hair.

TOES Well arched.

PADS Unusually large and well down on the ground.

supervision from humans, who were often left well behind the fast-moving hounds. This habit of depending on its own wits has contributed to the Afghan's independence and intelligence—its ability to figure things out for itself, sometimes to the discomfort of its owner.

Some of these hounds, then referred to as Persian Greyhounds, were taken to England by British soldiers in the late nineteenth and early twentieth centuries and in the 1920s some Afghan Hounds came to the U.S. from the U.K.

As with all sight hounds, the Afghan requires regular exercise, preferably a good run within a fenced area, though it can adjust to long walks on a leash. It should not be allowed to run freely except in a fenced area because, once running, it is quite reluctant to return when called.

GENERAL APPEARANCE
An aristocrat, the Afghan's whole appearance is one of dignity and aloofness, with no trace of plainness or coarseness. The head is carried proudly and the eyes seem to gaze into the distance.

CHARACTERISTICS
An exotic or "Eastern" expression, long silky topknot, peculiar coat pattern, very prominent hipbones, large feet, the impression of an exaggerated bend of stifle due to profuse trousering—all give the Afghan the appearance of a king of dogs that has held true to tradition throughout the ages.

TEMPERAMENT
The Afghan is aloof and dignified, yet gay and loyal with its family.

GAIT/MOVEMENT
When running, the Afghan moves at a gallop, with great elasticity and spring in its smooth, powerful stride. On a loose leash, the Afghan can trot rapidly; it appears to place its hindfeet directly in the footprints of the forefeet, all four feet being thrown straight ahead. Moving with head and tail high, the Afghan possesses great style and beauty.

COAT
The hindquarters, flanks, ribs, forequarters, and legs are well covered with thick, silky hair, very fine in texture. Ears and all four feet are well feathered. From in front of the shoulder, and backward from the shoulders along the saddle from the flanks and the ribs upward, the hair is short and close, forming a smooth back in mature dogs—this is a traditional characteristic of the Afghan Hound. Short hair on cuffs on either forelegs or hindlegs is permissible. The head is surmounted by a topknot of long, silky hair. **KC/FCI/ANKC** No clipping.

COLOR
All colors are permissible. White markings, especially on the head, are undesirable.

SIZE
HEIGHT

males	females
27 in (67.5cm)	25 in (62.5cm)

Both plus or minus 1 in (2.5cm).

KC/FCI/ANKC Up to 1 in (2.5cm) higher.

WEIGHT (approximate)

males	females
60 lb (27.3kg)	50 lb (27.7kg)

BODY AND TOPLINE
Strong, powerful loins, slightly arched and falling away toward the stern, with hipbones very pronounced. Well ribbed and tucked up in flanks. Backline appears practically level from shoulders to loins. Height at shoulder equals distance from chest to buttocks.

TAIL
Not set too high, has a ring or curve at the end. Should never be curled over, nor rest on the back, nor be carried sideways, and should never be bushy.
KC/FCI/ANKC Ring end required.

HINDQUARTERS
Powerful and well muscled.
HINDLEGS Great length between hip and hock. Hocks well let-down, with good angulation of both stifle and hock. Slightly bowed from hock to crotch.

BASENJI

Among the oldest of breeds, and basically unchanged for thousands of years, the Basenji is fairly primitive. It cannot bark like other dogs, and females have only one estrus cycle a year. Basenjis were found living with pygmy tribesmen by an English explorer in the Congo in the 1890s. The tribes valued the dogs highly for their courage, intelligence, and hunting ability. As with many hound breeds, the Basenji was prized for its ability to work successfully alone, or with other dogs, but with no direction from humans. This independent intelligence is still evident in the dog's behavior and attitudes.

The Basenji needs plenty of mental and physical exercise. The former can be met by training for obedience, agility, or tricks, the latter by frequent play in a fenced yard plus long walks on a leash. Most Basenjis are very gentle with well behaved children in their own family.

GENERAL APPEARANCE
A small, shorthaired hunting dog, the Basenji is short backed and lightly built, appearing high on the leg compared to its length. A balanced structure and smooth musculature enable it to move with ease and agility.

CHARACTERISTICS
The Basenji should not bark but it is not mute. The wrinkled forehead, tightly curled tail, and swift, effortless gait are typical of the breed.

TEMPERAMENT
Intelligent and independent, but affectionate and alert; can be aloof with strangers.

GAIT/MOVEMENT
The Basenji moves at a swift, tireless trot. The stride is long, smooth, and effortless; the topline remains level. Coming and going, the straight column of bones from shoulder joint to foot, and from hip joint to pad, remains unbroken, converging toward the centerline under the body.

COAT
The coat is short and fine, and the skin is very pliant.

COLOR
The coat is chestnut red, pure black, tricolor (pure black and chestnut red); or brindle (black stripes on a background of chestnut red), all with white feet, chest, and tail tip. White legs, blaze, and collar are optional. The amount of white should never predominate over primary color. Colors should be rich, clear, and well defined.

SIZE
HEIGHT (from front of chest to point of buttock)

males	females
17 in (42.5cm)	16 in (40cm)

WEIGHT (approximate)

males	females
24 lb (10.9kg)	22 lb (10kg)

KC/FCI/ANKC Prefer females 1 lb (0.5kg) lighter.

EYES AND EARS
EYES COLOR Dark hazel to dark brown. SHAPE Almond shaped, obliquely set and farseeing. Rims dark.
EARS Small, erect, and slightly hooded, of fine texture and set well forward on top of head.

HEAD AND SKULL
Head is proudly carried. Skull is flat, well chiseled, and of medium width, tapering toward the eyes. Foreface tapers from eye to muzzle, with a perceptible stop. When ears are erect, wrinkles appear on forehead which are fine and profuse. Side-wrinkles are desirable but should never become a dewlap.
NOSE Black is greatly desired.

MOUTH AND JAWS
MUZZLE Shorter than skull, neither coarse nor snipy, but with rounded cushions.
JAWS Evenly aligned.
BITE Scissor.

BODY AND TOPLINE
Body balanced, short coupled, with a definite waist. Ribs moderately sprung, deep to elbows, and oval. Slight forechest in front of point of shoulder. Chest of medium width. Back level.

TAIL
Set high on topline, bending acutely forward, and lying well curled over to either side.

NECK
Of good length, well crested.

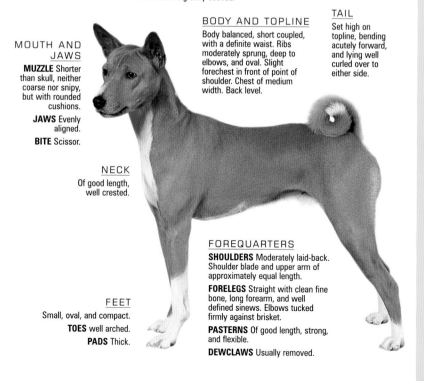

FOREQUARTERS
SHOULDERS Moderately laid-back. Shoulder blade and upper arm of approximately equal length.
FORELEGS Straight with clean fine bone, long forearm, and well defined sinews. Elbows tucked firmly against brisket.
PASTERNS Of good length, strong, and flexible.
DEWCLAWS Usually removed.

FEET
Small, oval, and compact.
TOES well arched.
PADS Thick.

HINDQUARTERS
Medium wide, strong, and muscular.
HINDLEGS Hocks well let-down and turned neither in nor out, with long second thighs and moderately bent stifles.
DEWCLAWS Usually removed.

BASSET HOUND

Early authorities are agreed that the first Basset appeared in litters of normal-sized hounds; essentially it was a genetic mistake. These early dwarf dogs were retained (basset is French for dwarf, or low-set), and bred to establish a distinct strain. By the seventeenth century, the breed had gained fame as a gun dog; its low stature, heft, and dense coat enabling it to push through heavy cover to flush game. It was imported into England in 1866, where it was subsequently developed to perfection by Sir John Everett Millais.

As a family pet, the Basset is one of the most popular of the hound breeds. Its hunting instincts are still very strong so it should not be allowed to roam loose; it does require ample exercise. Training may require patience, because it seems to mull over any command before responding. It makes an excellent companion for adults and children alike.

GENERAL APPEARANCE

The Basset is a short-legged dog, heavier in bone than any other breed. Movement is deliberate, but never clumsy. The dog is capable of great endurance in the field.

CHARACTERISTICS

This dog is heavy-boned, with short legs and a Bloodhound-like head, with drooping ears and extra skin. It typically moves with its tail flagging gaily.

TEMPERAMENT

The Basset is mild-mannered, never sharp or timid, equable in temper, and extreme in its devotion. It is generally a happy dog which gets on well with everyone. Although independent and a slow learner, it retains lessons well.

GAIT/MOVEMENT

The correctly built Basset moves smoothly, powerfully. A scenting dog with short legs, it tends to hold its nose to the ground. Gait is absolutely true, with hindfeet following in line with forefeet and hocks well bent. Forelegs do not paddle, weave, or overlap, and the elbows must lie close to the body.

COAT

The coat is hard, smooth, and short, with sufficient density to offer some protection from brush and weather. The skin is loose and elastic.

COLOR

Any recognized hound color is acceptable, and the distribution of color and markings is of no importance.

SIZE

14 in (35cm)

KC/FCI/ANKC Up to 15 in (38cm).

DISQUALIFICATIONS

- Height more than 15 in (37.5cm) at the highest point of the shoulder blade
- Knuckling over forelegs
- Distinctly long coat

EYES AND EARS

EYES Soft, sad, and slightly sunken, showing a prominent haw. COLOR Brown, preferably dark brown. A lighter colored eye conforming to the dog's general coloring is acceptable but not desirable.

EARS Extremely long, low-set, and folding well over end of nose when drawn forward. Velvety texture, hanging in loose folds with ends curling slightly inward. Set far back on head at the base of skull, but appear to be set on neck in repose.

HEAD AND SKULL

Head large and well proportioned. Length from occiput to muzzle greater than width at the brow. Skull is domed, with a pronounced occipital protuberance. Length from nose to stop approximates the length from the stop to the occiput.

Sides flat and free from cheek bumps. Toplines of muzzle and skull straight and lying in parallel planes, with a moderately defined stop. Skin over the whole head loose, falling in distinct wrinkles over the brow when head is lowered.

NOSE Darkly pigmented, preferably black, with large, wide-open nostrils.

BODY AND TOPLINE

Rib structure long, smooth, and extending well back. Ribs well sprung. Topline straight, level, and free from any tendency to sag or roach.

NECK

Powerful, of good length, and well arched. Dewlap is very pronounced.

TAIL

Not docked. Should be carried gaily with a slight curvature. Hair on underside coarse. **KC/FCI/ANKC** Never gay but saber fashion.

MOUTH AND JAWS

MUZZLE Deep, heavy.

LIPS Darkly pigmented, pendulous, falling squarely in front, in loose, hanging flews.

TEETH Large, sound, and regular.

BITE Scissor or even.
KC/FCI/ANKC Scissor only.

FOREQUARTERS

Chest deep and full, with prominent sternum. Shoulders and elbows set close against ribs. Distance from deepest point of chest to ground should allow free movement and must be no more than one-third the total height at the withers in an adult.

SHOULDERS Well laid-back and powerful.

FORELEGS Short, powerful, heavy in bone, with wrinkled skin.

DEWCLAWS May be removed.

HINDQUARTERS

Very full and well rounded, approximately equal to the shoulders in width. Not light in relation to the overall depth of the body.

HINDLEGS Dog stands firmly on its hindlegs, with a well let-down stifle and no tendency toward a crouching stance. Hocks turning neither in nor out.

DEWCLAWS May be removed.

FEET

Paws massive and heavy. Forefeet inclining equally outward, balancing shoulder width. Hindfeet pointing straight ahead.

PADS Tough, heavy.

TOES Never splayed.

BEAGLE

Hounds were probably the first dogs to hunt with man, and of the hounds, a dog like the Beagle or Foxhound was surely among the earliest types. The Talbot Hounds that were brought from Europe to Britain by William the Conqueror in the eleventh century were the ancestors of the Southern (England) Hound, which in turn produced the Beagle/Foxhound.

Even earlier, so the historians tell us, the Greeks, and later the Romans, kept packs of hounds which were the progenitors of the Foxhounds and Beagles. Successful hound packs existed in pre-Roman Britain; the Welsh Celts kept a medium-sized white hound which was said to have no peer at the time. Henry VIII and his daughter Elizabeth I, both great lovers of the hunt, kept packs of hunting Beagles. Deforestation of the English countryside in the seventeenth and eighteenth centuries provided more open country for horseback riding, and though the deer population decreased with the loss of cover, foxes and hares still provided good

HEAD AND SKULL
Skull should be fairly long, slightly domed at occiput, with broad, full cranium.
NOSE Nostrils large and open.

NECK
Rises free and light from shoulders. Throat clean and free from skin folds. A slight wrinkle below the angle of the jaw may be allowable.

EYES AND EARS
EYES Large, set well apart, and soft, gentle, and houndlike. COLOR Brown or hazel.

EARS Set-on moderately low. Long, reaching nearly to end of nose when drawn out. Fine textured, fairly broad, almost entirely lacking erectile power. Set close to head, with rounded edge slightly inturning to cheek, and rounded at tip.

MOUTH AND JAWS
MUZZLE Medium length, straight and square-cut, the stop moderately defined.

LIPS Free from flews.

JAWS Level.

BITE Not specified.
KC/FCI Scissor.

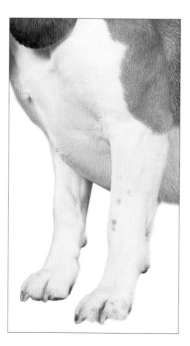

FOREQUARTERS
FORELEGS Straight, with plenty of bone in proportion to size of the hound.

PASTERNS Short and straight.

hunting. By the nineteenth century Beagles were present in several sizes, including one as small as 9 inches (22.5cm) high. These "pocket Beagles" became very popular, even with the royal family. From 1880 onward Beagles were imported to the U.S., and over time they developed into the more familiar larger hounds. Beagles bred for the show ring in the U.S. have benefited from concerted efforts to produce the beautiful, sound dog of today.

Modern field Beagles are still excellent, happy hunters. This breed is not aggressive; it is small enough to travel easily and large enough to fill a spot on the sofa. A clean little dog, it is very responsive to fair and consistent training.

→ GENERAL APPEARANCE

A miniature Foxhound, the Beagle is solid and big for its inches, with the wear-and-tear look of a hound that can last in the chase and follow its quarry to the death.

→ CHARACTERISTICS

The Beagle is a square hound, with a soft expression and a gaily carried tail.

→ TEMPERAMENT

Merry and equable. A keen hunter but otherwise not aggressive. Some bark excessively and all will roam to hunt if allowed.

→ COAT

The coat is close and hard, and of medium length.

→ COLOR

The Beagle is found in any true hound color.

→ SIZE

In the U.S., Beagles are divided into two varieties—Under 13 inches and Over 13 inches but Not Exceeding 15 inches.

HEIGHT

13 in   15 in
(32.5cm)   (37.5cm)

KC/FCI/ANKC Only one variety, 13–16 in (32.5–40cm).

→ DISQUALIFICATION

■ Height over 15 inches

BODY AND TOPLINE

Shoulders sloping, clean, muscular, not heavy or loaded. Chest deep and broad. Back short, muscular, and strong. Loins broad and slightly arched. Ribs well sprung.

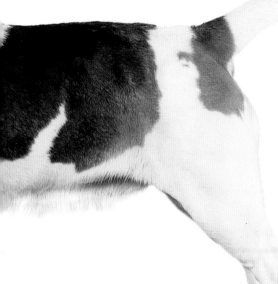

TAIL

Set moderately high, carried gaily, but not turned forward over the back; with a slight curve. Short compared with size of the hound, and a brush. **KC/FCI** Tip of tail white.

HINDQUARTERS

Hips strong and well muscled.

HINDLEGS Thighs strong and well muscled. Stifles strong and well let-down. Hocks firm, symmetrical, and moderately bent.

FEET

Close, round, and firm.
PADS Full and hard.

BLOODHOUND

It is known that Bloodhounds were found around the Mediterranean and came to Europe from Constantinople (modern-day Istanbul). The Bloodhound was long used for deer-hunting in the Ardennes region of France, and both black and white hounds were bred at the Flemish monastery of St. Hubert (this breed is called the Chien de Saint Hubert by the FCI). In the 1100s, the most powerful members of European society kept packs of Bloodhounds with which they rode to hunt. Because of the great care taken to keep the pedigrees of these hounds pure, the dogs came to be called the "blooded" (meaning "aristocrats") hounds. The Bloodhound is a stubborn, strong, and tough animal, and while not popular as a pet, it has proved invaluable as a search-and-rescue dog, and as a police-trailer. It needs a lot of exercise, preferably within a fenced area or on leash.

HEAD AND SKULL

Head narrow in proportion to length, and long in proportion to body, tapering slightly from temples to end of muzzle. Appears flattened at the sides and nearly equal in width throughout the entire length. Topline of skull nearly in same plane as foreface. Length from end of nose to stop not less than from stop to back of occipital peak.

WRINKLE The head is furnished with an amount of loose skin, which in nearly every position appears superabundant, but more so when the head is carried low. Skin falls into loose, pendulous ridges and folds, especially over forehead and sides of face.

NOSE Nostrils large and open.

TAIL

Tail is long and tapering, set-on rather high.

EYES AND EARS

EYES Deeply sunk in their orbits. Lids assume a lozenge shape, due to weight of heavy flews. **KC/ANKC** Eyes neither sunken nor prominent. COLOR Deep hazel (preferred) to yellow, corresponding to general tone of the animal.

EARS Thin and soft to touch, extremely long, set very low, falling in graceful folds.

BODY AND TOPLINE

Shoulders muscular and well sloped backward. Ribs well sprung. Chest well let-down between forelegs, forming a deep keel. Back and loins strong, the latter deep and slightly arched.

NECK

Long.

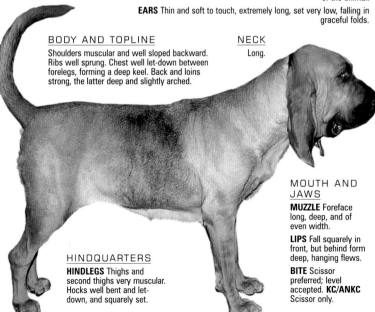

MOUTH AND JAWS

MUZZLE Foreface long, deep, and of even width.

LIPS Fall squarely in front, but behind form deep, hanging flews.

BITE Scissor preferred; level accepted. **KC/ANKC** Scissor only.

HINDQUARTERS

HINDLEGS Thighs and second thighs very muscular. Hocks well bent and let-down, and squarely set.

GENERAL APPEARANCE

The Bloodhound possesses, to a marked degree, every point and characteristic of those dogs which hunt by scent. It is very powerful and stands over more ground than is usual with hounds of other breeds.

CHARACTERISTICS

This is a medium-sized dog of determination and great strength,whose loose skin (especially about the head and neck) and gaily carried stern are distinctive. The skin is thin to the touch.

TEMPERAMENT

The Bloodhound is extremely affectionate, neither quarrelsome with companions nor with other dogs. By nature it is somewhat shy and equally sensitive to kindness or correction by its master, but is strong-willed and can be stubborn.

GAIT/MOVEMENT

The gait is elastic, swinging and free, with the stern carried high, but not too much curled over the back.

COAT

Not mentioned in standard.

COLOR

Colors are black-and-tan, liver-and-tan, and red. A small amount of white is permissible on the chest, feet and tip of stern.

SIZE

HEIGHT (mean average)

males	females
26 in	24 in
65cm	60cm

HEIGHT (range)

males	females
25–27 in	23–25 in
(62.5–67.5cm)	(57.5–62.5cm)

The greater height is preferred, provided that character and quality are also combined.

WEIGHT (average)

males	females
90–110 lb	80–100 lb
(40.9–50kg)	(36.4kg–45.5kg)

FCI Slightly taller and heavier males and females preferred.

FOREQUARTERS

FORELEGS Straight and large in bone; with elbows squarely set.

FEET

Strong and well knuckled-up.

BORZOI

The Borzoi was originally known as the Russian Wolfhound in the United States and is identified as the "Borzoi—Russian Hunting Sighthound" by the FCI. The breed dates from about 1650, when the first standard was written by Russian aristocrats, although the history of the Borzoi arguably goes farther back. By the late eighteenth century, the sole purpose of hunts run by members of the Russian aristocracy was to test their Borzoi. These grand hunts lasted until the Russian Revolution in 1917, when most Borzoi were killed. In the 1890s a few Borzoi had been imported into the U.S. and the Borzoi of today is little changed from those which chased and held wolves on the Russian steppes. It still enjoys long runs, and a concerned owner will arrange one at least weekly, along with daily walks on leash. Very intelligent and highly trainable, the Borzoi is an excellent obedience competitor and a pleasant household companion.

→ GENERAL APPEARANCE

Originally bred to course wild game on open terrain, the Borzoi needed a particular structure to chase, catch, and hold its quarry. Special emphasis is placed on sound running gear, strong neck and jaws, courage, and agility.

→ CHARACTERISTICS

The Borzoi is a dog of elegance, graceful in motion or repose. It is a large dog, with obvious strength. It is instantly recognizable by its flowing coat and lines, coupled with its gently arched topline and long head.

→ TEMPERAMENT

A strong and active dog outdoors, the Borzoi is a gentle and quiet companion in the house, noted for its intelligence, dignity, and obedience.

→ GAIT/MOVEMENT

The forelegs must reach well out in front, with the pasterns strong and springy. There should be noticeable drive, with a ground-covering stride from well angulated stifles and hocks, allowing a double-suspension gallop. The dog should give an overall impression of power, endurance, speed, agility, smoothness, and grace.

→ COAT

The coat is long and silky, with feather on the neck, hindquarters, tail, and belly. Seasonal shedding can be heavy.

→ COLOR

Any color or combination of colors is acceptable. **FCI** Not combinations including blue and brown (chocolate).

→ SIZE

HEIGHT

males	females
28 in (70cm)	26 in (65cm)

FCI males 30–33.5in (75–85cm); females 27–31in (68–78cm).

Measurements are the minimum for mature animals. Sizes above these limits should not compromise quality and balance.

WEIGHT

males	females
75–105 lb (34.1–47.4kg)	60–85 lb (27.3–38.6kg)

EYES AND EARS

EYES Set somewhat obliquely, with inner corner midway between tip of nose and occiput. COLOR Dark, with dark eye rims. SHAPE Never round.

EARS Small and fine, lying back on neck when in repose. Raised when at attention.

HEAD AND SKULL

Skull slightly domed, long and narrow, with a barely perceptible stop. Roman-nosed.

NOSE Large and black.

NECK

Clean, free from throatiness, slightly arched, very powerful.

BODY AND TOPLINE

Chest rather narrow, with great depth of brisket. Ribs only slightly sprung, but very deep. Back rising a little at the loins in a graceful curve. Loins extremely muscular, but rather tucked up, owing to the great depth of chest and comparative shortness of back and ribs.

MOUTH AND JAWS

JAWS Long, powerful, and deep.

TEETH Strong and clean. Missing teeth should be penalized.

BITE Even or scissor. **KC** Scissor only.

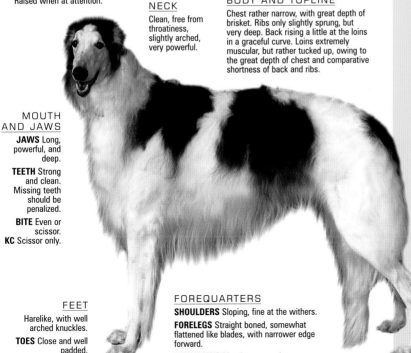

FEET

Harelike, with well arched knuckles.

TOES Close and well padded.

FOREQUARTERS

SHOULDERS Sloping, fine at the withers.

FORELEGS Straight boned, somewhat flattened like blades, with narrower edge forward.

DEWCLAWS May be removed.

HINDQUARTERS

Long, very muscular and powerful. Somewhat wider than the forequarters.

HINDLEGS Strong first and second thighs. well bent stifles. Hocks clean and well let-down.

DEWCLAWS Generally removed.

TAIL

Long, set on, and carried low in a graceful curve.

↓ DACHSHUND

The Dachshund's personality has put it among the most popular of Hounds and consistently in the top ten of AKC breeds. In Germany, the Dachshund's home country, the breed was used to hunt a variety of game and vermin, the name Dachs meaning badger, and Hund, dog. Its structure, unique among dogs, serves it admirably in these pursuits. It can hunt all day, trailing game through rough cover and over long distances. It can maneuver in very tight quarters with no loss of strength or agility, so that it can pursue, seize, and hold its prey until the hunter digs through the earth to find it. There are two sizes, Standard and Miniature, each size found in Smooth, Longhaired, and Wirehaired coat types. In the U.S., unlike Canada, the U.K., Australia, and Europe, all three varieties and two sizes may be interbred. The FCI publishes the German standard for this breed which is very detailed and names three sizes for the Dachshund in addition to the three coat types.

Quite intelligent, the Dachshund responds well to fair and consistent training. Despite its short stature, it requires regular exercise.

ABOVE Wirehaired Standard.
BELOW Wirehaired Miniature.

BODY AND TOPLINE
Trunk long and fully muscled. Abdomen slightly tucked-up. Back level with slightly arched loin. Flat topline impedes rear movement. Breastbone strongly prominent in front so that a dimple appears on either side. Thorax oval, extending downward to the mid-point of forearm. Ribs well sprung. Keel merges gradually into line of abdomen and extends well beyond forelegs, so that lowest point of breastline is covered by front leg.

LEFT Smooth Miniature.
BELOW Smooth Standard.

HINDQUARTERS
Pelvis, thigh, second thigh, and metatarsus ideally the same length, forming a series of right angles. Croup long, rounded, and full, sinking very slightly toward the tail.
HINDLEGS Turn neither in nor out.
DEWCLAWS Should be removed.

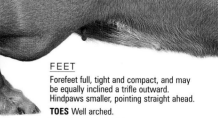

TAIL
Extending without kinks, twists, or pronounced curvature, and not carried too gaily.

FEET
Forefeet full, tight and compact, and may be equally inclined a trifle outward. Hindpaws smaller, pointing straight ahead.
TOES Well arched.
PADS Tough and thick.

ABOVE Longhaired Standard.
RIGHT Longhaired Miniature.

EYES AND EARS

EYES Medium sized. Bridge bones over eyes strongly prominent. COLOR Very dark, with dark rims. SHAPE Almond.

EARS Set near top of head, not too far forward. Moderate length, rounded.

HEAD AND SKULL

Head tapers to tip of nose, in wedge shape. Skull slightly arched, little perceptible stop.

NOSE Preferred color is black. Nostrils should be well open.

NECK

Long, muscular, without dewlap, slight arched at nape.

MOUTH AND JAWS

MUZZLE Slight Roman arch.

LIPS Tightly stretched, covering the lower jaw.

JAWS Open wide and hinged well back of the eyes, with strongly developed bones and teeth.

BITE Scissor. Even bite is a minor fault.

FOREQUARTERS

For effective underground work, front must be strong, deep, long, and cleanly muscled.

SHOULDERS Long, broad, well laid-back, closely fitting at withers and furnished with hard, pliable muscles.

FORELEGS Upper arm same length as and at right angles to shoulder blade, lying close to ribs, with elbows close to body. Forearm short, with hard, yet pliable muscles; slightly curved inward. Joints between forearms and feet (wrists) closer together than shoulder joints, so that foreleg is not perfectly straight.

DEWCLAWS May be removed.

→ GENERAL APPEARANCE

Though short-legged, the Dachshund should never appear crippled, awkward, or cramped in its movement. It is well balanced and robust. Its hunting spirit, good nose, loud tongue, and distinctive build make it well suited for below-ground work.

→ CHARACTERISTICS

Low to ground, long in body, and short of leg, the Dachshund is agile, very quick, and fluid in movement.

→ TEMPERAMENT

Clever, lively, and courageous to the point of rashness. It is never shy or overly aggressive.

→ GAIT/MOVEMENT

Gait is fluid and smooth. If the shoulder assembly is correct, the forelegs reach well forward, freely and without much lift. Correct propulsion of hindlegs is seen when the rear pads are clearly exposed during rear extension.

→ COAT

There are three varieties of coat— Smooth, Wirehair, and Longhair. Each of these varieties is shown in two sizes—Standard and Miniature. Special characteristics of the three coat varieties follow.

SMOOTH—coat short and smooth. (Ears not leathery.)

WIREHAIR—with the exception of jaw, eyebrows, and ears, the whole body is covered with a rough, hard outercoat with finer, somewhat softer, shorter hairs (undercoat). Facial furnishings include a beard and eyebrows.

LONGHAIR—straight or wavy hair is longer under neck and on forechest, underside of body, ears, and behind legs. Hair attains its greatest length on tail and forms a veritable flag.

→ COLOR

All three varieties are found in a wide range of colors and patterns.

→ SIZE

There are two sizes—Standard (usually 16–32 lb [7–14.5kg]) and Miniature (under 11 lb [5kg] as adult).

FCI Follows German standard, which names three chest circumference sizes— Standard (35cm [14in]), Miniature (30–35cm [12–14in]), and Rabbit (up to 30cm [12in]).

→ DISQUALIFICATIONS

- Knuckling-over of forelegs

GREYHOUND

The earliest evidence of the Greyhound's existence is the carvings of Greyhounds hunting that were found in ancient Egyptian tombs dating as far back as 2900 B.C. Around the time of the Bible, Greyhounds were conveyed from the valleys of the Tigris and Euphrates rivers, through Babylon and Persia (modern-day Iraq and Iran), to Afghanistan and Russia. The ancient Celts are believed to have taken these dogs with them through present-day France and Germany, and from there to England, where the Greyhound standard was developed. The Greyhound has chased and caught a wide variety of game over the centuries; most often, hares. In the 1800s, coursing with Greyhounds became the favorite sport of the wealthy in England. Later, with the invention of the mechanical lure for use in circular tracks, Greyhound racing

HEAD AND SKULL
Head long and narrow, fairly wide between the ears, with a scarcely perceptible stop. Little or no development of nasal sinuses.

EYES AND EARS
EYES Bright and intelligent. COLOR Dark.

EARS Small and fine in texture, thrown back and folded (rose-shaped). Semipricked when excited.

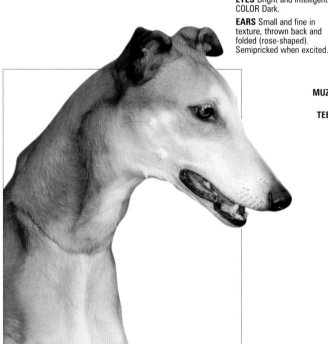

MOUTH AND JAWS
MUZZLE Of good length and powerful, without coarseness.

TEETH Very strong and even in front.

BITE Scissor.

NECK
Long, muscular, without throatiness, slightly arched, and widening gradually into the shoulder.

FOREQUARTERS
SHOULDERS Placed as obliquely as possible. Muscular without being loaded.

FORELEGS Perfectly straight, set well into the shoulders, neither turned in nor out.

PASTERNS Strong.

FEET
Hard and close, rather more harelike than catlike, and well knuckled-up, with good strong nails.

became very popular with the public, especially in the U.S. Unfortunately the popularity of Greyhound racing led to a vast increase in breeding and alleged abuse of surplus dogs.

The prototype of all sighthounds, this speedy, svelte dog, with its long, aristocratic history, can be aloof, but is unstintingly devoted to its family. It needs regular exercise, but not the long runs required by some sporting dogs. Greyhounds enjoy the company of other sight hounds, and most can be taught to tolerate living with smaller animals inside the house.

GENERAL APPEARANCE
The Greyhound is a medium-sized, short-haired dog, obviously built for great speed.

CHARACTERISTICS
The Greyhound is an elegant, strong, and svelte coursing hound. Long and lean in body, graceful and agile in motion.

TEMPERAMENT
Aloof with strangers. Devoted to family.

GAIT/MOVEMENT
Long strides, especially in double-suspension gallop.

COAT
The coat is short, smooth, and firm.

COLOR
Any color or combination is accepted.

SIZE
WEIGHT

males	females
65–70 lb	60–65 lb
(29.5–31.8kg)	(29.5–29.5kg)

KC/FCI/ANKC Males 28–30 in (71–76cm); females 27–28 in (69–71cm).

BODY AND TOPLINE
Chest deep and as wide as consistent with speed. Ribs fairly well sprung. Back muscular and broad. Loins have good depth of muscle, well arched and tucked up.

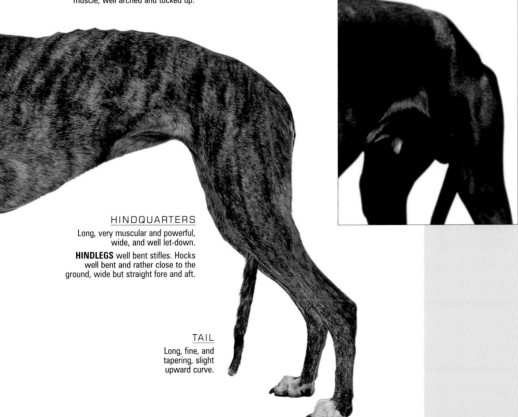

HINDQUARTERS
Long, very muscular and powerful, wide, and well let-down.
HINDLEGS well bent stifles. Hocks well bent and rather close to the ground, wide but straight fore and aft.

TAIL
Long, fine, and tapering, slight upward curve.

IRISH WOLFHOUND

In about 170 B.C., the Roman consul Quintus Aurelius wrote of seven Irish Greyhounds he had received as a gift. Rome was impressed by these giant dogs who could fight as well as they could hunt. The Irish hounds were valued by the Celts for their prowess in hunting the big game that still thrived in the Irish forests. The disappearance of big game in Ireland, and the frequent exportation of the hounds, almost led to the breed's extinction. In the mid-nineteenth century, the breed was restored by George Graham, a British army captain, and the standard for the Irish Wolfhound was established.

The Irish Wolfhound remains the tallest dog breed and, with its rough coat, shaggy brows, and beard, is very impressive. It is a failure as a guard dog because it seems to trust everyone, friend or stranger. It is happiest in the midst of its human family, although serious consideration should be given before acquiring an Irish Wolfhound because of its great size. It must have daily exercise including long walks on a leash and regular romps and runs in a spacious fenced area.

GENERAL APPEARANCE
A rough-coated, Greyhoundlike breed, the Irish Wolfhound is very muscular and strong though gracefully built.

CHARACTERISTICS
Of great size and commanding appearance, the Irish Wolfhound is remarkable in combining power and swiftness with keen sight. It is the largest and tallest of the galloping hounds.

TEMPERAMENT
An equable and calm dog, very devoted and loyal to family. Friendly to all. Generally non-aggressive but may inadvertently cause injury due to size and weight.

GAIT/MOVEMENT
Easy, active, graceful movement. Double- suspension gallop.

COAT
The hair is rough and hard on the body, legs, and head, and especially wiry and long over eyes and underjaw.

COLOR
The recognized colors include gray, brindle, red, black, pure white, fawn, or any other color that appears in the Scottish Deerhound.

SIZE
The following are the minimum requirements for animals over 18 months old. Great size, including height at the shoulder and proportionate length of body, is to be aimed at.

HEIGHT (at shoulder)

males	females
32 in (80cm)	30 in (75cm)

WEIGHT

males	females
120 lb (54.5kg)	105 lb (47.7kg)

BODY AND TOPLINE
Chest very deep. Breast wide. Back long rather than short. Loins arched. Belly well drawn up.

HEAD AND SKULL
Head long. Frontal bones of forehead very slightly raised, with very little indentation between the eyes. Skull not too broad. Head carried high.

HINDQUARTERS
HINDLEGS Muscular thighs, and second thigh long and strong as in the Greyhound. Hocks well let-down and turning neither in nor out.

EYES AND EARS
EYES Moderately full COLOR Dark. **KC** Eyelids black.

EARS Small, Greyhound-like carriage. **KC** "Rose" shaped.

MOUTH AND JAWS
MUZZLE Long, moderately pointed.

BITE Not specified. **KC** Scissor. **FCI/ANKC** Scissor, level acceptable.

NECK
Rather long, very strong, and muscular, well arched, without dewlap or loose skin about the throat.

FEET
Moderately large and round, neither turned inward nor outward.

TOES Well arched and closed.

NAILS Very strong and curved.

FOREQUARTERS
SHOULDERS Muscular, sloping, giving breadth of chest.

FORELEGS Elbows well under, neither turned inward nor outward. Forearm muscular, and whole leg strong and quite straight.

TAIL
Long, slightly curved, moderately thick, well covered with hair.

NORWEGIAN ELKHOUND

The Norwegian Elkhound originated when people lived in caves and dogs earned their keep. It is built as it is because its conformation and behavior helped it to succeed at the hunt. In western Norway, in a cave near Jaeren, two dog skeletons dating from 4000–5000 B.C were found and identified as being definite Elkhound type. A Spitz-type dog, its body shape and heavy coat helped it survive in the very harsh climate and topography of Norway, to act as a guardian of home and flocks, and as a tracker of large game. The Elkhound needed to be hardy, intelligent, and courageous—as it still is.

The Elkhound is a versatile hunting and tracking dog. True to its heritage, it must be trained when young or it may assume the dominant position in the home. It can be a roamer, so needs a fenced yard.

HEAD AND SKULL

Head broad at the ears, wedge-shaped, strong, and dry. Forehead and back of skull only slightly arched. Stop not large, yet clearly defined.

NOSE Bridge straight, parallel to and about the same length as skull.

EYES AND EARS

EYES Medium sized, not protruding. COLOR Very dark. SHAPE Oval.

EARS Set high, firm and erect, yet very mobile. Comparatively small.

BODY AND TOPLINE

Body short, closely-coupled. Rib cage accounts for most of length. Chest deep, moderately broad. Brisket level with points of elbows. Ribs well sprung. Loins short and wide, with very little tuck-up. Topline straight and strong.

NECK

Medium length, muscular, with a slight arch and no loose skin on the throat.

TAIL

Set high, tightly curled, and carried over centerline of back. Thickly and closely haired, with no brush.

MOUTH AND JAWS

MUZZLE Thickest at base and tapering evenly without being pointed.

LIPS Tightly closed.

BITE Scissor bite.

FOREQUARTERS

SHOULDERS Sloping with elbows closely set-on.

FORELEGS Well under body, medium in length, and substantial, but not coarse in bone. Legs straight.

PASTERNS Strong and only slightly bent.

HINDQUARTERS

HINDLEGS Straight and strong. Thighs broad and well muscled. Moderate angulation at stifle and hock.

FEET

Paws comparatively small, slightly oval. Forefeet turned neither in nor out.

TOES Tightly closed.

PADS Thick.

→ GENERAL APPEARANCE

The Norwegian Elkhound is a hardy, gray hunting dog. A typical northern dog, it is of medium size and substance, square in shape, close-coupled and balanced in proportions.

→ CHARACTERISTICS

A broad head with prick ears and a gray coat. The tail is tightly curled over the back.

→ TEMPERAMENT

Bold and energetic, the Elkhound is an effective guardian yet normally friendly. It has great dignity and independence of character.

→ GAIT/MOVEMENT

The gait is characteristic of an active dog constructed for agility and endurance. At a trot the stride is even and effortless, and the back remains level.

→ COAT

The coat is thick, hard, weather-resistant, and smooth-lying. It is made up of a soft, dense, wooly undercoat and coarse, straight covering hairs. It is short and even on the head, ears, and front of legs, and longest on the back of the neck, buttocks, and underside of the tail. The coat is not altered by trimming, clipping, or artificial treatment. Trimming of whiskers is optional.

→ COLOR

Gray, preferably medium gray. The undercoat is clear, light silver, as are the legs, stomach, buttocks, and the underside of the tail. The gray body hair is darkest on the saddle and lighter on the chest, mane, and distinctive harness mark (a band of longer guard hairs from shoulder to elbow). The muzzle, ears, and tail tip are black, the muzzle shading to lighter gray over the forehead and skull.

→ SIZE

Animals should be square in profile.

HEIGHT

males	females
20½ in (51.25cm)	19½ in (48.75cm).

WEIGHT (approximate)

males	females
55 lb (25kg)	48 lb (21.8kg)

KC/FCI/ANKC Males 51 lb (20kg); females 44 lb (17lb).

→ DISQUALIFICATION

■ Any overall color other than gray

PETIT BASSET GRIFFON VENDÉEN

A recent addition to the Hound Group in the U.S., the Petit Basset Griffon Vendéen is an old French breed. The breed's name also describes it—petit ("small"), basset ("dwarf" or "low set"), griffon ("rough or wire coat"), and Vendéen is the region where the breed developed. The Vendée region has rocky terrain and coarse, wild brush. To hunt there successfully a dog needed a rough, protective coat, short stature, a solid body to push through rough cover, but sufficient height to chase rabbits in the open. All this describes the Petit.

This dog is not a wirehaired Basset Hound, nor is it a dwarf. Rather, it is a miniature version of the Grand Basset Griffon Vendéen, in both size and shape. There are twenty-eight breeds of hunting hounds in France; many, like the Petit and Grand Basset Griffon Vendéen, are two size variations of the same breed. They were generally bred for hunting in a specific area and a written standard was not considered crucial, even for dog show judging. The first official standard was written in 1898 and included both Grand and Petit. A

TAIL
Medium in length, set-on high, strong at the base, and tapering regularly. Well furnished with hair and carried proudly like the blade of a saber. Tip of tailbone should reach approximately to hock joint.

HINDQUARTERS
HINDLEGS well defined second thigh. Moderate angulation at stifle and hock. Strong and muscular, with good bend of stifle. Hocks short and well angulated, perpendicular from hock to ground.
DEWCLAWS May be removed.

FEET
Not too long. Slight turnout of forefeet acceptable. Hindfeet must point straight ahead.
PADS Hard and tight.
NAILS Strong and short.

BODY AND TOPLINE
Muscular, somewhat longer than tall. Chest deep, with prominent sternum. Ribs moderately rounded, extending well back. Loins strong, muscular. Topline level with a slight arch over loins. Withers and croup should be equidistant from the ground.

new standard was written in 1909, dividing the Petit and Grand into two types. At that time they were differentiated by size and by the fact that some Petits had crooked forelegs. In 1950 the Petit Basset Griffon Vendéen was designated a separate breed in France with its own standard, but until 1975 the two breeds could still be interbred, resulting in both sizes appearing in one litter.

The Petit is a very appealing dog with a passion for hunting. More like a terrier than a typical hound in outlook, it is curious, determined, and quite intelligent—in short, not a dog drawn to inactivity. Its exercise requirements are met by long daily walks, plus a romp in a safely fenced yard. It responds well to consistent training.

GENERAL APPEARANCE

A scent hound developed to hunt small game over difficult terrain. Compact, tough, and robust in construction. It has an alert outlook, lively bearing, and a good voice which is freely used.

CHARACTERISTICS

The rough, unrefined outline, proudly carried head with long eyebrows, beard, and mustache, and the compact, casual, and rather tousled appearance, with no part exaggerated and all parts in balance, distinguish this breed.

TEMPERAMENT

The Petit Basset is a happy extrovert, bold and independent yet willing to please.

GAIT/MOVEMENT

Movement should be free at all speeds. The front action is straight, with good reach, and the hind action is parallel, with great drive.

COAT

The coat is rough, long without exaggeration, and harsh with a thick, shorter undercoat. It is never silky or wooly. The overall appearance is casual and tousled. Clipping or scissoring are prohibited.

COLOR

The color is white with markings in any combination of lemon, orange, black, tricolor, or grizzle.

FCI Colors: hare, wolf, badger, or wild boar.

SIZE

The dog is approximately 50 percent longer than tall when measured from sternum to buttocks versus withers to ground.

HEIGHT

males	females
13–15 in (32.5–37.5cm)	13–15 in (32.5–37.5cm)

A ½ in (1.25cm) tolerance in either direction is allowed.

FCI 34–38 cm (13–15in) ±1cm (2½ in).

DISQUALIFICATION

- Height of more than 15½ in (38.75cm) at the withers

HEAD AND SKULL

Head carried proudly. Longer than wide, in a ratio of approximately 2:1. Skull domed and oval-shaped. Well cut away under the eyes, with a well developed occipital protuberance. Stop clearly defined.

NOSE Black and large.

EYES AND EARS

EYES Surmounted by long eyebrows, standing forward, but not obscuring eyes. COLOR Large and dark, showing no white. Red of lower eyelids should not show.

EARS Supple, narrow, and fine, covered with long hair, folding inward. Leathers reach almost to end of nose. Set-on low, not above line of eyes.

NECK

Long and strong, without throatiness.

MOUTH AND JAWS

MUZZLE Slightly shorter than length of head from stop to occiput.

LIPS Covered by long hair, forming a beard and mustache.

JAWS Underjaw strong and well developed.

BITE Scissor preferred; level acceptable. **FCI** Scissor only.

FOREQUARTERS

SHOULDERS Clean and well laid-back.

FORELEGS Upper arm approximately equal in length to shoulder blade. Elbows close to body. Length of leg from elbow to ground should be slightly less than half the length from withers to ground. Should be straight, but a slight crook is acceptable. Leg is strong and well boned.

PASTERNS Strong and slightly sloping.

DEWCLAWS May be removed.

RHODESIAN RIDGEBACK

Developed by Boer farmers in South Africa, the dog now known as the Rhodesian Ridgeback probably came from crosses of dogs brought from Europe in the seventeenth and eighteenth centuries, including Bloodhounds, Foxhounds, Greyhounds, Great Danes, Mastiffs, Pointers, and assorted terriers. The farmers needed an all-purpose dog, equally adept at flushing out game birds, assisting in hunts for large animals, and guarding home and family, while at the same time being a devoted companion.

In the 1700s, a semiwild dog kept by the Hottentot people provided valuable attributes to the developing breed. This dog excelled at hunting and added hardiness—an ability to handle drastic temperature changes, limited water, and the physical hardships of this wild country. It had a characteristic ridge of hair growing in the reverse direction along its spine—like a cowlick. This ridge became a defining characteristic of the new breed.

Some Boer dogs went to big-game hunters in Rhodesia in 1877 and proved very valuable in hunting lions from

HEAD AND SKULL

Skull flat and rather broad between the ears. Stop reasonably well defined. Face free of wrinkles when in repose.

NOSE Color should harmonize with color of body hair and eyes—black nose with dark eyes and darker coat; brown or liver nose with amber eyes and the lighter wheaten coat.

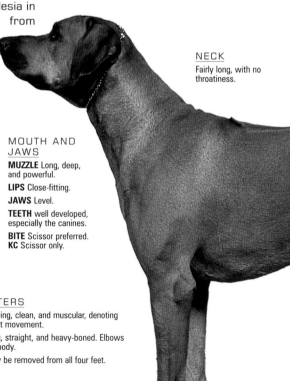

EYES AND EARS

EYES Set well apart, bright, and showing intelligence. COLOR Dark with black nose and darker coat; amber with brown or liver nose and lighter wheaten coat. SHAPE Round.

EARS Set high, medium-sized, wide at base, tapering to rounded point, and carried close to head.

MOUTH AND JAWS

MUZZLE Long, deep, and powerful.

LIPS Close-fitting.

JAWS Level.

TEETH well developed, especially the canines.

BITE Scissor preferred. **KC** Scissor only.

NECK

Fairly long, with no throatiness.

FOREQUARTERS

SHOULDERS Sloping, clean, and muscular, denoting speed and efficient movement.

FORELEGS Strong, straight, and heavy-boned. Elbows must be close to body.

DEWCLAWS May be removed from all four feet.

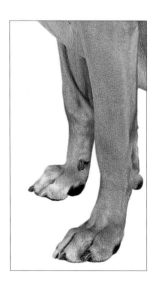

FEET

Compact.

TOES Well arched, with hair between them.

PADS Round, tough, and elastic.

horseback; the dogs chased and harassed lions until the hunters approached. This required great courage, intelligence, speed, and endurance—all of which the breed still has in abundance.

The Ridgeback is the only breed in the Hound group considered a guard dog in addition to having hunting capability, both by sight and scent, as befits its heritage. It makes an excellent companion for an experienced dog owner. It requires obedience training and regular exercise to avoid behavior problems. This is a very strong dog, and it can be determined to the point of dominating a careless or inconsistent owner.

GENERAL APPEARANCE

A strong, powerful, and active dog, symmetrical and balanced in outline. It should be slightly longer than it is tall. An adult should be handsome and athletic, capable of great endurance with a goodly amount of speed.

CHARACTERISTICS

The ridge is considered the characteristic feature of the breed.

TEMPERAMENT

A typical adult Ridgeback has an even, dignified temperament. The Ridgeback is devoted to its family and somewhat reserved with strangers. It tends not to be excessively noisy. It responds well to consistent and fair training, which it needs in order to be a satisfactory companion. This dog is strong and determined (as follows from its developmental history) and can dominate an uncertain or inconsistent owner.

GAIT/MOVEMENT

At a trot, the back remains level, and the stride is efficient, unrestricted, long and free. Reach (with the forelegs) and drive (with the hindlegs) show power. Shows great endurance and balance at the run.

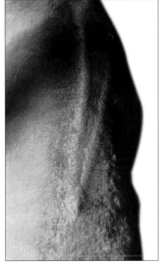

COAT

The coat should be short and dense, sleek and glossy in appearance, but neither wooly nor silky.

COLOR

The only permitted colors are light wheaten to dark red wheaten over the entire body. A little white on the chest and toes is permissible, but excessive white there, on the belly, or above the toes, is undesirable. Less white is generally preferred. Some dogs have black hairs interspersed on the head or muzzle, which is acceptable unless the black covers the eyes, forming a mask.

SIZE

HEIGHT

males	females
25–27 in (62.5–67.5cm)	24–26 in (60–65cm)

WEIGHT

males	females
85 lb (38.6kg)	70 lb (31.8kg)

FCI/ANKC Males 80 lb (36.5kg); females 70 lb (32 kg).

DISQUALIFICATIONS

- Absence of ridge

BODY AND TOPLINE

Chest not wide, but very deep. Ribs moderately well sprung, never rounded. Back powerful, firm, strong, muscular with slightly arched loins. Preferred condition is hard and muscular, giving the appearance of strength and endurance.

TAIL

Strong at base and tapering to end. Carried with a slight curve upward, never curled over the back or gay.

HINDQUARTERS

Muscles clean and well defined.
HINDLEGS Hocks well let-down.

RIDGE

The hallmark of this breed, the ridge along the spine must be clearly defined, tapering, and symmetrical. It should start immediately behind the shoulder blades and continue to a point between the prominence of the hips. It should contain two identical crowns (whorls) directly opposite each other and at the top edge of the ridge. The crowns should not extend down more than one-third of the ridge.

SALUKI

The Saluki has been called the Royal Dog of Egypt, but its history goes back long before the time of the Pharaohs. The Saluki was bred for centuries, and the breed of today is essentially the same as that depicted on tomb carvings in the Upper Nile Valley, dating back thousands of years. The Arabs continued the tradition of breeding for perfection of form, stamina, and hunting ability. Treasured for its functional beauty and because, as a hunter, it provided meat for its owner, it was allowed inside the Bedouin's tent and was treated as a valuable member of the family.

Despite its fragile appearance, the Saluki is very tough and hardy. As a sight hound it locates game through vision, but it also has a good nose. It runs with great speed and agility, jumping and climbing in pursuit of game. It is docile and fairly easy to train, but as a sight hound, it should never be allowed to roam. It is very gentle with considerate children, but may prove too undemonstrative as a playmate.

GENERAL APPEARANCE
A medium-sized dog of grace and symmetry. Its great speed and endurance, coupled with strength and agility, enable it to catch and kill gazelle or other quarry over deep sand or rocky mountains.

CHARACTERISTICS
A graceful and elegant dog, the Saluki is also strong and active. It is Greyhound-like in outline, but with elegant feathers on ears, legs, and tail.

TEMPERAMENT
The Saluki is gentle and dignified, aloof with strangers, but devoted and quietly affectionate with its owners.

GAIT/MOVEMENT
A sound Saluki has great speed, endurance, agility, and jumping ability. Double-suspension gallop. Trot is slightly springy.

COAT
The coat is smooth, soft, silky, and of moderate length. There are slight feathers on the legs and the back of the thighs, and sometimes a slight wooly feather on the thigh and shoulder. The smooth variety is similar but is completely lacking in feathering.

COLOR
The colors of both varieties are white, cream, golden, red, grizzle-and-tan, tricolor (white, black and tan), and black-and-tan.

SIZE
HEIGHT
males
23–28 in
(57.5–79cm)

Females may be considerably smaller, this being very typical for the breed.

EYES AND EARS
EYES Large, but not prominent. COLOR Dark to hazel. SHAPE Oval.

EARS Long, covered with long, silky hair hanging close to skull, and mobile.

HEAD AND SKULL
Head long and narrow. Skull moderately wide between ears, not domed. Stop not pronounced.
NOSE Black or liver.

HINDQUARTERS
Strong, with hipbones well set apart and stifle moderately bent.
HINDLEGS Hocks low to ground, showing galloping and jumping power.

BODY AND TOPLINE
Chest deep and moderately narrow. Back fairly broad, with muscles slightly arched over loins.

MOUTH AND JAWS
TEETH Strong and level.

NECK
Long, supple, and well muscled.

FOREQUARTERS
SHOULDERS Sloping and set well back, well muscled without being coarse.

FORELEGS Straight and long from elbow to knee.

TAIL
Long, set-on low, and carried naturally in a curve. Well feathered on underside, with long silky hair, not bushy.

FEET
Of moderate length, the whole being strong and supple.
TOES Long, well arched, and well feathered between the toes.

SCOTTISH DEERHOUND

Another breed showing clear Greyhound ancestry, the Scottish Deerhound's (called the Deerhound by the KC, ANKC, and FCI) main function was in the hunt. Dogs resembling Greyhounds were found in Britain by the third century A.D., and already some were being used on large game; those that became Irish Wolfhounds on wolves, bear and deer in Ireland, and those that became Deerhounds on large stags in Scotland. Both these dogs were bred for strength and speed. The exclusivity of ownership in Scotland almost led to the breed's demise, however, until the McNeil brothers set about saving the breed. Succeeding breeders have worked to maintain the historic type of Scottish Deerhound with much success. A very easy dog to live with, despite its large size, the Scottish Deerhound is content merely to be with its owner. However, because of its hunting instincts, it should never be allowed to roam unsupervised.

GENERAL APPEARANCE

The Deerhound resembles a rough-coated Greyhound, but is of larger size and bone.

CHARACTERISTICS

This dog is a shaggy, gray coursing hound of great size.

TEMPERAMENT

An active and willing courser outdoors, but quiet indoors. It is gentle and devoted to its family, but aloof with strangers. It is very sensitive and never aggressive or argumentative.

GAIT/MOVEMENT

Movement should be easy, active, and true.

COAT

The hair on the body, neck, and quarters is harsh and wiry, and about 3–4 in (7.5–10cm) long. On the head, breast, and belly it is much softer. There should be a slight fringe on the insides of the forelegs and hindlegs but nothing approaching "feather." The ideal coat is thick, close-lying, ragged, and crisp to the touch.

COLOR

Dark blue-gray is the preferred color. Next come the darker and lighter grays and brindles (darker shades preferred), or the yellow and sandy red, or red fawn with black ears and muzzle. White is condemned, but a white chest and white toes are acceptable.

SIZE

HEIGHT

males	females
30–32 in (75–80cm)	28 in (70cm)

Larger size is not faulted as long as symmetry is maintained, without coarseness.

WEIGHT

males	females
85–100 lb (38.6–45.5kg)	75–95 lb (34.1–43.2kg)

DISQUALIFICATIONS

■ White blaze on head or white collar

HEAD AND SKULL

Head long, broadest at ears, narrowing slightly to eyes, with muzzle tapering more decidedly to nose. Skull flat rather than rounded, with very slight rise over eyes but nothing approaching a stop.

NOSE Black (blue in some blue-fawns) and slightly aquiline. A good mustache of rather silky hair and a fair beard.

EYES AND EARS

EYES Moderately full. COLOR Dark, dark brown, brown, or hazel. Rims of eyelids must be black.

EARS Set-on high. Folded back, Greyhound-like, when in repose. Raised above head in excitement, without losing the fold. Soft, glossy, like a mouse's coat to touch, and the smaller the better. Must be black or dark colored..

NECK

Should be long, but not extreme, and strong. Nape very prominent where head is set on. Throat clean.

BODY AND TOPLINE

General formation of body like a Greyhound, but of larger size and bone. Chest deep rather than broad, not too narrow or slab-sided. Loins well arched.

MOUTH AND JAWS

MUZZLE Should be pointed.

BITE Teeth and lips level.

KC/FCI Scissor.

FOREQUARTERS

SHOULDERS Well sloped. Shoulder blades well back with not too much width between them.

FORELEGS Broad and flat, with good broad forearms and elbows. Must be as straight as possible.

TAIL

Tolerably long, tapering, and reaching to within 1½ in (3.75cm) of ground and about the same below hocks. Dropped down or curved when dog is still; curved when dog is in motion or excited, but in no case lifted out of line of the back.

HINDQUARTERS

Drooping and as broad and powerful as possible. Hips set wide apart.

HINDLEGS Stifles well bent, with great length from hip to hock, which should be broad and flat. All this facilitates the double-suspension gallop of these running hounds.

FEET

Close and compact.

WHIPPET

The Whippet is among the youngest of the sight hound breeds. It was developed in England in the late 1800s from a combination of small Greyhounds and various rat terriers. Much later, Italian Greyhound crosses were added, giving the flowing lines and elegance found in today's Whippet. The Whippet was bred in the coal-mining districts of England, initially for poaching rabbits and other small game for the family table. Wagers were placed on the dogs in "snap-dog" competitions, the winner being the dog that snapped up the greater number of rabbits in a confined space.

Later, when the Industrial Revolution forced many of these miners into the cities, where rabbits were unavailable, Whippet racing became popular. The Whippet was first brought to the U.S. by English millworkers, and for many years the area around Lawrence and Lowell, Massachusetts, with their huge fabric mills, was the center of American Whippet racing. Later the sport moved south to Baltimore, Maryland. Races are run over short distances; although the Whippet is among the fastest of animals (getting up to 35 miles/5km per hour), it can sustain this speed only briefly.

The Whippet does far more than race. It is easy to train, doing very well in obedience competition. This willingness to please also makes it simple for a novice to handle at dog shows. An eager rabbit courser, it is also an adept ratter. More importantly, it is a delightful family companion, quiet and clean. Not given to excessive barking, it still performs as a

BODY AND TOPLINE
Back broad, firm, and well muscled, having length over the loins. Backline runs smoothly from withers with a natural arch, not too accentuated, beginning over loins and carrying through over croup—arch is continuous without flatness. Brisket very deep, reaching almost to elbow. Ribs well sprung, but no suggestion of barrel shape. Space between forelegs filled in so that there is no appearance of a hollow between them. Definite tuck-up.

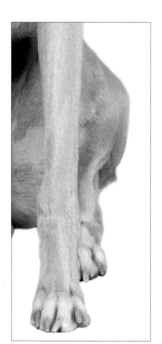

HINDQUARTERS
Long and powerful.
HINDLEGS Thighs broad and muscular. Stifles well bent; muscles long and flat, and carry well down toward the hock. Hocks well let-down and close to the ground.
DEWCLAWS May be removed.

FEET
More harelike than catlike, but both acceptable.
TOES Should be long, close, and well arched.
NAILS Strong.

TAIL
Long and tapering, reaching to hipbone when drawn between hindlegs. Carried low with only a gentle curve upward when dog is in motion. Should not be carried higher than top of back.

GENERAL APPEARANCE

A medium-sized sight hound, giving the appearance of elegance and fitness, denoting great speed, power and balance without coarseness. The dog is built for speed and work, and all forms of exaggeration should be avoided.

CHARACTERISTICS

Symmetry of outline, muscular development, and a powerful gait are characteristic. The dog should convey an impression of beautifully balanced muscular power and strength.

TEMPERAMENT

Amiable, friendly, and gentle; capable of great intensity during sporting pursuits.

GAIT/MOVEMENT

The gait is low, free-moving, and smooth, with good reach in the forequarters and strong drive in the hindquarters. The forelegs move forward close to the ground to give a long, low reach, and the hind legs have strong propelling power.

COAT

The coat is short, close, smooth, and firm.

COLOR

Immaterial.

SIZE

Length from forechest to buttocks should be equal to or slightly greater than height at withers. Moderate bone throughout.

HEIGHT (ideal)

males	females
19–22 in (47.5–55cm)	18–21 in (45–52.5cm)

KC/FCI/ANKC Prefer slightly smaller.

DISQUALIFICATIONS

- Deviation of more than ½ in (1.25cm) above or below stated height limits
- Blue or wall eyes
- Undershot or overshot ¼ in (0.5cm) or more
- Any coat other than short, close, smooth, and firm in texture

watch dog, warning of approaching strangers. It tends to be very sensitive, both physically and emotionally, so definitely avoid rough treatment.

Its grace, charm, and temperament account for the Whippet being the most popular of the sight hounds. A Whippet's coat requires very little care; a weekly rub-down with a hound glove should suffice. Weekly teeth, ear, and nail care finish the job. Its comfort and well-being will be assured by regular exercise, affectionate care, and a soft, draft-free bed—preferably close to its owner's.

NECK
Long, clean, muscular. Well arched with no suggestion of throatiness.

HEAD AND SKULL
Keen, intelligent, alert expression. Skull long and lean, fairly wide between ears, with stop scarcely perceptible.

NOSE Entirely black. **KC/FCI/ANKC** Color of nose to suit coat color.

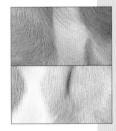

EYES AND EARS
EYES COLOR Large and dark. Both must be the same color. Fully pigmented eyelids desirable.

EARS Rose ear, small and fine-textured. Thrown back and folded along neck in repose. Fold should be maintained at attention.

MOUTH AND JAWS
MUZZLE Long and powerful, denoting great strength of bite, without coarseness.

TEETH White and strong.

BITE Tight scissor.

FOREQUARTERS
SHOULDERS Shoulder blade long and well laid-back, with flat muscles, allowing for moderate space between shoulder blades at peak of withers. Upper arm of equal length, placed so that elbow falls directly below withers. Points of elbows should point straight back.

FORELEGS Straight, appearing strong and substantial.

PASTERNS Strong, slightly bent, flexible.

DEWCLAWS May be removed from all four feet.

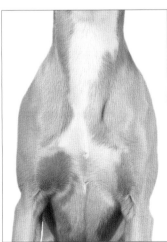

AKITA

One of many Spitz-type breeds from Japan, the Akita almost became extinct several times. The largest and best-known of the Japanese breeds, it can be very swift and is also a powerful swimmer.

The modern Akita probably traces its beginning to a project started by a Japanese noble who was exiled to the island of Honshu centuries ago. The Akita Prefecture, at the northern end of the island, has fiercely cold and snowy winters. The newly exiled ruler issued a challenge to his nobles to breed a hunting dog of size and strength, with great versatility, intelligence, and the hardiness needed to thrive in that harsh climate. They produced the Akita.

The Akita in the seventeenth and eighteenth centuries was valued as a hunter of bear, deer, and wild boar. Members of the nobility developed the breed and only nobles could own it. Great ceremony surrounded the care and feeding of the Akita. A special vocabulary was used to discuss the dogs, and each dog had an assigned and elaborately costumed caretaker. After World War II, many American servicemen who saw and admired Akitas in Japan brought the dogs home with them, and thus the breed became established in the U.S.

This is an intelligent, dominant breed that is also independent, stubborn, and strong. It is aggressive toward other dogs unless trained to tolerance when young and well controlled as an adult. The Akita totally focuses its devotion on its family and will guard it to the best of its ability. This is

TAIL

Large and full, set high and carried over back or against flank in a three-quarter, full, or double curl, always dipping to or below level of back. On a three-quarter curl, tip drops well down flank. Root large and strong. Tailbone reaches hock when let-down. Hair coarse, straight, and full, with no appearance of a plume.

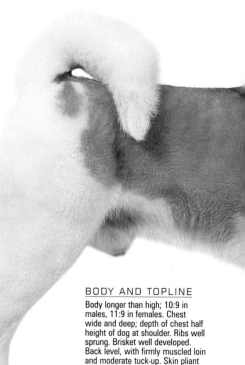

HINDQUARTERS

Width, muscular development, and bone comparable to that of forequarters.

HINDLEGS Upper thighs well developed. Stifle moderately bent. Hocks well let-down, turning neither in nor out.

DEWCLAWS Generally removed.

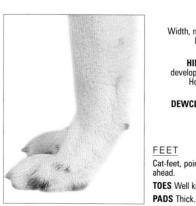

FEET

Cat-feet, pointing straight ahead.

TOES Well knuckled-up.

PADS Thick.

BODY AND TOPLINE

Body longer than high; 10:9 in males, 11:9 in females. Chest wide and deep; depth of chest half height of dog at shoulder. Ribs well sprung. Brisket well developed. Back level, with firmly muscled loin and moderate tuck-up. Skin pliant but not loose.

not a dog for everyone, but in the hands of an experienced owner who is willing and able to train and control it consistently and fairly, an Akita can be an excellent companion.

The Akita needs regular exercise, either a daily run in a safely fenced area or a long jog on a leash. If it receives sufficient exercise and training, it should not be obstreperous in the house. It should never be forced to live tied up or penned in because it needs constant interaction with its owners to maintain the best relationship.

GENERAL APPEARANCE
Large, powerful, and alert, with much substance and heavy bone.

CHARACTERISTICS
The broad head, forming a blunt triangle, with a deep muzzle, small eyes, and erect ears is characteristic of the breed, as is the large, curled tail.

TEMPERAMENT
Alert and responsive, dignified and courageous, but aggressive toward other dogs.

GAIT/MOVEMENT
The gait is brisk and powerful, with strides of moderate length. The back remains strong and level.

COAT
The Akita has a double coat, the undercoat being thick, soft, dense, and shorter than the outercoat. The outercoat is straight, harsh, and standing somewhat off the body. Hair on the head, legs, and ears is short. That at the withers and rump is approximately 2 in (5cm), slightly longer than on rest of body, except the tail, where the coat is longest and most profuse.

COLOR
Any color, including white, brindle, or pinto, is acceptable. Colors should be brilliant and clear, and markings well balanced, with or without a mask or blaze. The undercoat may be a different color from the outercoat.

SIZE
HEIGHT

males	females
26–28 in (65–70cm)	24–26 in (60–65cm)

DISQUALIFICATIONS
- Butterfly nose or total lack of pigmentation on nose
- Drop or broken ears
- Noticeable undershot or overshot
- Sickle or uncurled tail
- Deviation of more than 1 in (2.5cm) below preferred height

NECK
Thick, muscular, and comparatively short. A pronounced crest blends in with base of skull.

HEAD AND SKULL
Head massive but in balance with body. Skull flat between ears and broad. Head forms blunt triangle when viewed from above. Stop well defined. A shallow furrow extends well up forehead.

NOSE Broad and black. Liver permitted on white Akitas, but black preferred.

EYES AND EARS
EYES Small, deep set. Eye rims black and tight. COLOR Dark brown. SHAPE Triangular.

EARS A characteristic of the breed. Strongly erect and small in relation to rest of head. Triangular, slightly rounded at tip, wide at base. Set wide on head, but not too low, and carried slightly forward over eyes in line with back of neck.

MOUTH AND JAWS
MUZZLE Broad and full.

LIPS Black and not pendulous; tongue pink.

TEETH Strong.

BITE Scissor preferred; level acceptable.

FOREQUARTERS
SHOULDERS Strong and powerful, with moderate layback.

FORELEGS Heavy boned and straight.

DEWCLAWS Not generally removed.

PASTERNS Angle 15 degree forward from vertical.

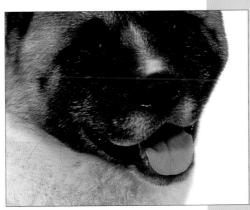

ALASKAN MALAMUTE

Another breed in the Spitz group, the Alaskan Malamute is built to haul heavy freight over rough ground, through deep snow, and for long distances. It is a fairly large dog, very strong and hardy, though not known for speed. This dog was developed and used, probably for centuries, by the tribe of Mahlemet (now Malamute), part of the Inuit (Eskimo) people who lived in northern Canada and in what is now Alaska. The dog's job began when the hunt ended, as it hauled the heavy carcass of seal or polar bear back to the tribal village. With the discovery of Alaskan gold in 1896, the pure Malamute was almost lost. The breed was eventually preserved by the determined efforts of two American breeders, Milton and Eva ("Short") Seeley.

A well trained Malamute is affectionate and faithful to its family. It is strong and determined, so it is important for the owner to establish a position of control when the dog is young, through group obedience classes and consistently fair, firm treatment.

GENERAL APPEARANCE
This substantially built dog has a deep chest and a strong, well muscled body. Heavy-boned with sound legs, good feet, and powerful shoulders.

CHARACTERISTICS
Face markings consist of a cap over the head, the face being either all white or marked with a bar and/or mask. The tail is well furred, plume-like, and carried over the back.

TEMPERAMENT
Affectionate, friendly, loyal, devoted, and playful, but generally impressive by its dignity after maturity.

GAIT/MOVEMENT
The gait is steady, balanced, and powerful. The Malamute is agile for its size. Hindquarters exhibit a strong drive. Forequarters show a smooth, reaching stride.

COAT
The thick, coarse guard coat is never long and soft. The undercoat is dense, from 1–2 in (2.5–5cm) in depth, oily and wooly. Guard coat and under-coat vary in length. Trimming is not acceptable, except to shape feet.

COLOR
Colors range from light gray to black, sable, and shadings of sable to red. The only solid color allowed is all white. White is always the predominant color on the underbody, parts of the legs, the feet and part of the face markings. A white blaze on the forehead and/or collar, or a spot on the nape, is acceptable. Broken colors extending over the body or uneven splashing are unacceptable.

SIZE
A natural range of size exists. Length of body from point of shoulder to rear point of pelvis is longer than height from ground to top of withers.

HEIGHT

males	females
25 in (62.5cm)	23 in (57.5cm)

KC Prefers a slight larger dog—males 25–28 in (62.5–70cm); females 23–26 in (57.5–65cm).

WEIGHT

males	females
85 lb (38.6kg)	75 lb (34kg)

DISQUALIFICATIONS
- Blue eyes

EYES AND EARS
EYES Obliquely placed in skull and medium-sized. COLOR Brown. SHAPE Almond.

EARS Small in proportion to skull. Triangular in shape and slightly rounded at tips. Set wide apart on outside back edges of the skull, on line with upper corner of eye.

HEAD AND SKULL
Head broad and deep. Skull broad, moderately rounded between ears, gradually narrowing and flattening as it approaches eyes, rounding to moderately flat cheeks. Slight furrow between eyes.

BODY AND TOPLINE
Chest well developed. Body compactly built but not short-coupled. Back straight and gently sloping to hips. Loin hard and well muscled.

NECK
Strong and moderately arched.

TAIL
Carried over back when dog is not working. Not curled tight against the back. Well furred, with the appearance of a waving plume.

MOUTH AND JAWS
MUZZLE Large in proportion to skull, diminishing slightly in width and depth from junction with skull.

LIPS Close fitting.

JAWS Broad.

BITE Scissor.

FOREQUARTERS
SHOULDERS Moderately sloping; **FORELEGS** Heavily boned and muscled, straight to the pasterns. **PASTERNS** Short, strong, and slightly sloping.

HINDQUARTERS
HINDLEGS Broad and heavily muscled through thighs. Stifles and hock joints moderately bent. Hocks well let-down.

DEWCLAWS Should be removed.

FEET
Large, of "snow-shoe" type.

TOES Tight, well arched, giving firm, compact appearance. Protective growth of hair between toes.

PADS Thick and tough.

NAILS Short and strong.

BERNESE MOUNTAIN DOG

One of four Swiss Mountain Dogs, and arguably the most popular, the Bernese is the only one with a longish coat. The Berner probably originated from the large Mastiff-type dogs that accompanied the Roman armies when they invaded Switzerland two thousand years ago. These were bred with native flock-guarding dogs to produce a large, sturdy dog capable of surviving the Alpine weather. The offspring of these crosses proved adept at a variety of tasks—as drovers and herders, cart-pullers, and guardians of flocks and farms. The Bernese Mountain Dog is a courageous watchdog, and some are now used in avalanche control.

Nowadays primarily a family pet, it is sensitive, intelligent, and very responsive to consistent training. It is reserved with strangers, yet very gentle and affectionate with its family. Most are compatible with other animals. As a house pet, it needs ample indoor space and is most content in the midst of family activities.

GENERAL APPEARANCE
A sturdy, balanced, and large dog. It is intelligent, strong, and agile enough to perform draft and droving work. Males appear masculine and females distinctly feminine.

CHARACTERISTICS
A striking, tri-colored, large dog, the Bernese has a powerful body and a moderately long coat.

TEMPERAMENT
Self-confident, alert and good-natured, the Bernese is never sharp nor shy. It should stand steady, though it may remain aloof to the attentions of strangers.

GAIT/MOVEMENT
The natural working gait is a slow trot. However, in keeping with its use in draft and droving work, it is capable of speed and agility. There is good reach in front and the powerful drive from the rear. There is no wasted action.

COAT
The coat is thick, moderately long, and slightly wavy or straight. Undue trimming is discouraged.

COLOR
The Bernese is tri-colored, the ground color being jet black and the markings rich rust and clear white. Symmetry of markings is desirable. There is a white blaze and a muzzle band. A white marking on the chest typically forms an inverted cross. The tail tip is white. White on the feet is desirable but must not extend higher than the pasterns.

SIZE
HEIGHT

males	females
25–27 in (62.5–67.5cm)	23–26 in (57.5–65cm)

Though appearing square, it is slightly longer in body than it is tall.

DISQUALIFICATIONS
- Blue eye color
- Any ground color other than black

TAIL
Bushy and carried low when in repose. An upward swirl is permissible when dog is alert. Tailbones should reach to hock joint or below.

BODY AND TOPLINE
Chest deep and capacious, with well sprung, not barrel-shaped, ribs. Brisket reaches at least to the elbows. Back broad and firm. Loin strong. Croup broad, rounded to tail insertion. Topline level from withers to croup.

HEAD AND SKULL
Skull flat on top and broad, with a slight furrow and a well defined, but not exaggerated stop.
NOSE Always black.

NECK
Strong, muscular, and of medium length.

EYES AND EARS
EYES With close-fitting eyelids. COLOR Dark brown. SHAPE Oval.

EARS Medium-sized, set high, triangular in shape, gently rounded at tip. Ears hang close to head.

MOUTH AND JAWS
MUZZLE Strong and straight.

LIPS Clean. Flews only slightly developed.

TEETH Full dentition.

BITE Scissor.

HINDQUARTERS
HINDLEGS Thighs broad, strong, and muscular. Stifles moderately bent. Hocks well let-down and straight.

DEWCLAWS May be removed.

FEET
Round and compact, turning neither in nor out.

TOES Well arched.

FOREQUARTERS
SHOULDERS Moderately laid-back, flat-lying, well muscled, and never loose.

FORELEGS Straight and strong, with elbows well under shoulder when dog is standing.

PASTERNS Sloping very slightly, but never weak.

DEWCLAWS May be removed.

WORKING

BOXER

The modern Boxer is a powerfully built, streamlined, and elegant animal. It can be traced back to the Molossus (or Mastiff-type) dog that is the progenitor of most of the large, powerful breeds. These Mastiff-type dogs spread through Europe with the invading Roman armies, their job being to drive and guard the great herds of cattle necessary to feed the hungry legions. Early Boxer-type dogs were used either to hunt boar, deer, or bear, or in the "sports" of bull-baiting and dog-fighting, then popular throughout Europe. Later these dogs were employed by butchers to manage cattle before slaughter. By about 1900, Boxers had begun to gain favor for other purposes. While still courageous and protective, it is now a reliable family companion. This is a strong and protective breed, so it is very important to start obedience training when the dog is quite young.

GENERAL APPEARANCE
A medium sized, square-built dog of good substance, with a short back, strong limbs, and a short, tight-fitting coat. It combines strength and agility with elegance and style.

CHARACTERISTICS
The chiseled head, with its broad, blunt muzzle, is the distinctive feature, and great value is placed upon its being of proper form.

TEMPERAMENT
Instinctively a "hearing" guard dog, the Boxer's bearing is alert, dignified, and self-assured. It is fundamentally playful, yet patient and stoical with children. Deliberate and wary with strangers, it will exhibit fearless courage if threatened. Intelligent, loyal, and affectionate, it is receptive to training.

GAIT/MOVEMENT
The smoothly efficient, level-backed, ground-covering stride has powerful drive and adequate reach.

COAT
The coat is short and shiny, lying smooth and tight to the body.

COLOR
Colors are fawn and brindle. Fawn varies from light tan to mahogany. Brindle ranges from sparse but clearly defined black stripes on a fawn background to a heavy concentration of black stripes such that the fawn background barely, but clearly, shows through.

SIZE
HEIGHT

males	females
22½–25 in (56.25–62.5cm)	21–23½ in (52.5–58.75cm)

Distance from front of forechest to rear projection of upper thigh should equal height from top of withers to ground.

KC/ANKC Specifies weight—males 66–70 lb (30–32kg); females 55–60 lb (25–27kg).

DISQUALIFICATIONS
- Any color other than fawn or brindle
- Total of white markings exceeding a third of entire coat

RIGHT Uncropped ears
BELOW Cropped ears

BODY AND TOPLINE
Forechest well defined and visible from the side. Brisket deep, reaching down to elbows. Depth of body at brisket equals half the height of dog at withers. Ribs extend far to rear, well arched but not barrel-shaped. Back short, straight, and muscular. Loin short and muscular. Slight tuck-up. Topline smooth, firm, and slightly sloping.

HEAD AND SKULL
Head should be clean, with no deep wrinkles. Wrinkles are on forehead when ears are erect, and folds run downward from lower edge of stop on both side of muzzle. Top of skull slightly arched. Forehead shows slight indentation between eyes and forms a distinct stop. Cheeks relatively flat.

NOSE Broad and black.

EYES AND EARS
EYES Not too small, too protruding, or too deep set. COLOR Dark brown.

EARS Set at highest point of sides of skull. Cropped, cut rather long and tapering. Raised when alert.

NECK
Round, of ample length, muscular, clean, without dewlap. Elegant arch.

TAIL
Set high, docked, and carried upward.

HINDQUARTERS
In balance with forequarters.

HINDLEGS Thighs broad and curved. Breech musculature hard and strongly developed. Upper and lower thighs long. Well angulated stifle. Well let-down hock.

DEWCLAWS None.

MOUTH AND JAWS
MUZZLE Top of muzzle not concave. Tip of nose slightly higher than root of muzzle. Chin perceptible.

LIPS Meet evenly in front. Upper lip thick and padded.

JAWS Upper jaw broad, very slightly tapering to front. Lower jaw undershot.

BITE Canines far apart and of good length to keep front of muzzle broad and squarish. Incisors of lower jaw are in a straight line.

FOREQUARTERS
SHOULDERS Long and sloping. Upper arm long, approaching a right angle to shoulder blade.

FORELEGS Long, straight, and firmly muscled.

PASTERNS Strong and distinct, slightly slanting, but almost perpendicular to ground.

DEWCLAWS May be removed.

FEET
Compact, turning neither in nor out.

TOES Well arched.

↓
BULLMASTIFF

The Bullmastiff breed results from a fairly recent combination of the Mastiff and the English Bulldog, and was developed to protect gamekeepers from attacks by poachers on large estates and game preserves. What was needed was a large, strong, swift dog that would wait silently with the keeper, give chase on command, and subdue but not bite the poacher. The Mastiff had proved to be too slow and not sufficiently aggressive for this task. The Bulldog of that time, though fast and aggressive, was too small to stop an adult man. A combination of these two breeds proved an excellent solution. Bullmastiffs were breeding true to type and accepted for registration by the KC in 1924. Because of their eventual size and heft, this dog must be trained while young. It will probably be stronger than its owner by the age of one year, so obedience and leash training is crucial to prevent management problems with the adult dog.

EYES AND EARS

EYES Medium-sized. **COLOR** Dark.

EARS Medium-sized, V-shaped and carried close to cheeks. Set-on wide and high, level with occiput and cheeks, giving a square appearance to skull. Darker in color than the body.

HEAD AND SKULL

Skull large, with a fair amount of wrinkle when alert. Broad, with well developed cheeks. Forehead flat. Stop moderate.

NOSE Black, with large, broad nostrils.

BODY AND TOPLINE

Body compact. Chest wide and deep, with ribs well sprung and well set down between forelegs. Back short. Loin wide, muscular, and slightly arched, with fair depth of flank. Topline straight and level between withers and loin.

NECK

Slightly arched, of moderate length, very muscular, and almost equal in circumference to skull.

TAIL

Set on high, strong at root, and tapering to hocks. May be straight or curved, but never carried hound-fashion.

MOUTH AND JAWS

MUZZLE Broad and deep; length approximately a third that of entire head. Dark muzzle preferred.

LIPS Flews not too pendulous.

JAW Preferably level or slightly undershot.

TEETH Canines large and set wide apart.

FOREQUARTERS

SHOULDERS Muscular but not loaded, sloping.

FORELEGS Straight, well boned, and set well apart. Elbows turn neither in nor out.

PASTERNS Straight.

→ GENERAL APPEARANCE

Shows great strength, endurance, and alertness, and is powerfully built. It should appear to be 60 percent Mastiff and 40 percent Bulldog.

→ CHARACTERISTICS

A very powerfully built dog with a distinctive head that clearly shows its progenitors' influence.

→ TEMPERAMENT

Fearless and confident, yet docile, the Bullmastiff combines reliability and intelligence with a willingness to please.

→ GAIT/MOVEMENT

Gait is free, smooth, and powerful. Reach and drive indicate maximum use of the dog's moderate angulation. The back remains firm and level and there is no twisting in or out at the joints.

→ COAT

The coat is short and dense.

→ COLOR

Colors are red, fawn, or brindle. A very small white spot on the chest is allowed.

KC/FCI Any shade of red, fawn, or brindle. Black muzzle essential with dark marking around the eyes contributing to expression.

→ SIZE

HEIGHT

males	females
25–27 in (62.5–67.5cm)	24–26 in (60–65cm)

WEIGHT

males	females
110–130 lb (50–59kg)	100–120 lb (45.5–54.5kg)

The more substantial dog is preferred, within stated limits. Nearly square in proportion.

HINDQUARTERS

Broad and muscular, with well developed second thighs.

HINDLEGS Moderate angulation at hocks.

FEET

Medium-sized.

TOES Round and well arched.

PADS Thick and tough.

NAILS Black.

DOBERMAN PINSCHER

In the 1880s, Herr Louis Dobermann was a tax-collector in Thuringia, Germany. He decided to develop a breed of dog to protect him on his collecting rounds. In a relatively short time, and using a combination of the old German Shepherd, Rottweiler, German Pinscher ("terrier" in German) and Manchester Terrier, he had his Doberman Pinscher. He later added either Weimaraner or Pointer, and also Greyhound for more speed and elegance. By 1899, the (German) National Doberman Pinscher Club was organized; a year later the breed standard was written and agreed on, and the breed was given official recognition. In 1908, Dobermans were

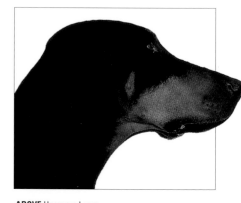

ABOVE Uncropped ears
BELOW and LEFT Cropped ears

HEAD AND SKULL
Head long and dry, resembling a blunt wedge, and widening gradually toward base of ears. Top of skull flat, with slight stop. Cheeks flat and muscular.

NOSE Solid black in black dogs, dark brown in reds, dark gray in blues, dark tan in fawns.

NECK
well arched neck proudly carried, well muscled, and dry. Length proportional to body and head.

EYES AND EARS
EYES Moderately deep set. COLOR Iris, of uniform color, ranging from medium to darkest brown in black dogs. In reds, blues, and fawns the color of the iris blends with that of the markings. The darkest shade is always preferred. SHAPE Almond.

EARS Normally cropped and carried erect. Upper attachment of ear is on a level with top of skull. If not cropped, set high and hang folded close to cheek.

MOUTH AND JAWS
MUZZLE Topline extends parallel to topline of skull.

LIPS Lying close to jaws.

JAWS Full and powerful, well filled under eyes.

TEETH Strongly developed and white.

BITE True scissor, with 42 correctly placed teeth; 22 in lower jaw and 20 in upper jaw.

FOREQUARTERS
Chest broad, with forechest well defined.

SHOULDERS Shoulder blade sloping forward and down at 45 degree angle to ground, meeting upper arm at angle of about 90 degrees. Length of upper arm and shoulder blade equal. Height from elbow to withers approximately equal to height from ground to elbow.

FORELEGS Straight, muscled, and sinewy, with heavy bone. Elbows close to brisket.

PASTERNS Firm, almost perpendicular to ground.

DEWCLAWS May be removed.

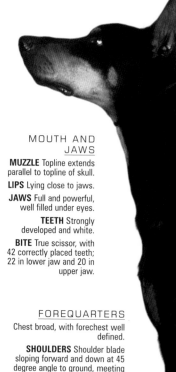

imported into the U.S. Serious importation to the U.K. did not occur until 1948, after World War II. Wherever Herr Dobermann's dogs went, they were met with acclaim because of their intelligence and devotion to their owner.

A well bred Doberman is aristocratic in bearing, its clearly etched outline being both beautiful and functional. Always ready to defend its owner, it is very affectionate, loyal, and obedient with its own family. Very quick to learn, it is an outstanding obedience competitor. Since the Doberman can be dominant, a wise owner will initiate training when the puppy is young, and maintain it through the dog's life.

→ GENERAL APPEARANCE
A medium-sized dog, square in body, the Doberman is compact, muscular, and powerful, and capable of great endurance and speed.

→ CHARACTERISTICS
Elegant in appearance, this short-coated, athletic dog usually has cropped ears and a docked tail.

→ TEMPERAMENT
The Doberman is energetic, watchful, determined, alert, fearless, loyal, and obedient.

→ GAIT/MOVEMENT
The free gait is balanced and vigorous, with good reach and drive. The back remains strong and firm.

→ COAT
The coat is smooth-haired, short, hard, thick, and close-lying. An invisible gray undercoat on neck permissible.

→ COLOR
Permitted colors include black, red, blue, and fawn (Isabella). Sharply defined rust on all colors. A white patch on the chest, not exceeding half an inch (1.27cm) square, is permissible.

→ SIZE

HEIGHT

males	females
26–28 in (65–70cm)	24–26 in (60–65cm)

HEIGHT (ideal)

males	females
27½ in (68.75cm)	25½ in (63.75cm)

→ DISQUALIFICATIONS
- Overshot more then ³⁄₁₆ in (0.47cm), undershot more than ⅛ in (0.3cm)
- Four or more missing teeth
- Not of an allowed color

BODY AND TOPLINE
Withers pronounced, forming highest part of body. Back short, firm, muscular at loin, extending in a straight line from withers to slightly rounded croup. Ribs well sprung but flattened at lower end to permit elbow clearance. Brisket reaching to elbow. Belly well tucked up. Loin wide and muscled. Hips broad, breadth of hips being approximately equal to breadth of body at rib cage and shoulders.

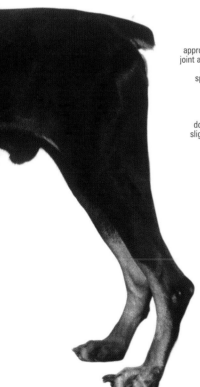

TAIL
Docked at approximately second joint and appears to be a continuation of spine. Carried only slightly above horizontal when dog is alert. **KC** Customarily docked. Undocked: slightly raised when dog is moving.

HINDQUARTERS
Angulation balances that of front. Hip bone falls away from spinal column at an angle of about 30 degrees, for a slightly rounded, well filled-out croup.

HINDLEGS Upper shanks at right angle to hip bones. Long, wide, and well muscled on both sides of thigh. Stifles clearly defined. Upper and lower shanks of equal length.

DEWCLAWS Generally removed.

FEET
Well arched, compact, catlike, turning neither in nor out.

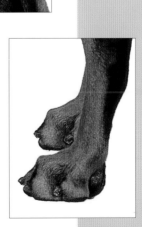

GIANT SCHNAUZER

The Giant Schnauzer is thought to have been developed in southern Bavaria. Local farmers were impressed with the Standard Schnauzer's abilities as a guardian and sheepherder, but they needed a larger dog to work with their cattle and drive them to market. Therefore, they combined larger, smooth-coated drover dogs, rough-coated sheepdogs, black Poodles, black Great Danes and the Bouvier des Flandres with the Standard Schnauzer. Later, Giant Schnauzers were used as guard dogs. Their excellence at this task led to their employment as police dogs in Germany, for which they are still used. Eventually they were valued as companions. The Giant does best with an experienced owner who can provide obedience training when the dog is young.

ABOVE Uncropped ears
BELOW Cropped ears

EYES AND EARS

EYES Medium sized, deep set. Lids tight-fitting. Eyes not hidden by overlong eyebrows. COLOR Dark brown. SHAPE Oval.

EARS When cropped, identical in shape and length, with pointed tips. Set high on skull. When uncropped, V-shaped, button ears of medium length and thickness, set high, and carried rather high and close to head.

HEAD AND SKULL

Head strong, rectangular, elongated; narrowing slightly from ears to eyes, and again from eyes to top of nose. Skull moderately broad between ears. Occiput not prominent. Top of skull flat. Skin unwrinkled. Cheeks flat.

NOSE Large and black.

BODY AND TOPLINE

Body substantial, short-coupled, strong, with great power and agility. Height at withers equals body length from breastbone to point of rump. Loin well developed, as short as possible. Back short, straight, strong, and firm.

NECK

Strong and well arched, of moderate length. No dewlap.

TAIL

Set moderately high and carried high in excitement. Docked to second, or not more than third, joint (approximately 1½–3 in (3.75–7.5cm) long at maturity). **KC** Customarily docked. Undocked: in balance with rest of dog.

MOUTH AND JAWS

MUZZLE Strong. Parallel and equal in length to topskull, ending in a moderately blunt wedge.

LIPS Tight but not overlapping. Black.

TEETH Full complement of sound white teeth (6/6 incisors, 2/2 canines, 8/8 premolars, 4/6 molars).

BITE Scissor.

FOREQUARTERS

Chest medium in width. Ribs well sprung but oval. Breastbone plainly discernible. Brisket descends to elbows.

SHOULDERS Flat, somewhat sloping. High withers; strongly muscled, well laid-back, forming as nearly as possible a right angle with upper arm.

FORELEGS Straight with strong pasterns and good bone. Elbows set close to body.

DEWCLAWS May be removed.

GENERAL APPEARANCE

Should resemble a larger and more powerful version of the Standard Schnauzer. Robust, strongly built, and nearly square in proportions, it is active, sturdy, and well muscled.

CHARACTERISTICS

A large dog, with distinguishing facial furnishings, this dog has a harsh, dense, weather-resistant body coat, in black or pepper-and-salt.

TEMPERAMENT

Combines spirit and alertness with intelligence and reliability. Composed, watchful, courageous, and easily trained, it is deeply loyal to family, playful, amiable in repose, and a commanding figure when aroused.

GAIT/MOVEMENT

The trot is free, balanced, and vigorous, with good reach in front and good drive behind. The back remains strong and flat.

COAT

Hard, wiry, and very dense with a soft undercoat and a harsh outercoat that stands slightly up off the back. There is coarse hair on the top of head, and a harsh beard and eyebrows.

COLOR

Color is solid black or pepper-and-salt—which is a combination of banded hairs. A small white spot on the breast is permitted. All shades from dark iron-gray to silver-gray are acceptable. Every shade of coat has a dark facial mask.

SIZE

HEIGHT

males	females
25½–27½ in	23½–25½ in
(63.75–68.75cm)	(58.75–63.75cm)

The medium sizes are preferred.

FCI Weight 16–20 lb (35–45kg).

DISQUALIFICATIONS

- Overshot or undershot.
- Markings other than specified in standard

HINDQUARTERS

Strongly muscled, in balance with forequarters. Not higher than shoulders. Croup full and slightly rounded.

HINDLEGS Upper thighs slanting and well bent at stifle. Legs from hock joint to feet short, perpendicular to ground.

DEWCLAWS Should be removed.

FEET

well arched, compact, and catlike, turning neither in nor out.

PADS Thick and tough.

NAILS Dark.

GREAT DANE

Dogs resembling the modern Great Dane can be traced back to the fifth century B.C. in Greece and the third century B.C. in Egypt. These dogs were probably the progenitors of early Mastiffs and Irish Wolfhounds, which ultimately spread across Europe with the Romans and Celts, and formed the basis of most of the giant dog breeds we know today. Used as a hunting dog in the pursuit of wild boar, the Great Dane became the national dog of Germany in 1876. An excellent guard and watchdog, the Great Dane is easy to train, requiring no stronger a reprimand than a sharp "No." It is best to avoid rough games with a young Great Dane because it will soon become much larger and could inadvertently cause harm. It gets on well with children but, again because of its size, could injure the very young.

EYES AND EARS

EYES Medium-sized, deep set. Lids tight, with well developed brows. COLOR Dark. SHAPE Almond.

EARS Set high, medium-sized, and of moderate thickness. Folded forward close to cheek. Topline of folded ear should be level with skull. If cropped, length is in proportion to head size and ears are carried uniformly erect.

ABOVE Uncropped ears
BELOW Cropped ears

BODY AND TOPLINE

Withers slope smoothly into a short level back with a broad loin. Chest broad, deep, and well muscled. Forechest well developed. Brisket extends to elbow. well sprung ribs. Underline tightly muscled with a well defined tuck-up. Croup broad and very slightly sloping.

HEAD AND SKULL

Rectangular, expressive, finely chiseled. A strong stop. Planes of skull and of muzzle straight and parallel. Masculinity pronounced in males; female is delicate. Cheek muscles not prominent.
NOSE Bridge as wide as possible.

NECK

well arched, long, muscular. Underline of neck should be clean.

TAIL

Broad at base, tapering uniformly down to hock joint. Falls straight when dog is at rest. When dog is excited it may curve upward, but never above level of back.

MOUTH AND JAWS

MUZZLE Length from tip of nose to center of stop should equal length from center of stop to slightly developed occiput.

TEETH Strong, clean, and with full dentition.

BITE Scissor.

FOREQUARTERS

Strong and muscular.
FORELEGS Shoulder blade strong and sloping, forming close to right angle with upper arm; both should be same length. Elbow half the distance from withers to ground.

PASTERNS Strong, sloping slightly.

DEWCLAWS May be removed.

HINDQUARTERS

Strong, broad, muscular, and well angulated.
HINDLEGS Hocks well let-down.

GENERAL APPEARANCE

A regal appearance, combining dignity, strength, and elegance with great size and a powerful, smoothly muscled body.

CHARACTERISTICS

This giant, majestic dog is so well balanced that it never appears clumsy.

TEMPERAMENT

Spirited, courageous, friendly, and dependable; never timid or aggressive.

GAIT/MOVEMENT

The gait denotes strength and power with long, easy strides. The backline should be level, and there should be a long reach and powerful drive. The elbow or hock joints should not twist in nor out.

COAT

Short, thick, clean, and glossy.

COLOR

BRINDLE—a yellow-gold base, always brindled with strong, black cross-stripes in a chevron pattern. A black mask is preferred.

FAWN—yellow-gold with a black mask.

BLUE—pure steel blue.

BLACK—glossy black; white markings at the chest and toes not desirable.

HARLEQUIN—a pure white base, with black torn patches, well distributed over the entire body.

MANTLE—black and white, with a solid black blanket extending over the body. The skull is black with a white muzzle; a white blaze is optional.

SIZE

HEIGHT (minimum)

males	females
30 in (75cm)	28 in (70cm)

HEIGHT (preferred)

32 in (80cm)	30 in (75cm)

Males more massive throughout than females. Body square in ratio between body height and length. In females a somewhat longer body is permissible. Coarseness or lack of substance are equally undesirable.

DISQUALIFICATIONS

- Danes under minimum height
- Split nose
- Docked tail
- Color other than those described in standard

FEET

Round and compact.
TOES Well arched, pointing neither in nor out.
NAILS Short, strong and dark. May be lighter in harlequins.

Recognized → AKC, ANKC, CKC, FCI, KC

GREAT PYRENEES

The primary function of the Great Pyrenees (called the Pyrenean Mountain Dog by the KC, ANKC, and FCI), another descendent of the old Roman Mastiffs and local herding breeds, was to guard flocks of sheep from predatory bears and wolves, and humans. The dogs worked in pairs on the steep slopes of the Pyrenees Mountains in France and northern Spain. By the fourteenth century, the French nobles of the great fortress chateaux were keeping packs of Great Pyrenees for protection against surprise attacks and to assist jailers in guarding prisoners. The Great Pyrenees was used in World War I for pack service over snow-covered trails, a development of its long-established use as a carrier of contraband between France and Spain. Loyal to its family, the Great Pyrenees learns quickly but may not be easy to train because it tends to think for itself. In the U.S., the breeding of the Great Pyrenees and its recognition by the AKC did not occur until the early 1930s.

GENERAL APPEARANCE
Great overall size and majesty. The Great Pyrenees is sound enough to perform the work of guarding flocks on the slopes of the Pyrenees mountains.

CHARACTERISTICS
The white, or nearly white, weather-resistant coat and double dewclaws on the hindfeet are typical.

TEMPERAMENT
Confident, gentle, and protective. Strong-willed and reserved, the Great Pyrenees is also attentive and fearless.

GAIT/MOVEMENT
Moves smoothly and elegantly, exhibiting both power and agility. Has good reach and strong drive. Ease and efficiency of movement are more important than speed.

COAT
The weather-resistant double coat consists of a long, flat outercoat of coarse hair, straight or slightly waved, lying over a dense, fine, wooly undercoat. The coat is more profuse around the neck and shoulders, forming a ruff or mane. Longer hair on the tail forms a plume, and feathering along the backs of the forelegs and thighs gives a "pantaloon" effect. Correctness of coat is more important than its abundance.

COLOR
Color is white, or white with markings of gray, badger, reddish brown, or varying shades of tan. The undercoat may be white or shaded.

SIZE

HEIGHT

males	females
27–32 in (67.5–80cm)	25–29 in (62.5–72.5cm)

WEIGHT

males	females
100lb (45.5kg)	85lb (38.6kg)

Weights are for a 27 in (67.cm) male and a 25 in (62.5cm) female.

EYES AND EARS
EYES Medium sized, set slightly obliquely. Eyelids are close fitting with black rims. COLOR Rich dark brown. SHAPE Almond.

EARS Small to medium in size, V-shaped, with rounded tips. Set on at eye level. Carried low and close to head.

HEAD AND SKULL
Wedge-shaped with slightly rounded crown. Width and length of skull approximately equal. Slight furrow between eyes. No apparent stop. Bony eyebrow ridges only slightly developed.

NOSE Black.

BODY AND TOPLINE
Chest moderately broad. Ribcage well sprung, oval, and reaching to elbows. Back and loin broad and strongly coupled with some tuck-up. Croup slopes gently with tail set on just below level of back. Backline level.

NECK
Strongly muscled, of medium length, and with minimal dewlap.

TAIL
Tailbones reach to hock. Tail well plumed, carried low in repose, and may be carried over back when aroused. When gaiting, tail may be carried either over back or low; both are equally correct.

HINDQUARTERS
Angulation similar to that of forequarters.

HINDLEGS Upper and lower thighs of same length. Stifle and hock moderately angulated.

PASTERNS Medium length and perpendicular to ground as dog stands naturally.

DEWCLAWS Double dewclaws.

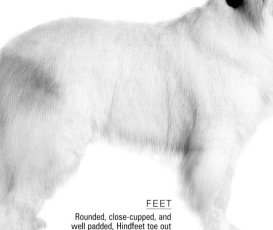

FEET
Rounded, close-cupped, and well padded. Hindfeet toe out slightly (not to be confused with cowhocks).

TOES Well arched.

MOUTH AND JAWS
MUZZLE Approximately equal in length to backskull.

LIPS Tight fitting with the upper lip just covering the lower. Black.

JAWS Strong lower jaw.

TEETH Dropped (receding) lower central incisor teeth are not unusual.

BITE Scissor preferred; level acceptable.

FOREQUARTERS
SHOULDERS Well laid-back, muscular. Upper arm meets shoulder blade at a right angle; they are approximately equal in length. Height from ground to elbow appears approximately equal to height from elbow to withers.

FORELEGS Of sufficient bone and muscle to balance with frame. Elbows close to body.

PASTERNS Strong and flexible.

DEWCLAWS Single.

GENERAL APPEARANCE

A large, massive, and well knit dog. Males are more massive than females. Positive qualities of type and soundness are equally important.

CHARACTERISTICS

Massive, heavy-boned, and powerful. It is a dog of dignity and great power.

TEMPERAMENT

A combination of grandeur, good nature, courage, and docility. Dignity, rather than gaiety is its correct demeanor. Shyness or viciousness should not be condoned.

GAIT/MOVEMENT

The gait denotes power and strength. The rear should have good drive with good reach in front.

COAT

The outercoat is straight, coarse, and moderately short. The undercoat is dense, short, and close-lying. It should not be so long as to produce a "fringe" on the belly, tail, or hindlegs.

COLOR

Colors are fawn, apricot, or brindle. Brindle should have apricot or fawn as a background color, covered by very dark stripes. The muzzle, ears, and nose must be dark, with a similar color around the eye orbits and extending upward between them. A small patch of white on the chest is permitted.

SIZE

HEIGHT (minimum, at shoulder)

males	females
30 in (75cm)	27½ in (68.75cm)

Body rectangular, length from fore-chest to rump being somewhat longer than height at withers. Height should come from depth of body rather than length of leg. Males or females below minimum height a fault.

KC/FCI/ANKC No sizes specified.

MASTIFF

When Caesar invaded Britain in 55 B.C., he encountered Mastiffs fighting alongside their masters. He subsequently sent some back to Rome, where they fought in the huge arenas, designed to entertain the citizenry, and defeated all other fighting dogs. They were also matched against gladiators, as well as bulls, bears, lions, and tigers.

However, the Mastiff's popularity, which has endured for over two thousand years, is due more to its ability as a protector than as a fighter. Later, the Mastiff became popular in Europe, the U.K., and the U.S. as a fighting dog, and in bull- and bear-baiting. By the 1800s, society's view of animals was changing, and these vicious "sports" were banned in England in 1835, though they continued almost unabated for another two decades.

The Mastiff develops its typical personality only through living with maximum human contact and is very good with children. It is easy to train, but because of its extreme bulk it must be well trained before reaching six months.

HEAD AND SKULL

Gives a massive appearance from any angle. Skull broad and somewhat flattened between ears. Forehead slightly curved, showing marked wrinkles. Brows moderately raised. Muscles of temples well developed and those of cheeks extremely powerful. Stop well marked but not abrupt.

NOSE Broad and always dark.

EYES AND EARS

EYES Set wide apart, medium-sized, not prominent. No haw showing. COLOR Brown, the darker the better.

EARS Small in proportion to skull, and V-shaped, with rounded tips. Leather moderately thin. Set widely apart at highest points on sides of skull, lying close to cheeks. Dark in color, the blacker the better.

NECK

Powerful, very muscular, slightly arched, and of medium length. Moderately dry.

BODY AND TOPLINE

Chest deep, wide, well let-down between forelegs, extending at least to elbows. Forechest deep, with breastbone extending in front of point of shoulder. Ribs well rounded. Reasonable tuck-up. Slight rounding over the hips. Loin wide and muscular. Topline straight, level and firm.

MOUTH AND JAWS

MUZZLE Half length of skull. Muzzle broad under eyes and nearly equal in width to end of nose. Dark in color; the darker the better.

LIPS Sufficiently pendulous to show a modified square profile.

JAWS Powerful. Underjaw is broad to the end and slightly rounded. Moderately undershot should not be faulted provided that teeth are not visible when mouth is closed.

BITE Scissor preferred.

FOREQUARTERS

SHOULDERS Moderately sloping, powerful, and muscular, with no looseness. Front and rear angulations should match.

FORELEGS Heavy-boned, straight, strong, and set wide apart. Elbows parallel to body.

PASTERNS Strong and bent only slightly.

HINDQUARTERS

Broad, wide, and muscular.

HINDLEGS Wide apart. Second thighs well developed, leading to strong hock joint. Stifle moderately angulated.

TAIL

Set-on moderately high and reaching to hocks or a little below. Wide at root, tapering to end. Hangs straight in repose, but never carrid over the back when dog is in motion.

FEET

Large, round, and compact.

TOES Well arched.

NAILS Black preferred.

NEWFOUNDLAND

This breed developed on the island of Newfoundland, off the southeastern coast of Canada. Being a strong swimmer, with webbed feet and an oily coat, it could stay longer in the water than other dogs, and had great size and strength, plus intelligence and tractability. The Newfoundland is credited with saving humans from the icy sea, swimming through waters so rough that no human could take a lifeline to a stranded vessel. The Newfoundland thrived on the island and many were exported to England. It became the darling of the British upper classes, treasured as much for its imposing size and gentle demeanor as for its intelligence and docility. Ferocious only when provoked, it was greatly trusted. The Newfoundland is very patient with children, very rarely quarrelsome with other dogs, and tends to watch over other animals and smaller dogs.

GENERAL APPEARANCE

Capable of draft work and possesses natural lifesaving abilities. A large, heavily coated, well balanced dog that is deep-bodied, heavily boned, muscular, and strong.

CHARACTERISTICS

A dog of great size, with a heavy coat and webbed feet.

TEMPERAMENT

Sweetness of temperament is the hallmark of a Newfoundland.

GAIT/MOVEMENT

The dog has good reach, strong drive. Gait is smooth, rhythmic, and ground covering. When moving, there is a characteristic slight roll of the skin.

COAT

The adult Newfoundland has a flat, water-resistant double coat. The outercoat is coarse, moderately long, and full, either straight or with a wave. The undercoat is soft and dense, though less dense in summer or in warmer climates. The hair on the face and muzzle is short and fine. The backs of the legs are feathered and the tail is covered with long, dense hair.

COLOR

Color is secondary to type, structure, and soundness. Colors include black, brown, and gray. The Landseer has a white base coat with black markings. Clear white or white with minimal ticking is preferred.

KC/FCI/ANKC Does not include gray.

SIZE

HEIGHT

males	females
28 in (70cm)	26 in (65cm)

WEIGHT (adult, approximate)

males	females
130–150lb (59–68.2kg)	100–120lb (45.5–54.5kg)

Large size is desirable, but never at the expense of balance, structure and correct gait. Slightly longer than tall when measured from point of shoulder to point of buttocks and from withers to ground.

DISQUALIFICATIONS

■ Colors or combinations of colors not specifically described

EYES AND EARS

EYES Relatively small, deep set, and spaced wide apart. Eyelids fit closely with no inversion. COLOR Dark brown. (Brown and gray dogs may have lighter eyes and should be penalized only to the extent the color affects expression.)

EARS Relatively small and triangular, with rounded tips. Set on skull level with, or slightly above, brow and lying close to head.

BODY AND TOPLINE

Back is strong, broad, muscular, and level from just behind the withers to the croup. Chest is full and deep, with brisket reaching at least to elbows. Ribs well sprung. Flank deep. Croup broad and slopes slightly.

HEAD AND SKULL

Head massive with a broad skull, slightly arched crown, and strongly developed occiput. Cheeks well developed. Free of wrinkles. Slope of stop moderate but brow well developed.

TAIL

Broad at base and strong, without kinks; bone reaches to the hock. Hangs straight or with a slight curve at end when dog is standing relaxed. Carried out, but not curling over back when dog is in motion or excited.

NECK

Strong and long enough for proud head carriage.

MOUTH AND JAWS

MUZZLE Clean-cut, broad throughout its length, and deep. Length from tip of nose to stop, only slightly less than that from stop to occiput. Top of muzzle rounded, and bridge straight or only slightly arched.

TEETH Dropped lower incisors in an otherwise normal bite are only a minor deviation.

BITE Scissor or level.

FEET
Webbed; cat-foot.

FOREQUARTERS

SHOULDERS Muscular, well laid-back. Elbows lie directly below highest point of withers.

FORELEGS Muscular, heavily boned, straight. Distance from elbow to ground equals about half the dog's height.

PASTERNS Strong and slightly sloping.

DEWCLAWS May be removed.

HINDQUARTERS

Rear assembly powerful, muscular, and heavily-boned.

HINDLEGS Thighs broad and fairly long. Stifles and hocks well bent. Hocks well let-down.

DEWCLAWS Should be removed.

PORTUGESE WATER DOG

In centuries past, hardly a Portugese fishing boat left harbor without a Water Dog as part of the crew. Once a common sight along the entire Portugese coast, it is now found in its homeland primarily in the Algarve region. They were taught to herd fish into nets, to retrieve broken nets, and even to carry messages between boats, or between boat and shore. In the 1930s, a wealthy shipping magnate, Dr. Vasco Bensuade, decided to promote the breed as a companion and show dog. Through his efforts, breed clubs were formed, and a breed standard written. The breed was accepted by the AKC in 1981. The Water Dog enjoys the company of adults and children, and is a loyal companion and an alert guard. It wants to be a hard-working dog and requires not only daily exercise but also a job—even if only retrieving a thrown stick.

HEAD AND SKULL

Head distinctively large with exceptional breadth of topskull. Skull slightly longer than muzzle. Top of skull appears domed, with a slight depression in the middle. Forehead prominent, with a central furrow. Occiput and stop well defined.

NOSE Broad, with well flared nostrils. Black in dogs with black, black-and-white, or white coats; various shades of brown in dogs with brown coats.

EYES AND EARS

EYES Medium-sized, set well apart, oblique. Neither prominent nor sunken. COLOR Black or various tones of brown in color. Darker eyes preferred. SHAPE Roundish.

EARS Set well above line of eye. Leathers heart-shaped and thin. Tips do not reach below lower jaw.

MOUTH AND JAWS

MUZZLE Substantial. Wider at base than at nose.

JAWS Strong.

LIPS Thick. No flew. Lips and mucous membranes of roof of mouth, under tongue, and gums quite black, or well ticked with black or with various tones of brown to match coat color.

TEETH Not visible when mouth closed.

BITE Scissor or level.
KC/ANKC Scissor only.

BODY AND TOPLINE

Chest broad and deep, reaching down to elbow. Ribs long and well sprung. Abdomen well held up. Back broad and well muscled. Loin short. Croup only slightly inclined. Topline level and firm.

TAIL

Not docked; thick at base and tapering. Set on slightly below line of back and should not reach below hock.

NECK

Straight, short, round, and held high. Strongly muscled. No dewlap.

FOREQUARTERS

SHOULDERS Well inclined, very strongly muscled.

FORELEGS Strong and straight, with long, well muscled forearms.
PASTERNS Long and strong.
DEWCLAWS May be removed.

HINDQUARTERS

Powerful, well balanced with forequarters. Buttocks well developed.

HINDLEGS Very strongly muscled in upper and lower thighs. Tendons and hocks strong. Metatarsus long.
DEWCLAWS None.

GENERAL APPEARANCE

This medium-sized dog has a robust build that allows for a full day's work in and out of the water. It is a swimmer and diver of exceptional ability and stamina, with a ruggedly built body, and a powerful, thickly-based tail that it uses as a rudder.

CHARACTERISTICS

The Curly or Wavy coat and the long, thick tail with a full-length flag at the end, are characteristic of this breed.

TEMPERAMENT

Spirited, self-willed, brave, and very resistant to fatigue. Intelligent and loyal.

GAIT/MOVEMENT

Short, lively steps when walking. The trot is forward-striding and well balanced.

COAT

The profuse coat of strong, healthy hair covers the whole body evenly, except where the forearm meets the brisket and in the groin area, where it is thinner.

CURLY—cylindrical curls, somewhat lusterless. The hair on the ears is sometimes wavy.

WAVY—falls gently in waves, not curls, and has a slight sheen.

Two clips are acceptable and no preference is given to either.

LION—the middle part and hindquarters, as well as the muzzle, are clipped. The hair at the end of the tail is left at full length.

RETRIEVER—the entire coat is scissored or clipped to follow the outline of the dog, leaving a blanket of hair no longer than 1 in (2.5cm). The hair at the end of the tail is left at full length.

COLOR

Black, white, and various tones of brown; also combinations of black or brown with white. In animals with black, white, or black and white coats, the skin is bluish.

SIZE

HEIGHT

males	females
20–23 in (50–57.5cm)	17–21 in (42.5–52.5cm)

HEIGHT (ideal)

22 in (55cm)	19 in (47.5cm).

WEIGHT

males	females
42–60lb (19.1–27.3kg)	35–50lb (15.9–22.7kg)

Proportion off-square; slightly longer than tall when measured from prosternum to rearmost point of buttocks, and from withers to ground.

KC/ANKC Slightly smaller at top end of scale.

↓
ROTTWEILER

The progenitors of the Rottweiler were the Mastiff-type dogs of Asia that came to Germany with the invading Roman legions somewhere about 74 A.D. Crossing the Alps into southern Germany, the Romans found an area well suited to agriculture and livestock farming. It was here, near the Neckar river, that some of the Romans, with their drover dogs, settled permanently.

The dogs were originally used to guard cattle and as drovers. Their duties included hauling freight carts, guarding the herds at night, preventing straying, driving the herd to market, and then carrying home the master's purse, tied around their neck, on the premise that only a fool would attempt to steal it.

In the mid-1800s, after the advent of railroads, the driving of cattle was prohibited and soon the hauling was taken over by donkeys. As the need for the Rottweiler declined, breeding almost stopped and the population decreased dramatically. In 1921, the Allegmeine Deutsche Rottweiler Klub was formed in an effort to retrieve the breed and the first stud book was published in 1924. The

EYES AND EARS

EYES Medium-sized, with well fitting lids. Moderately deep set, neither protruding nor receding. COLOR Uniform dark brown preferred. SHAPE Almond.

EARS Medium-sized, pendant, triangular in shape. When alert, ears are level with top of skull and appear to broaden it. Set well apart, hanging forward with inner edge lying tightly against head and terminating at approximately mid-cheek.

HEAD AND SKULL

Of medium length, broad between ears. Forehead line moderately arched. Zygomatic arch and stop well developed. Ratio of backskull to muzzle is 3:2. Forehead dry, but some wrinkling may occur when dog is alert.

NOSE Broad rather than round. Always black.

MOUTH AND JAWS

MUZZLE Bridge straight and broad at base, with slight tapering toward tip. End of muzzle broad with well developed chin.

JAWS Strong, broad upper and lower jaws.

LIPS Always black. Corners closed. Preferred inner mouth pigment is dark.

TEETH Strong, correctly placed. 42 in number (20 upper and 22 lower).

BITE Scissor.

NECK

Powerful, well muscled, moderately long, slightly arched, and without loose skin.

FOREQUARTERS

SHOULDERS Long and well laid-back. Upper arm equal in length to shoulder blade. Elbows well under withers. Equal distances from withers to elbows and elbows to ground.

FORELEGS Strongly developed, with straight, heavy bone.

PASTERNS Strong, springy, and almost perpendicular to ground.

DEWCLAWS May be removed.

FEET

Round and compact. Hindfeet somewhat longer.

TOES Well arched, turning neither in nor out.

NAILS Short, strong, and black.

Rottweiler was recognized by the AKC in 1931, and a standard was adopted in 1935. The American Rottweiler Club was formed in 1971, and the breed has grown steadily in popularity since. The breed has retained its basic character and conformation. The Rottweiler is strong, very intelligent, and retains considerable working ability. It is a formidable guard of family and home, and not overly excitable or given to unnecessary barking.

While the Rottweiler makes an excellent companion for an involved and experienced owner/trainer, it is not a dog for everyone. A wise owner will begin obedience training with the young puppy and continue it consistently. The Rottweiler needs exercise daily on leash and relishes mental stimulation. It also needs constant human companionship to reinforce bonding, and for it to be a satisfactory companion.

GENERAL APPEARANCE
A medium-large, robust, and powerful dog, black with clearly defined rust markings.

CHARACTERISTICS
A solid dog, with a docked tail and the appearance of compact strength and agility.

TEMPERAMENT
Calm, confident, and courageous, the Rottweiler has a self-assured aloofness that does not lend itself to immediate and indiscriminate friendships. Has an inherent desire to protect its home and family, and is an intelligent dog of extreme hardness and adaptability.

GAIT/MOVEMENT
This dog is a trotter. Its movement should be balanced, with strong reach and powerful drive. The imprint of the hindfeet should touch that of the forefeet.

COAT
The outercoat is straight, coarse, dense, of medium length, and lying flat. The undercoat should be present on the neck and thighs; it should not show through the outercoat. The coat is shortest on the head, ears, and legs, and longest on breeching. No trimming is allowed.

COLOR
Always black, with rust to mahogany markings. Demarcation between black and rust is clearly defined. The undercoat is gray, tan, or black. Quantity and location of rust markings is important and should not exceed 10 percent of the body color.

SIZE
HEIGHT

males	females
24–27 in	22–25 in
(60–67.5cm)	(55–62.5cm)

Preferred size is mid-range for each. Body slightly longer than height at withers. The ratio of height to length is 9:10. Neither coarse nor shelly. Depth of chest is approximately 50 percent of the dog's height.

KC The taller the better, provided symmetry is maintained.

DISQUALIFICATIONS
- Entropion, ectropion
- Overshot, undershot, or wry mouth
- Unilateral cryptorchid or cryptorchid dogs
- Long coat
- Any base color other than black
- Absence of all markings
- A dog that, in the opinion of the judge, attacks any person in the ring
- Two or more missing teeth

BODY AND TOPLINE
Chest broad and deep, reaching to elbows. Pronounced forechest and well sprung, oval ribs. Back straight and strong. Loin short, deep, and well muscled. Croup broad, of medium length, and only slightly sloping. Slight tuck-up. Back firm and level, extending in a straight line from behind withers to the croup.

TAIL
Tail docked short, close to body, leaving one or two tail vertebrae. Set of tail more important than length. Properly set, it gives an impression of elongation to topline, carried slightly above horizontal when dog is excited or moving. **KC/ANKC** Customarily docked. Undocked: carried as docked but may hang when dog is at rest.

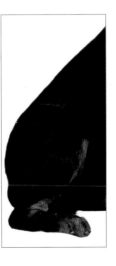

HINDQUARTERS
Angulation balances with forequarters.

HINDLEGS Upper thigh fairly long, very broad, well muscled. Stifle joint well turned. Lower thigh long, broad and powerful, with extensive muscling and a strong hock joint.

PASTERNS Rear pasterns nearly perpendicular to ground.

DEWCLAWS Must be removed.

SAINT BERNARD

The Saint Bernard has been used for over eight hundred years by farmers in the mountain valleys of Switzerland, where it was used as a farm guard, cattle-drover, and to pull carts. It is believed to be descended from the old Asian Molossian dogs (Mastiff-type) dogs that came to Switzerland with the Romans. The dog came to the Hospice of Saint Bernard between 1660 and 1670 and was originally used to pull carts and as a guard dog. The monks found this dog to have an excellent sense of direction, which was especially valuable in the fog and snow typical of high mountain passes. Its keen nose and independent intelligence were invaluable in locating and rescuing travelers lost in the snow. A Saint Bernard should be calm and dignified. It tends to be gentle with children, though not playful. It tends to respond to commands in slow motion. Though stubborn, it is fairly easy to train.

HEAD AND SKULL

Massive skull is wide, slightly arched, with sides sloping in a gentle curve into high cheekbones. Moderate occiput. Supraorbital ridge very strongly developed. Skin of forehead forms noticeable wrinkles. Stop sudden and rather steep.

NOSE Very substantial, broad, and always black.

BODY AND TOPLINE

Withers strongly pronounced. Chest moderately deep, not reaching below elbows. Back very broad, straight to haunches, from there gently sloping to rump; very powerful loin section; slight tuck-up.

EYES AND EARS

EYES Medium-sized, set moderately deep. Lower eyelids form an angular wrinkle toward inner corner. COLOR Dark brown.

EARS Medium-sized and set rather high. Standing slightly away from head at base, then dropping with a sharp bend to side and clinging to head. Flap forms a rounded triangle.

NECK

Set high, very strong, and carried erect when dog is alert. Nape very muscular, appearing rather short. Dewlap of throat and neck pronounced.

MOUTH AND JAWS

MUZZLE Short, does not taper, depth at root must be greater than length. Bridge straight. A wide, well marked shallow furrow runs from over bridge of muzzle root up to occiput.

JAWS Flews of upper jaw are strongly developed and slightly overhanging. Flews of lower jaw must not be deeply pendant.

BITE Scissor or even. Undershot is allowed but not preferred. Black roof to mouth.

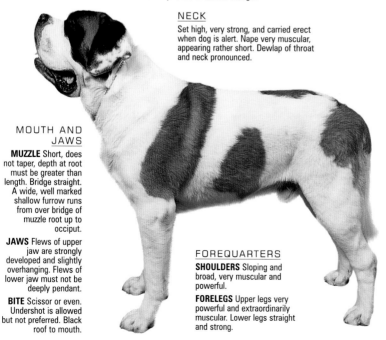

FOREQUARTERS

SHOULDERS Sloping and broad, very muscular and powerful.

FORELEGS Upper legs very powerful and extraordinarily muscular. Lower legs straight and strong.

→ GENERAL APPEARANCE

A powerful, proportionately tall dog, strong and muscular in every part, with a powerful head and intelligent expression.

→ CHARACTERISTICS

This is a large and imposing dog, with either a short or a long coat in a combination of white with red.

→ TEMPERAMENT

Intelligent, independent, calm and gentle. Stubborn.

→ GAIT/MOVEMENT

Not specified.

→ COAT

The coat is very dense. The Short-haired type's coat lies smooth and tough, without feeling rough to the touch. Its thighs are slightly bushy. The root of the tail has longer and denser hair which tapers to the tip. The tail appears bushy. The Longhaired type resembles the Shorthaired, except for the coat, which is of medium length, plain to slightly wavy, never rolled or curly. The hair is wavier on the back, from the haunches to the rump. The tail has dense hair of moderate length. The forelegs are only slightly feathered and the thighs are very bushy.

→ COLOR

Colors are white with various shades of red, red with white, or brindle patches with white markings. Red and brown-yellow are of equal value. It is never of one color or without white.

→ SIZE

HEIGHT (at shoulder, minimum)

males	females
27½ in (68.75cm)	25½ in (63.75cm)

Females are of finer and more delicate build.

TAIL

Starts broad and powerful. Long, very heavy, and ending in a powerful tip. Hangs straight down in repose. Should not be carried erect or rolled over back.

HINDQUARTERS

Well developed.

HINDLEGS Very muscular. Hocks of moderate angulation.

DEWCLAWS Not desirable; if present, they must not obstruct gait. Of no use to dog and may be removed by surgery.

FEET

Broad.

TOES Strong, moderately closed, with rather high knuckles.

SAMOYED

This dog lived for many centuries with a nomadic tribe that left central Asia, roamed through what is now northern Europe, and finally settled in the tundra area near the Arctic Circle. It is from this tribe that the dog gets its name.

Its role was to herd and guard the reindeer that were essential to the tribe's survival and to pull the heavy sleds. It also shared the family's shelter, sleeping with the children to keep them warm in the icy Arctic nights. This long and interdependent relationship between dog and man has given the Samoyed a need for human companionship, and it is only happy when living in the midst of its human family. The breed arrived in the U.K. in around 1900, where Queen Alexandra became a devoted fan and did much to promote it. The first Samoyeds came to the U.S. in 1906; since then the breed has grown in popularity because of its shining white beauty, tractability, and smiling face.

GENERAL APPEARANCE

The Samoyed should present a picture of beauty, alertness, and strength, with agility, dignity, and grace. The coat is heavy. The body is muscular, with a deep chest and well sprung ribs.

CHARACTERISTICS

A Spitz-type breed, the Samoyed has a white or near-white, stand-away double coat and prick ears.

TEMPERAMENT

Intelligent, gentle, loyal, and adaptable, the Samoyed is also alert, full of action, eager to serve, and friendly.

GAIT/MOVEMENT

The Samoyed should trot, not pace. It has a quick, agile stride, with good reach in front and good drive in the rear. The back remains level when trotting.

COAT

The coat is double. The body is well covered with an undergrowth of soft, short, thick, close wool, with longer and harsh hair growing through it to form the outercoat, which stands straight out from the body. Coat forms a ruff round the neck and shoulders (more on males than females). The coat is weather-resistant and quality is considered more important than quantity. Females do not carry as long a coat, and it is softer in texture.

COLOR

Samoyeds should be pure white, white and biscuit, cream, or all biscuit.

KC Does not give "all biscuit" as option.

SIZE

HEIGHT

males	females
21–23½ in	19–21 in
(52.5–58.75cm)	(47.5–52.5cm)

Bone is heavier than would be expected for a dog of this size. Not so heavy as to appear clumsy, nor so light as to appear racy.

DISQUALIFICATIONS

- Any color other than pure white, cream, biscuit, or white and biscuit
- Blue eyes

BODY AND TOPLINE

Chest deep, with ribs well sprung but not barrel-chested, reaching point of elbows. Back is straight to loin, medium in length, very muscular. Loin strong and slightly arched. Dog is approximately 5 percent longer than height. Females slightly longer in body than males. Belly tightly muscled. Croup full and slightly sloping.

EYES AND EARS

EYES Placed well apart and deep set, with lower lid slanting toward base of ears. Dark eye rims preferred. COLOR Dark. SHAPE Almond.

EARS Strong and thick, erect, triangular, and slightly rounded at tips. Should not be large nor pointed, nor small and "bear-eared". Ears mobile, with inside well covered with hair.

HEAD AND SKULL

Skull wedge-shaped, broad, slightly crowned. Stop well defined but not too abrupt.

NOSE Black preferred, but brown, liver or a Dudley nose not penalized. Color of nose can change with age or weather.

NECK

Strong, well muscled, and carried proudly erect with a graceful arch.

TAIL

Moderately long, reaches to hock when let-down. Profusely covered with long hair, carried over back or side when alert, but may be dropped when at rest. Should be mobile and loose, not tight over back.

HINDQUARTERS

HINDLEGS Strong, well developed, turning neither in nor out. Upper thighs and hocks well developed. Stifles well bent.

FEET

Large, long, flattish— a hare-foot, slightly spread but not splayed. Turning neither in nor out, but may turn in slightly when dog is pulling. Feathers on feet not essential but more profuse on females than males.

TOES Arched.

PADS Thick and tough, with protective hair between toes.

MOUTH AND JAWS

MUZZLE Medium length and width. Should taper toward nose. Must have depth. Whiskers not to be removed.

LIPS Black preferred. Slight upward curving at corners of mouth gives the "Samoyed Smile".

BITE Scissor.

FOREQUARTERS

SHOULDERS Long and sloping, with a layback of 45 degrees.

FORELEGS Parallel and straight to pasterns. Length from ground to elbow should approximate 55 percent of dog's total height.

PASTERNS Strong and straight, but flexible with some spring.

SIBERIAN HUSKY

The Siberian Husky was developed by the Chukchi, a nomadic people of northeastern Asia. The Chukchi ranged far and wide, relying primarily on hunting for their survival. By crossing a variety of indigenous dogs, they produced a dog that had the necessary strength, speed, and stamina to travel long distances at moderate speed, while hauling a moderate load, in a harsh and cold climate. Having achieved this goal, the Chukchi guarded the breed's purity. These dogs are the basis of the present Siberian Husky.

The Siberian is a very sociable dog, and greets everyone as its friend, and is therefore not an effective watchdog. Typically gentle, affectionate, and responsive to training, it is also independent, stubborn, and outgoing.

GENERAL APPEARANCE

This medium-sized working dog is quick and light on its feet, and free and graceful in action.

CHARACTERISTICS

A moderately compact and well furred body, erect ears, and a brush tail.

TEMPERAMENT

Friendly and gentle, alert and outgoing, the Siberian Husky does not display the possessive qualities of a guard dog, nor is it overly suspicious of strangers or aggressive with other dogs. Mature dogs tend to be reserved and dignified, intelligent, tractable, and eager.

GAIT/MOVEMENT

The gait is characteristically smooth The Husky is quick and light on its feet with good reach in front and good drive in the rear. The topline remains level when moving.

COAT

The coat is double and medium in length, giving a well furred appearance, but never so long as to obscure the outline of the dog. The undercoat is soft and dense. Guard hairs are straight and somewhat smooth-lying. The absence of an undercoat during the shedding season is normal.

COLOR

All colors from black to pure white are allowed. A variety of markings on the head is common, including many striking patterns not found in other breeds.

SIZE

HEIGHT

males	females
22–23½ in (55–58.75cm)	20–22 in (50–55cm)

WEIGHT

males	females
45–60 lb (20.45–27.27kg)	35–50 lb (15.9–110kg)

There is no size preference within these ranges. Length of body from point of shoulder to rear point of croup is slightly longer than height of body from ground to top of withers.

DISQUALIFICATIONS

- Deviation of more than ½ in (1.25cm) above preferred height

BODY AND TOPLINE

Chest deep and strong, but not too broad, with deepest point just behind and level with elbows. Ribs well sprung. Back straight and strong, with level topline from withers to croup; of medium length. Slight tuck-up. Croup slopes away from spine.

HEAD AND SKULL

Skull medium-sized, slightly rounded on top, and tapering from widest point to eyes. Stop well defined.

NOSE Black in gray, tan, or black dogs; liver in copper dogs; may be flesh-colored in pure white dogs. Pink-streaked "snow nose" is acceptable.

TAIL

well furred tail of fox-brush shape set on just below level of topline. Usually carried over back in a graceful sickle curve when dog is at attention. When carried up, tail does not curl to either side, nor does it snap flat against back. Hangs down when dog is in repose. Hair on tail is of medium length, approximately the same length on top, sides, and bottom.

EYES AND EARS

EYES Moderately spaced and set a trifle obliquely. COLOR Brown or blue in color; one of each. or parti-colored. is acceptable. SHAPE Almond.

EARS Medium-sized, triangular in shape, and set high on head. Thick, well furred. Strongly erect, with slightly rounded tips pointing straight ahead.

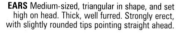

NECK

Medium in length, arched.

MOUTH AND JAWS

MUZZLE Medium length and width, tapering gradually to nose.

LIPS Well pigmented and close fitting.

BITE Scissor.

HINDQUARTERS

HINDLEGS Upper thighs well muscled and powerful. Stifles well bent. Hock joint well defined, set low to the ground.

DEWCLAWS Should be removed.

FEET

Oval but not long, medium in size, compact and well furred between toes and pads.

PADS Tough and thickly cushioned.

FOREQUARTERS

SHOULDERS Shoulder blade well laid-back. Upper arm angles slightly backward from point of shoulder to elbow.

FORELEGS Elbows close to body. Length of leg from elbow to ground slightly more than distance from elbow to top of withers.

PASTERNS Slightly slanted, strong, but flexible. Bone substantial but never heavy.

DEWCLAWS May be removed.

STANDARD SCHNAUZER

Of the three Schnauzers, the Standard is the oldest and formed the basis for the other two. Standard Schnauzer history dates to fifteenth- and sixteenth-century Germany, and the breed probably resulted from crosses between the black Poodle, the gray Wolf Spitz, and the Wirehaired Pinscher. Its original role was as home and yard guardian, rat catcher, and hunting companion. The Standard Schnauzer is very intelligent and makes an excellent obedience student; the Germans describe it as having a "human brain." Its innate bravery and apparent ability to sense approaching danger account for its frequent use as a personal guard and companion.

ABOVE Uncropped ears
BELOW Cropped ears

BODY AND TOPLINE

Body compact, strong, and substantial, to permit great flexibility and agility. well sprung ribs; oval. Breastbone plainly discernible. Brisket descends to elbows. Belly moderately drawn up. Topline should have a slight slope from the withers to the croup and set-on of tail. Back strong, firm, straight, and short. Distance from last rib to hip as short as possible.

EYES AND EARS

EYES Medium sized, turned forward. Neither round nor protruding. Vision not impaired nor eyes hidden by too long an eyebrow. COLOR Dark brown. SHAPE Oval.

EARS Set high, evenly shaped, carried erect when cropped. If uncropped, of medium size, V-shaped and mobile, breaking at skull level and carried forward with inner edges close to cheek.

HEAD AND SKULL

Head rectangular, narrowing slightly from ears to eyes and again to nose tip. Skull width not exceeding two-thirds its length. Skull flat. Slight stop, accentuated by wiry brows. Cheeks well developed but not coarse.

NOSE Large, black, and full.

MOUTH AND JAWS

MUZZLE Strong. Parallel and equal in length to topskull, ending in a blunt wedge; wiry whiskers accentuate the rectangular shape of head.

LIPS Black, tight, and not overlapping.

TEETH Full complement.

BITE Scissor.

NECK

Strong, of moderate length, elegantly arched. No wrinkles or dewlap.

FOREQUARTERS

SHOULDERS Strongly muscled, sloping, well laid-back. Shoulder blades meet upper arm at nearly a right angle.

FORELEGS Straight. Set moderately apart, heavy boned. Elbows set close to body.

DEWCLAWS May be removed.

FEET

Cat foot.

TOES Well closed and arched, pointing straight ahead.

PADS Thick.

NAILS Strong and black.

TAIL

Set moderately high, carried erect. Docked to not less than 1in (2.5cm) nor more than 2in (5cm).

GENERAL APPEARANCE

A robust, heavy-set dog, sturdily built with good muscle and plenty of bone.

CHARACTERISTICS

A rugged body, dense, harsh coat, and bristly mustache, eyebrows, and whiskers are characteristic of this breed.

TEMPERAMENT

Has highly developed senses, aptitude for training, intelligence, fearlessness, endurance, and resistance to weather and illness. It combines a high-spirited temperament with extreme reliability.

GAIT/MOVEMENT

The gait is strong, quick, free and level, with powerful hindquarters that reach out, balanced by the reach of the forelegs. At a trot, the back remains firm and level.

COAT

Tight, hard, wiry, and as thick as possible. It is composed of a soft, close undercoat and a harsh outercoat, which slightly stands off the back. The outercoat is trimmed by plucking to accent the body outline. Coat texture is of the greatest importance. The coat on the ears, head, neck, chest, belly, and under tail may be closely trimmed. On the muzzle and over the eyes, the coat lengthens to form the beard and eyebrows. The hair on the legs is longer than that on the body. These "furnishings" should be of harsh texture and not so profuse as to detract from the dog's working capabilities.

COLOR

Colors are pepper-and-salt or pure black. All shades of pepper-and-salt, and dark iron gray to silver gray are acceptable. A darker facial mask, harmonizing with the coat color, is desirable. Black dogs should have a black undercoat.

SIZE

HEIGHT (ideal, at highest point of shoulder blades)

males	females
18½–19½ in (46.25–48.75cm)	17½–18½ in (43.75–46.25cm)

Height at highest point of withers should equal length from breastbone to point of rump.

DISQUALIFICATIONS

- Deviation of more than ½ in (1.25cm) above or below preferred height
- Vicious dogs

HINDQUARTERS

Strongly muscled, in balance with forequarters, never appearing higher than shoulders.

HINDLEGS Thighs broad. Stifles well bent. Hock joint clearly defined.

DEWCLAWS Generally removed.

AIREDALE TERRIER

Known as the "King of Terriers," the Airedale Terrier is certainly the tallest in this group. The breed was established by the late 1870s, probably from a mixture of the Old English, or Black and Tan Terrier, the Welsh Harrier, and later the Irish and Bull Terriers, and certainly the Otterhound. The Airedale was bred originally to hunt river otters but became a versatile hunting dog, being used on fox, badger, water rats, and small game in the area between the Aire and Wharfe rivers in Yorkshire, England.

A handsome and upstanding dog, it quickly became popular throughout Europe and the U.S. It was used for police work in Germany, for big-game hunting in Africa, India and North American game lands and it was an outstanding dispatch carrier for the military in both world wars. However, it was always most valued as a family guardian and faithful companion.

The Airedale tends to be dominant and may react strongly to a perceived threat by another dog, though if it is introduced to other household pets while young, it can be taught to accept them reliably. Obedience training should start quite early,

HEAD AND SKULL
Skull long and flat, not too broad between ears, narrowing slightly to eyes. No wrinkles. Stop hardly visible. Foreface deep, powerful.

NECK
Of moderate length and thickness. Skin tight.

EYES AND EARS
EYES Small, not prominent. COLOR Dark.
EARS Small, V-shaped, and carried to the side of head, not pointing to eyes. Topline of folded ear should be above level of skull.

MOUTH AND JAWS
BITE Level or scissor.
KC/FCI/ANKC Scissor only.

FOREQUARTERS
SHOULDERS Long, sloping, flat.
FORELEGS Straight, with plenty of muscle and bone. Elbows perpendicular to body, moving freely.

→ GENERAL APPEARANCE
A medium-sized dog, basically square in shape, with a docked tail.

→ CHARACTERISTICS
The dense double wire coat and natural ear are typical of the breed.

→ TEMPERAMENT
Bold, intelligent, dominant, affectionate.

→ GAIT/MOVEMENT
The gait is free, strong, and well balanced, the feet turning neither in nor out.

→ COAT
The double coat consists of hard, dense, wiry guard hairs, lying close. The body hair may be crinkled or slightly wavy. The undercoat is short and soft. The hair on the legs is a little softer and longer, and the facial furnishings consist of a distinctive beard and eyebrows.

→ COLOR
This is basically a tan dog with a black saddle. The head, legs up to the thighs and elbows, the underpart of the body and the chest are tan, the ears being a darker tan. The sides and upper part of the body are black or grizzle. A red mixture is often found in the black and a small white blaze on the chest is allowed.

→ SIZE
HEIGHT (approximate, at shoulder)

males

23 in (57.5cm)

Females slightly less. Both sexes should be sturdy, with good muscle and bone.

beginning with a "puppy kindergarten" class and then more formal instruction. Though intelligent, an Airedale may prefer to set its own agenda, and can be stubborn.

It is very devoted to its own family but tends to be aloof with others. It enjoys playing with children and games with its owner. An Airedale that gets a fair amount of exercise will be content in any size dwelling, as long as it is able to share quality time with its family every day. The attractive show coat results from artful stripping and hand-plucking—and it's a big job. Pets are usually clipped about every two months.

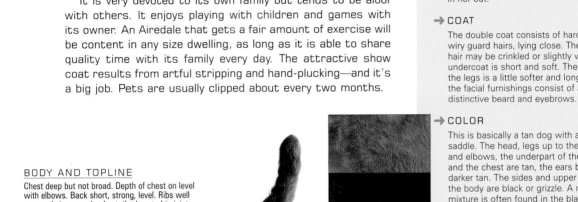

BODY AND TOPLINE
Chest deep but not broad. Depth of chest on level with elbows. Back short, strong, level. Ribs well sprung. Loin muscular. Last rib close to hip joint.

TAIL
Docked. Root set well up on back. Carried gaily but not curled over back.

HINDQUARTERS
Strong and muscular with no droop.
HINDLEGS Thighs long, powerful, well muscled. Stifles well bent. Hocks well let-down.

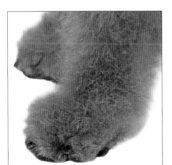

FEET
Small, round, and compact
TOES Moderately arched, turning neither in nor out.

AMERICAN STAFFORDSHIRE TERRIER

The American Staffordshire Terrier is of medium size, but is among the strongest of all dogs. It was developed originally in England through a combination of the Old English Bulldog, and the English Terrier or the Old English Black and Tan Terrier (forerunner of today's Manchester Terrier) in the 1820s. The aim was to produce a dog that would excel at those barbaric "sports" that involved setting a strong and tenacious dog against a bull or bear, or another dog in a pit. These new "Bull and Terriers" fulfilled the expectations of their breeders, but the cruelties associated with the "baiting sports" grew so extreme that, in 1835, they were banned in Britain by an act of Parliament, though dog-fighting continues in hidden corners, even today.

Unfortunately, because of its reputation as a pit-fighter, the Amstaff tends to attract a generally unsavory segment of society as part of its following. Yet under its tough exterior lurks a kinder nature; this dog will become deeply attached to its owner and is gentle with its own people. If trained when young, it can readily tolerate other dogs with no show of aggression. The American Staffordshire Terrier is an excellent home guardian, with a reputation for being able to discern between people with good and bad intentions. It is a grand companion for an owner who is able and willing to train it when young and control it as an adult.

HEAD AND SKULL
Medium length, deep, and broad skull, with very pronounced cheek muscles. Distinct stop.

BODY AND TOPLINE
Shoulders strong and muscular with blades wide and sloping. Back fairly short, slight slope from withers to rump with gentle short slope at rump to base of tail. Loin slightly tucked. Well-sprung ribs, deep in rear. All ribs close together.

TAIL
Short, low set, tapering to a fine point. Not curled or held over back. Not docked.

HINDQUARTERS
Well-muscled.
HINDLEGS Let-down at hocks, turning neither in nor out.

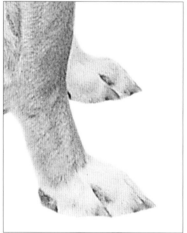

FEET
Of moderate size, well arched, and compact.

→ GENERAL APPEARANCE

This well put together dog gives the impression of great strength for its size. Though muscular, it is also agile and graceful, and not long-legged or racy in outline.

→ CHARACTERISTICS

The American Staffordshire is a stocky, very powerfully-built dog, with a short coat, and a distinctive head and muzzle.

→ TEMPERAMENT

Keenly alive. Dominant. Courageous.

→ GAIT/MOVEMENT

The gait is springy, but without roll or pace.

→ COAT

The coat is short, close, and stiff to touch.

→ COLOR

Any color, solid, parti or patched is permitted, but all-white, more than 80 percent white, and black-and-tan or liver are not encouraged.

→ SIZE

HEIGHT (preferred, at shoulder)

males	females
18–19 in	17–18 in
(45–47.5cm)	(42.5–45cm)

Height and weight should be in proportion.

The American Staffordshire and the Pit Bull Terrier are essentially the same dog, and together have borne the brunt of legislation attempting to ban them from many areas in the U.S. and U.K. The breed is not recognized by the KC. Living with an American Staffordshire Terrier in today's society can be a challenge because of how the breed is perceived by the public and legislatures. But to those who know the breed best, the Amstaff has no equal.

LEFT Uncropped ears.
RIGHT Cropped ears.

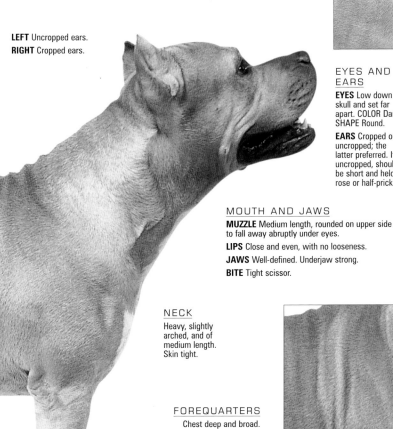

EYES AND EARS

EYES Low down in skull and set far apart. COLOR Dark. SHAPE Round.

EARS Cropped or uncropped; the latter preferred. If uncropped, should be short and held rose or half-pricked.

MOUTH AND JAWS

MUZZLE Medium length, rounded on upper side to fall away abruptly under eyes.

LIPS Close and even, with no looseness.

JAWS Well-defined. Underjaw strong.

BITE Tight scissor.

NECK

Heavy, slightly arched, and of medium length. Skin tight.

FOREQUARTERS

Chest deep and broad.

FORELEGS Straight, large or round-boned, set wide apart and without bend.

↓
BORDER TERRIER

Possibly one of the oldest of the terrier breeds, the Border Terrier worked for decades with the Border Foxhounds, a hunt club in the Cheviot Hills in the north of England, for which it was named. A true working terrier, it was valued by farmers and shepherds as well as by organized hunt clubs, and one or more Borders could be found on every farm in the region. The Border is higher on the leg than most terriers of the same general size, to enable it to follow the hounds on a hunt, yet is small enough to go down a burrow after a fox. It still retains all its hunting instincts and will happily take off on an expedition alone if allowed to roam unsupervised. Unusually for a terrier, it was bred to run and work with other dogs, and it is therefore less likely than many other terriers to be a fighter. Not a demonstrative dog, it is dignified and wants to please, needing only a verbal reprimand should it misbehave. It is generally a good student.

GENERAL APPEARANCE
This is an active working terrier, of medium bone, and rather narrow in the shoulder, body, and quarters.

CHARACTERISTICS
The "otter" head is unique in the terrier group.

TEMPERAMENT
The Border has a typical terrier temperament, being good-tempered, affectionate, obedient, and easily trained. In the field it is hard as nails and driving in attack.

GAIT/MOVEMENT
The gait is straight and rhythmical before and behind, with good length of stride, and flexing of the hock and stifle. It is free, agile, and quick.

COAT
The short, dense undercoat is covered with a very wiry and somewhat broken topcoat that lies closely, with no tendency to curl or wave. Except for neatening the feet, head, and neck, the coat should not be trimmed. The hide is very thick and loosefitting.

COLOR
Colors are red, grizzle-and-tan, blue-and-tan, or wheaten. A small amount of white on the chest is allowed and a dark muzzle is desirable.

SIZE

males	females
13–15½ lb (6–7kg)	11½–14 lb (5–6.4kg)

Slightly higher than long.

EYES AND EARS
EYES Moderate in size,. neither prominent nor small and beady. COLOR Dark hazel.

EARS Small, V-shaped, and moderately thick. set-on side of head, not high, dropping forward close to cheeks, and not breaking above level of skull. Dark preferred.

HEAD AND SKULL
Similar to that of an otter. Skull moderately broad and flat, plenty of width between ears and between eyes. Slight, moderately broad curve at the stop. Cheeks slightly full.
NOSE Black and good sized.

BODY AND TOPLINE
Back strong but laterally supple, no dip at shoulders. Loin strong. Body deep, fairly narrow. Body should be capable of being spanned behind the shoulders. Brisket not excessively deep or narrow. Deep ribs carried well back and not oversprung. Underline fairly straight.

NECK
Clean, muscular.

MOUTH AND JAWS
MUZZLE Short and well filled. Dark color is characteristic and desirable.
TEETH strong and large.
BITE Scissor.

FOREQUARTERS
SHOULDERS Well laid back and of good length. Brisket is not excessively deep or narrow.
FORELEGS Straight and not too heavy boned; placed wider than those of a Fox Terrier.

FEET
Small and compact.
TOES Moderately arched and pointing forward.
PADS Thick.

TAIL
Moderately short, thick at base, and tapering. Not set too high. Carried gaily when alert, but not over the back. Tail may drop when dog is at ease.

HINDQUARTERS
Muscular and racy.
HINDLEGS Long thighs. Stifles well bent. Hocks well let-down.

↓ BULL TERRIER

With its cousins, the American Staffordshire Terrier and the Staffordshire Bull Terrier, the Bull Terrier was originally intended to be a fighting dog. It resulted from crosses of the old Bull and Terrier dog with the now extinct white English Terrier and old Bulldog, with later additions of Spanish Pointer to increase its size. The resulting all-white strain was developed in around 1860 and became popular as a companion with fashionable young men of the day, who wanted a tough, yet attractive dog that would never seek a fight, yet once attacked, would prevail. The Bull Terrier's behavior fits that description well, and the dog's popularity among the British of all classes grew, especially during World War II. It is highly valued as a guardian of home and family, and as a devoted companion, because of its charming personality and the affection it shows its family.

→ GENERAL APPEARANCE

Both the White Bull Terrier and the Colored Bull Terrier must be strong, muscular, symmetrical, and active.

→ CHARACTERISTICS

The head, in both varieties, is distinctive, being egg-shaped, with small ears and eyes.

→ TEMPERAMENT

The Bull Terrier is full of fire, but of sweet disposition and amenable to discipline.

→ GAIT/MOVEMENT

The dog moves smoothly, with free, easy strides. The forelegs have a good reach, while the hindlegs move smoothly at the hip and flex well at stifle and hock. Movement is jaunty, with agility and power.

→ COAT

The coat is short, flat, and harsh to the touch. The skin is tight-fitting.

→ COLOR

Bull Terriers are found in two varieties.

WHITE—all-white, though markings on the head are permitted. Markings elsewhere are severely faulted. Skin pigmentation is not penalized.

COLORED—any color other than white, or any color with white markings. All being equal, the preferred color for markings is brindle.

→ SIZE

Not specified.

→ DISQUALIFICATIONS

■ Blue eyes

EYES AND EARS

EYES Small, well sunken, and obliquely placed. Set close and high up on head. COLOR Dark. SHAPE Triangular.

EARS Small, thin, and close together. Held stiffly erect, pointed upward.

HEAD AND SKULL

Head should be long, strong and deep to end of muzzle, fully filled, and egg shaped. In profile, it curves down from tip of skull to tip of nose. Forehead flat between ears. Distance from tip of nose to eyes greater than from eyes to top of skull.

NOSE Black, with nostrils bent downward at tip.

BODY AND TOPLINE

Chest broad; great depth from withers to brisket, so that later is closer to ground than belly. Body well rounded with marked spring of ribs; back short and strong. Back ribs deep. Slight arch over loin.

NECK

Very muscular, long, arched, and free from loose skin.

MOUTH AND JAWS

JAWS Underjaw deep and well defined.

LIPS Clean and tight.

BITE Level or scissor. **KC/FCI** Scissor only.

FOREQUARTERS

No slackness or dip at withers. Underline from brisket to belly forms a graceful upward curve.

SHOULDERS Shoulderblades wide and flat, with very pronounced backward slope from bottom of blade to top edge.

FORELEGS Big boned but not coarse, of moderate length, and straight. Elbows turning neither in nor out

PASTERNS Strong and upright.

FEET

Round and compact. **TOES** Well-arched.

TAIL

Short, set low, fine, and carried horizontally. Thick as it joins body, tapering to a fine point.

HINDQUARTERS

HINDLEGS Thighs very muscular. Hocks well let-down. Stifle joint well bent with well developed second thigh.

PASTERNS Short and upright.

CAIRN TERRIER

The Cairn Terrier comes from the Scottish Highlands and Western Isles, where it was earlier called the Shorthaired Skye Terrier. From the fifteenth century onward, Cairns were kept by both owners of large estates and farmers on small crofts. In 1910, the breed gained its current name as a reflection of the work it performed: on the Isle of Skye, otters hid in cairns (piles of rocks on shore and hillside) and the dog's job was to flush them out. It was also very successful at keeping farms free of foxes, badgers, and rats. Until the Dandie Dinmont and Skye Terrier were recognized somewhere about 1870, all generic Scotch terriers had been lumped togther. The Cairn Terrier and the West Highland White (part of the Skye designation), which started out as the same breed, were finally separated in about 1910, but cross-breeding continued. In 1917, the AKC insisted that cross-breeding be stopped, but both were included in the group known as "Skyes," along with the Scottish Terrier, until 1870. All three had been developed in the western part of Scotland and nearby islands, and all three originally turned up in the same litters. Late in the nineteenth century, breeders of the dog that is now known as the Scottish Terrier broke off and established their own stud book.

HEAD AND SKULL
Broad in proportion to length, with a decided stop and well furnished with hair on top of head. This hair may be somewhat softer than body coat.
NOSE Black.

EYES AND EARS
EYES Set wide apart, rather sunken, with shaggy eyebrows, medium in size. COLOR Hazel or dark hazel, depending on body color.

EARS Small, pointed, set wide apart on side of head, and carried erectly. Free from long hairs.

MOUTH AND JAWS
MUZZLE Strong but not too long or heavy.
TEETH Large.
JAWS Neither undershot nor overshot.

FOREQUARTERS
SHOULDERS Sloping.
FORELEGS Of medium length, with good but not heavy bone, and covered with hard hair. Perfectly straight, not turning out at elbows.

TERRIER

An adventure-loving dog with hunting instincts still intact, the Cairn may be aggressive toward other dogs and will attack cats and small animals if the opportunity presents itself. Within these limits however, it is a good family dog, ready for a romp with the children or a snuggle on the sofa.

The Cairn's double coat should always look rather rough, though never ragged or unkempt. The hair on the feet can be kept neat by scissoring; otherwise no part of its coat should ever be cut or clipped. Dead hair is removed by plucking with finger and thumb or with a stripping comb.

→ GENERAL APPEARANCE

Active, hardy, small and short-legged working terrier. Strong but not heavily built, deep in ribs, presenting a well proportioned body with a medium length back, and a hard, weather-resistant coat.

→ CHARACTERISTICS

Head shorter and wider than any other terrier, well furnished with hair, giving a foxy expression. Profuse outercoat stands somewhat out from body.

→ TEMPERAMENT

Game, bold working terrier.

→ GAIT/MOVEMENT

Should move freely.

→ COAT

The hard, weather-resistant double coat comprises a profuse harsh outercoat and a short, soft, close, furry undercoat.

→ COLOR

Any color except white is acceptable. Dark ears, muzzle, and tail tip are desirable.

KC/FCI/ANKC Not solid black or white, nor black-and-tan.

→ SIZE

HEIGHT

males	females
10 in	9½ in
(25cm)	(23.75cm)

WEIGHT

males	females
14 lb	13 lb
(6.4kg)	(5.9kg)

KC/FCI/ANKC Prefer slightly heavier dogs.

Must be balanced; neither too leggy nor too close to ground.

BODY AND TOPLINE

Well-muscled, strong active body. Well-sprung ribs. Level back of medium length.

TAIL

In proportion to head, well furnished with hair but not feathery. Carried gaily but must not curl over back. Set on at level of back.

HINDQUARTERS

Strong.

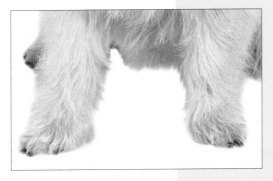

FEET

Forefeet larger than hindfeet and may turn out slightly.

PADS Thick and strong.

FOX TERRIER—SMOOTH

Smooth and Wire Fox Terriers were considered one breed with two varieties in the U.S. until 1985, when it was divided into two distinct breeds. In the minds of so many, the Fox Terrier is the Classic Terrier. The principal difference between them is the coat. Terriers have hunted foxes, badgers, rats, and other vermin for centuries. When fox-hunting from horseback became popular among the British gentry in the 1800s, a Fox Terrier was always carried in a saddle bag, ready to be released in order to flush out the fox from its lair. The Industrial Revolution only increased the breed's popularity—in towns as ratters and in the country for foxhunts. The Smooth Fox Terrier is a game, active companion, ready for a foxhunt or a hike at a moment's notice. It should never be allowed to roam unsupervised because most retain the breed's full hunting instincts and will consider cats and small animals fair game.

HEAD AND SKULL
Skull flat and moderately narrow, gradually decreasing in width to eyes. Minimal stop. Foreface gradually tapers from eye to muzzle and tips up slightly at junction with forehead, but does not "dish" or fall away below the eyes. Cheeks not full.
NOSE Black.

BODY AND TOPLINE
Back short, level, and strong. Chest deep and not broad. Brisket deep. Foreribs moderately arched, back ribs deep and well sprung. Loin, muscular and very slightly arched.

TAIL (stern)
Set on rather high, carried gaily but not over back or curled. Of good strength. Docked to three-quarter length.
KC/FCI/ANKC Customarily docked. Undocked: of moderate length to give balance.

NECK
Clean, muscular, dry, and of fair length.

HINDQUARTERS
Strong and muscular, free from droop or crouch.
HINDLEGS Thighs long and powerful. Stifles well curved, turning neither in nor out. Hocks well bent, near the ground, perfectly upright.

FEET
Round, compact, and not large, with hard, tough soles.
TOES Moderately arched, turning neither in nor out.

FOREQUARTERS
SHOULDERS Long and sloping, fine at points and clearly cut at withers.
FORELEGS Straight with strong bone. Elbows hang perpendicular to body.
PASTERNS Short and straight.

GENERAL APPEARANCE
The Smooth Fox Terrier has the general size, shape and contour of a dog that can gallop with horse and hound yet follow the fox to ground.

CHARACTERISTICS
A white, smooth-coated terrier with a distinctive head, elegant but not wedge shaped, and a gay tail.

TEMPERAMENT
Gay, intelligent, and active.

GAIT/MOVEMENT
The legs should carry straight forward, with propulsive power from the hindlegs When approaching, the forelegs should travel with the feet as far apart as the elbows.

COAT
The coat is smooth and flat, but also hard, dense, and abundant. The belly and underside of the thighs are not bare.

COLOR
White should be the predominant color. Brindle, red or liver markings are not desirable. Otherwise color or markings are of little importance.

SIZE
HEIGHT (maximum)
males
15½ in (38.75cm)
Females proportionately shorter. Maximum length of back from withers to root of tail is 12 in (30cm).
WEIGHT (for dogs of above size)

males	females
18 lb	16 lb
(8.2kg)	(7.3kg)

Margin of 1lb (0.5kg) either way.

DISQUALIFICATIONS
- Ears prick, tulip or rose
- Nose white, cherry or spotted to a considerable extent with either of these colors
- Mouth much undershot or overshot

EYES AND EARS
EYES Moderately small, rather deep set. COLOR Dark, with dark rims. SHAPE Circular.

EARS Small, V-shaped, and moderately thick, dropping forward close to cheeks. Topline of folded ear well above level of skull.

MOUTH AND JAWS
JAWS Upper and lower jaws strong and muscular.
BITE Tight scissor.

FOX TERRIER—WIRE

The Wire Fox Terrier has won more Best in Shows at Westminster KC than any other breed, and is a consummate show dog. Yet the Smooth Fox Terrier was seen at dog shows over twenty years before the Wire Fox Terrier.

The Wire closely resembles the Smooth, except for the wire coat. The two breeds were separated only in 1985 in the U.S. and in 1970 in the U.K., so it has a short history "on its own." The early ancestors of the Wire were probably the old rough-coated Black-and-Tan Terriers of Wales and Derbyshire, in the U.K. Later they were crossed with the Smooth to improve the head and gain the white color. Cross-breeding of the two varieties ceased in around 1900.

Usually good-tempered and reliable with older children, the Wire Fox Terrier is always ready for fun. Like the Smooth, it is a quick and willing student.

GENERAL APPEARANCE

In general, the Wire Fox Terrier resembles the Smooth, except for having a wiry coat and beard.

CHARACTERISTICS

White, wire-coated terrier, with a distinctive head, beard, and eyebrows, and a gay tail.

TEMPERAMENT

Alert, quick, and keen of expression. Affectionate with his family yet can be aggressive with other dogs or animals.

GAIT/MOVEMENT

As in the Smooth Fox Terrier, the legs move straight forward, and propulsion comes from the hindlegs.

COAT

The best coats are broken, the hairs twist and are dense and wiry. Under this coat is a short undercoat of fine, soft hair. The coat on the sides is not so hard as on the back and quarters. Some coats are "crinkly" or slightly waved, but never curly. The hair on the jaws should be crisp and only long enough to impart a look of strength to the foreface. The hair on the forelegs is dense and crisp. The coat should average ¾–1 in (1.88–2.5cm) in length on the shoulders and neck, and 1½ in (3.75cm) on the withers, back, ribs, and quarters.

COLOR

White should predominate. Red, liver, or slaty blue markings are undesirable. Otherwise color is of no importance.

SIZE

HEIGHT

males

15½ in (38.75cm)

Females are proportionately lower.

KC/FCI/ANKC Specify weight of 8.25kg (18 lb) for males; females slightly less.

DISQUALIFICATIONS

- Ears prick, tulip, or rose
- Nose white, cherry, or spotted to a considerable extent with either of these colors
- Mouth much overshot or much undershot

EYES AND EARS

EYES Moderately small, rather deep set, and not too far apart. COLOR Dark. SHAPE Circular.

EARS Small, V-shaped, and of moderate thickness, with flaps neatly folded over and dropping close to cheeks. Topline of folded ear should be well above level of skull.

HEAD AND SKULL

Length of head from back of occipital bone to nostrils should be 7–7¼ in (17.5–18.1cm); the female's head being proportionately shorter. Length of skull and foreface approximately equal. Top of skull almost flat, sloping slightly and decreasing in width toward eye.

BODY AND TOPLINE

Back short and level. Loin muscular and slightly arched. Short-coupled, females slightly longer coupled. Chest deep, not broad or narrow. Front ribs moderately arched, back ribs deep and well sprung.

TAIL

Set on rather high and carried gaily, but not curled. Docked to about three-quarters. Strong and substantial. **KC/FCI/ANKC** Customarily docked. Undocked: of good strength and fair balance.

NECK

Clean, muscular, and of fair length. Dry, with graceful curve.

MOUTH AND JAWS

MUZZLE Foreface gradually tapers from eye to muzzle, dipping slightly at juncture with forehead. It should not fall away quickly below eyes.

JAWS Well-developed, strong.

BITE Scissor.

FEET

Round, compact, and not large.

PADS Tough and well cushioned

TOES Moderately arched, turning neither in nor out.

FOREQUARTERS

SHOULDERS Slope steeply downward from withers. Long, well laid back.

FORELEGS Straight. Bone strong to the feet. Elbows hang perpendicular to body.

HINDQUARTERS

Strong and muscular; free from droop or crouch.

HINDLEGS Thighs long and powerful. Stifles well curved, turning neither in nor out. Hock joints well bent and near ground.

IRISH TERRIER

Once called the Irish Red Terrier to distinguish the breed from other terriers in Ireland, the Irish Terrier is thought to be the oldest terrier now extant. First recorded as a distinct breed in 1875, but mentioned by type long before, by 1929 it was ranked thirteenth among AKC breeds.

The progenitors of the Irish Terrier were probably the old wirehair Black-and-Tan Terrier, and a strain of Wheaten Terrier. Some breed histories point out the strong similarity between the body shape of this dog and that of the Irish Wolfhound, implying some connection between the breeds from long ago. The Irish Terrier is extremely loyal and is reputed to have a very long memory. Both contribute to the dog's desire to please and thus to the ease of training. Some are outstanding obedience prospects.

GENERAL APPEARANCE

A balanced, vital picture of symmetry, proportion and harmony, lithe and wiry in movement, with great animation. Sturdy, strong, and free from clumsiness. Speed, power, and endurance are essential.

CHARACTERISTICS

This self-colored reddish dog is moderately high on leg, with a graceful and racy outline.

TEMPERAMENT

Heedless when rushing an adversary, but affectionate and absolutely loyal to mankind, it guards its family with utter contempt for danger. Can be aggressive with other dogs and small animals.

GAIT/MOVEMENT

Front and hindlegs move straight forward, with the stifles never turning outward.

COAT

The dense, wiry coat has a broken appearance. Neither soft nor silky, nor so long as to alter body outline. It is harshest on the back and quarters. Undercoat is of fine hair, lighter in color.

COLOR

Color is bright red, golden red, red wheaten, or wheaten. A small patch of white on the chest is permissible but not desired. Puppies are sometimes born with black hair, which disappears before they are full grown.

SIZE

HEIGHT (approximate, at shoulder)

males	females
18 in (45cm)	18 in (45cm)

WEIGHT

males	females
27 lb (12.3kg)	25 lb (11.4kg)

KC Weight not specified.

EYES AND EARS

EYES Small, not prominent. COLOR Dark brown.

EARS Small, V-shaped, and moderately thick; dropping forward closely toward outside corner of eye. Top of folded ear should be well above level of skull.

HEAD AND SKULL

Head long, in proportion to body. Skull flat, narrow between ears, and more so toward the eyes. No wrinkle and stop barely noticeable. Foreface and skull from occiput to stop approximately equal in length.
NOSE Black.

NECK

Of fair length, gradually widening toward shoulder. Not throaty. Slight frill in hair at each side of neck extends almost to corner of ear.

BODY AND TOPLINE

Chest deep and muscular, not full or wide. Body moderately long. Back strong, straight. Loin strong and muscular; slightly arched. Ribs fairly sprung; deep, not round; reaching to elbows. Females may be slightly longer than males.

MOUTH AND JAWS

LIPS Close and well fitting, almost black in color.

JAWS Hair similar in quality and texture to body coat.

BITE Strong and even not over- or undershot.
KC Scissor.

TAIL (stern)

Should be docked by about a quarter. set-on rather high; not curled. Of good strength and substance. Well covered with harsh, rough hair.
KC/ANKC Customarily docked. Undocked: in balance, and carried so it will not be damaged when working.

HINDQUARTERS

Strong, muscular.

HINDLEGS Thighs powerful. Hocks near ground. Stifles moderately bent.

FEET

Strong, round, and moderately small.

TOES Arched, turning neither in nor out.

TOENAILS. Dark.

PADS Deep and sound.

FOREQUARTERS

SHOULDERS Fine, long, and sloping well into back.

FORELEGS Moderately long, straight, with plenty of bone and muscle. Elbows clear of sides. Free from feather and covered with same-textured hair as body.

PASTERNS Short, straight.

JACK RUSSELL TERRIER

The hunt terriers favored by a Victorian country parson came to be known by his name—the Jack Russell Terrier—the breed's full name in the U.K. is the Parson Russell Terrier. Russell, the parson, was an avid sportsman and developed a line of terriers ideally suited to foxhunts, all based on a rough-coated, predominantly white bitch that he had purchased while a student at Oxford. After Russell was ordained, he worked as a curate on the edge of Dartmoor in southwestern England, which was excellent foxhunting country. He was as dedicated to his dogs as he was to his parishioners, and when he died, over a thousand people attended his burial. The Jack Russell needs an experienced owner, able to spend a lot of time each day providing exercise and training. A bored Jack Russell can be destructive, but an untrained one can be a neighborhood nuisance. If allowed its freedom, it will roam to hunt adventure (and game).

HINDQUARTERS
Strong and muscular. **HINDLEGS** Good angulation and bend of stifle. Hocks near ground, parallel.

TAIL
Set high, strong, carried gaily but not over the back or curled. Docked so tip is approximately level with skull. **KC/FCI/ANKC** Customarily docked. Undocked: moderate in length to give balance.

BODY AND TOPLINE
Body appears approximately square; laterally flexible, allowing turns in confined space. Tuck-up moderate. Chest narrow, moderate depth, flexible and compressible. Ribs well sprung, oval, not round, extending only to elbow. Topline strong, level in motion, loin slightly arched.

EYES AND EARS
EYES Moderately sized, not protruding. COLOR Dark, with dark rims. SHAPE Almond.

EARS Button ear. Small, V-shaped, drop ears of moderate thickness, carried forward and close to head, pointing to eye. Fold level with top of skull or slightly above.

NECK
Clean, muscular, moderately arched, and of fair length.

HEAD AND SKULL
Strong. Skull flat, fairly broad between ears, narrowing slightly to eyes. Stop well defined but not prominent.

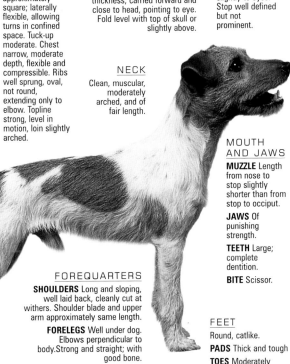

MOUTH AND JAWS
MUZZLE Length from nose to stop slightly shorter than from stop to occiput.

JAWS Of punishing strength.

TEETH Large; complete dentition.

BITE Scissor.

FEET
Round, catlike.

PADS Thick and tough

TOES Moderately arched, pointing forward.

FOREQUARTERS
SHOULDERS Long and sloping, well laid back, cleanly cut at withers. Shoulder blade and upper arm approximately same length.

FORELEGS Well under dog. Elbows perpendicular to body. Strong and straight; with good bone.

PASTERNS Firm and nearly straight.

89

TERRIER

→ GENERAL APPEARANCE
This basically square, medium-sized, predominantly white terrier has a smooth or broken coat, and resembles a smaller Fox Terrier.

→ CHARACTERISTICS
The smooth or broken coats, lack of excessive facial furnishings, and lightly built, flexible body are typical of this breed.

→ TEMPERAMENT
Bold, friendly, athletic, and clever, and a game, tenacious hunter at work. At home, it is playful, exuberant, and affectionate. Independent and energetic, it requires a lot of attention and training.

→ GAIT/MOVEMENT
Movement is free, lively, and well coordinated, with a straight action in front and behind.

→ COAT
There are two coat types. In both, the coat is double, coarse, and weatherproof, and the belly and underside of the thighs are not bare. Sculpting of the coat is prohibited.

SMOOTH—flat, but hard, dense, and abundant.

BROKEN—a short, tight jacket lies flat and close to the body and legs. The outline is clear, with only a hint of eyebrows and beard. There is no tendency to curl or wave.

→ COLOR
Colors are white, white with black or tan markings, or a combination of the three (tri-colored). Markings should be confined to the head and the root of the tail. Grizzle is allowed.

→ SIZE
HEIGHT

12–14 in (30–35cm)

Both sexes properly balanced at this height.

ANKC 10–12 in (25–30cm).

WEIGHT (working condition)

13–17 lb (5.9–7.7kg)

Overall balance is crucial. Height of body slightly more than length in ratio 6:5.

ANKC Weight is 1kg (2.2 lb) to each 5cm (2 in) in height.

→ DISQUALIFICATIONS
- Height below 12 in (30cm) or over 15 in (37.5cm)
- Prick ears
- Liver nose
- Four or more missing teeth
- Overshot, undershot or wry mouth
- Brindle markings
- Overt aggression toward other dogs or humans

TERRIER

KERRY BLUE TERRIER

The Kerry was developed in southwestern Ireland, centered around the Kerry peninsula, where it is claimed that they have been a pure breed since the late 1700s.

The Kerry was versatile and useful: it guarded sheep and cattle, hunted otter and badger, and kept the farm free of rats. Some also served as water retrievers—truly a one-man-band of a dog.

The breed was essentially unknown outside of Ireland until the 1920s, when it made a splash on the British dog show scene and, likewise, in around 1924, in the U.S. Since then, Kerry type and temperament have both stabilized. The Kerry responds happily to firm but kind training. It is a very affectionate dog and a delightful companion for an adult or older children.

GENERAL APPEARANCE
An upstanding dog, in good balance, with a well developed and muscular body.

CHARACTERISTICS
The overall blue-gray color, wavy soft coat, and full beard are unique.

TEMPERAMENT
Definite terrier style and character.

GAIT/MOVEMENT
The gait shows full freedom of action, with fore- and hindlegs moving straight forward.

COAT
The coat is soft, dense, and wavy. The body should be well covered but tidy and, except for the whiskers, the head, ears, and cheeks are clear.

COLOR
The color of a mature dog is any shade of blue-gray or gray-blue, from deep slate to light blue-gray. This should be fairly uniform throughout, but distinctly darker or black on the muzzle, head, ears, tail, and feet. The dog is born black, and the color gradually changes until about 18 months, when it should be as described.

SIZE
HEIGHT

males	females
18–19½ in	17½–19 in
(45–48.75cm)	(43.75–47.5cm)

WEIGHT (mature)

Males 33–40 lb (15–18.1kg)
Females weigh slightly less.

DISQUALIFICATIONS
- Solid black
- Dewclaws on hindlegs

HEAD AND SKULL
Head long but not exaggerated. Skull flat, with very slight stop, moderate breadth between ears, and narrowing slightly to eyes. Foreface full, moderately chiseled to avoid wedginess. Little difference between length of skull and foreface. Cheeks clean, level, free from bumpiness.
NOSE Black, with nostrils large and wide.

TAIL
Docked. Set on high, of moderate length, and carried gaily erect, the straighter the better.
KC/ANKC Customarily docked. Undocked: Set on high. Of moderate length to give an overall balanced appearance.

BODY AND TOPLINE
Back short, strong, level. Chest deep with only moderate breadth. Ribs fairly well sprung, deep rather than round. Slight tuck-up. Loin short and powerful.

EYES AND EARS
EYES Small, not prominent.
COLOR Dark.

EARS Moderately thick, V-shaped, and small but in proportion to size of dog. Carried forward close to cheeks with top of folded ear slightly above level of skull.

NECK
Clean and moderately long.

FOREQUARTERS
SHOULDERS Long and sloping, well laid back.
FORELEGS Straight. Elbows perpendicular to body.
PASTERNS Short, straight.

HINDQUARTERS
Strong and muscular, free from droop or crouch.
HINDLEGS Thighs long and powerful. Stifles well bent. Hocks near ground, upright.

FEET
Strong, compact, fairly round, and moderately small.
TOES Arched, turning neither in nor out.
NAILS Black.

MOUTH AND JAWS
JAWS Deep, strong and muscular.
BITE Strong, either level or slightly overlapping.
KC/ANKC Scissor.

MINIATURE SCHNAUZER

The Miniature Schnauzer is one of three German Schnauzer breeds. The Miniature was achieved through selectively breeding small Standard Schnauzers, and then crossing the resulting progeny with the Affenpinscher and Poodles. The Standard and Miniatures continued to be interbred until 1933; the Miniature remains in the Terrier Group; the Standard and Giant Schnauzers are in the Working Group. In the U.K. two are in the Utility Group; the Giant is in the Working Group. The Miniature Schnauzer is by far the most popular of the three, and one of the most popular of the AKC breeds. It is compact, muscular, and quite game. It is slightly suspicious of strangers and a good watchdog. Many bark excessively unless taught otherwise. It is a sweet pet, full of energy, which calls everyone known to it a friend and acts as if the entire household, rightfully, revolves around it.

EYES AND EARS

EYES Small and deep set. COLOR Dark brown. SHAPE Oval.

EARS Identical when cropped, with pointed tips. Set high on skull and carried perpendicularly at outer edges. When uncropped, small and V-shaped, folding close to skull. **KC/FCI** Never cropped.

ABOVE Uncropped ears.
BELOW Cropped ears.

BODY AND TOPLINE

Body short and deep, brisket extending at least to elbow. Ribs well sprung and deep, extending back to a short loin. No noticeable tuck-up. Back is straight, declining slightly from withers to base of tail. Length from chest to buttocks appears to equal height at withers.

HEAD AND SKULL

Strong and rectangular, width diminishing from ears to eyes, and again to nose tip. Forehead unwrinkled. Topskull flat and fairly long. Foreface parallel to and at least as long as topskull. Slight stop.

NECK

Strong and well arched. Skin fits tightly at throat.

TAIL

Set high and carried erect. Docked only long enough to be clearly visible over backline of body when dog is in proper coat.

When undocked:
FCI "Natural."
KC "Thick at root tapering to tip, straight as possible, carried jauntily."

MOUTH AND JAWS

MUZZLE Strong in proportion to skull, ending in moderately blunt manner, with thick whiskers accentuating head shape.

BITE Scissor.

FOREQUARTERS

SHOULDERS Muscled, yet flat, clean, and well laid back. Shoulder blades close together. Shoulder blades and upper arms are long, permitting depth of chest at brisket.

FORELEGS Straight, with good bone, separated by fairly deep brisket. Elbows close, ribs spread gradually from the first.

PASTERNS Strong.

FEET

Short and round

PADS Thick and black.

TOES Arched and compact.

GENERAL APPEARANCE

This robust, active dog, of terrier type, resembles its larger cousin, the Standard Schnauzer.

CHARACTERISTICS

The Miniature Schnauzer is a solidly built, square dog, with a close wiry coat and soft whiskers.

TEMPERAMENT

This dog is typically alert and spirited, yet obedient to command. Friendly, intelligent and willing to please, it should not be aggressive or timid.

GAIT/MOVEMENT

The forelegs, with the elbows close to the body, move straight ahead. The hindlegs also move straight forward. There is good reach in front and a strong drive from the rear.

COAT

The coat is double, with a hard, wiry outercoat and a close undercoat. The head, neck, ears, chest, tail, and body coat must be plucked. Furnishings are fairly thick but not silky.

COLOR

Recognized colors are salt-and-pepper, black-and-silver, and solid black. All colors have uniform skin pigmentation.

FCI Allows pure white.

SIZE

HEIGHT
12–14 in (30–35cm)

Nearly square in body, with no suggestion of toyishness.

DISQUALIFICATIONS

- Coat solid white (*see above*) or with white striping, patching or spotting, except for small white spot permitted on chest of black dogs
- Deviation above or below the stated height

HINDQUARTERS

HINDLEGS Strongly muscled, slanting thighs. Well bent at stifles.

PASTERNS Short, parallel, and perpendicular.

↓
SCOTTISH TERRIER

One of many short-legged, harsh-coated terriers from Scotland, the Scottish Terrier was found in greatest numbers in the Aberdeen region; and was for some years known as the Aberdeen Terrier. Among the oldest of terriers, it is closely related to, but distinct from, the West Highland White Terrier and the Cairn. The first Scotties were imported to the U.S. in 1883, and grew to become one of the most popular terriers until about 1950.

Proponents of the breed claim "Once a Scottie owner—always a Scottie owner." It is essentially a one-person dog, but gets on happily with other family members. From a rambunctious puppy, it becomes a dignified adult, stubbornly independent at times, yet quite happy to share its chosen master's pleasures or troubles.

President Franklin Roosevelt's beloved Scottie, "Fala," was his constant companion in life, and is buried next to the President in Hyde Park, New York. On one occasion, when Fala

HEAD AND SKULL
Long in proportion to overall size of dog. Skull and muzzle on parallel planes. Skull long, of medium width, slightly domed and covered with short, hard hair. Slight stop. Skull smooth with no prominences or depressions. Cheeks flat and clean.

NOSE Black; good sized, projecting somewhat over mouth.

EYES AND EARS
EYES Small, set wide apart, well in under the brow. COLOR Dark brown or nearly black. SHAPE Almond.

EARS Small, prick, set well up on skull and pointed, but never cut. Covered with short, velvety hair.

BODY AND TOPLINE
Body moderately short, with ribs extending well back into a short, strong loin, deep flanks and very muscular hindquarters. Ribs well sprung. Topline firm and level. Chest broad, very deep and well let-down between forelegs. Forechest extends well in front of legs and drops well down into brisket.

MOUTH AND JAWS
MUZZLE Approximately equal to length of skull, with a slight taper to nose.

TEETH Large.

BITE Scissor or level. **KC/FCI/ANKC** Scissor only.

NECK
Moderately short, strong, thick, and muscular.

FOREQUARTERS
SHOULDERS Well laid back.

FORELEGS Very heavy in bone, straight or slightly bent, with elbows close to body.

DEWCLAWS May be removed.

had traveled with Roosevelt to a military conference off the coast of Europe, the dog was left behind, causing great presidential consternation; when another naval ship was sent to retrieve the dog, the consternation came from the opposition party!

The Scottie is every inch a terrier, ready instantly to dispatch any small animal. It can be aggressive with other dogs. The Scottish Terrier needs daily exercise, either long walks on leash or vigorous play in a fenced area. A true hunter, it will seek adventure if allowed to roam.

The Scottie coat needs hand-stripping every four to five months, along with a thorough brushing and combing every two or three days, with special attention to the furnishings on head and legs.

→ GENERAL APPEARANCE

A small, short-legged, sturdily-built dog. It has a hard, wiry, weather-resistant coat, and a thick-set, cobby body on short, heavy legs.

→ CHARACTERISTICS

Its general build, erect ears and tail, piercing expression, and full beard set the Scottie apart.

→ TEMPERAMENT

Alert and spirited, but stable and steady-going, the Scottie is a determined and thoughtful dog. It can be loving and gentle with people, but aggressive with other dogs.

→ GAIT/MOVEMENT

The forelegs do not move in parallel planes, but rather incline inward because of the deep, broad forechest. Movement is free and agile, with drive from the rear and good reach in front. The hindlegs move squarely, with both hocks and stifles vigorously flexed.

→ COAT

A hard, wiry broken outercoat, and a soft, dense undercoat. The coat should be trimmed and blended into the furnishings to give the distinctive Scottie outline. The longer coat on the beard, legs, and lower body may be slightly softer than the body coat but never fluffy.

→ COLOR

Colors are black, wheaten, or brindle of any color. Many black and brindle dogs have sprinklings of white or silver hairs, which are normal. White is allowed only on the chest and chin, and only to a slight extent.

→ SIZE

HEIGHT

males	females
10 in	10 in
(25cm)	(25cm)

WEIGHT

males	females
19–22 lb	18–21 lb
(8.6–10kg)	(8.2–9.5kg)

Thick body and heavy bone. Length of back from withers to set-on of tail about 11 in (27.5cm).

TAIL
About 7in (17.5cm) long and never docked. Set on high and carried erect, either vertical or with a slight curve forward, but not over the back.

HINDQUARTERS
HINDLEGS Thighs very muscular and powerful. Stifles well bent and legs straight from hock to heel. Hocks well let-down.

FEET
Round, thick, and compact. Forefeet larger than hindfeet.
TOES Slight toeing out is acceptable but movement is straight ahead.
NAILS Strong.

SOFT COATED WHEATEN TERRIER

Ireland is the birthplace of the Kerry Blue, the Irish, and the Soft Coated Wheaten Terrier. The Wheaten is thought to have been the first on the scene, and is a progenitor of the other two. The Wheaten served as a general-purpose farm dog, herding and guarding cattle, and warring against all vermin. Basically a happy dog, it is alert, affectionate, and playful, especially with children. It is easy to train but, on occasion, its independence causes it to do things in its own way. It is more congenial than most terriers and gets on well with most other animals. It is a dog of moderation, both in its structure, show presentation, and personality. It is graceful, strong, and well coordinated in appearance, and not given to temper.

The Soft Coated Wheaten lacks the double coat of many terriers. Its single coat is soft and silky or wavy, growing to its greatest length on its chin and over its eyes. The coat is not shed and it will mat if not combed at least every two or three days.

→ GENERAL APPEARANCE
The Wheaten is a medium-sized, hardy, well balanced sporting terrier, square in outline.

→ CHARACTERISTICS
The soft, silky, gently waving single coat, of warm wheaten color, and a steady disposition, are typical of the Wheaten.

→ TEMPERAMENT
A happy, steady dog, gay and self-confident. It is alert and less aggressive than other terriers.

→ GAIT/MOVEMENT
Movement is free, graceful, and lively, with good reach in front and a strong drive behind. The tail must be kept erect when moving.

→ COAT
The abundant single coat covers the entire body, legs and head. On the head it falls forward to shade the eyes. The texture is soft and silky, with a gentle wave on mature dogs. The coat must never be clipped or plucked.

→ COLOR
Color is any shade of wheaten. Occasional red, white or black guard hairs may be found interspersed. Blue-gray shading may be present on the ears or muzzle.

→ SIZE
HEIGHT

males	females
18–19 in (45–47.5cm)	17–18 in (42.5–45cm

WEIGHT

males	females
35–40 lb (15.9–18.2kg)	30–35 lb (13.6–15.9kg)

Dog is square in outline.

HEAD AND SKULL
Rectangular, moderately long, powerful but not coarse. Skull flat. Cheekbones not prominent. Defined stop. **NOSE** Black and large.

EYES AND EARS
EYES Medium sized, set fairly wide apart. COLOR Dark reddish brown, with black rims. SHAPE Slightly almond.

EARS Small to medium, breaking level with skull and dropping slightly forward. Inside edge lying next to cheek and pointing to ground rather than eye.

BODY AND TOPLINE
Back strong and level. Body compact, relatively short-coupled. Chest deep. Ribs well sprung but not round.

TAIL
Docked; carried gaily, but never over the back. **KC/ANKC** Customarily docked. Undocked: tip may curl but all must be in balance.

MOUTH AND JAWS
MUZZLE Powerful. Skull and foreface of equal length. **LIPS** Tight and black. **BITE** Scissor or level. **KC** Scissor only.

NECK
Medium long, clean and strong, but not throaty.

FOREQUARTERS
SHOULDERS Well laid-back, clean. **FORELEGS** Straight and well boned. **DEWCLAWS** Removed.

FEET
Round and compact. **PADS** Black, with good depth. **NAILS** Dark.

HINDQUARTERS
HINDLEGS Well developed, with well bent stifles. Hocks well down and parallel.

STAFFORDSHIRE BULL TERRIER

Another of the breeds originally developed for the cruel "sports" of bull- and bear-baiting, and later for dog-fighting, the Staffordshire Bull Terrier's history is similar to that of the Bull, American Staffordshire, and Pit Bull Terriers.

In the early 1800s, the workers who moved to the cities of the U.K. as a result of the Industrial Revolution organized contests in which dogs were made to kill hundreds of rats in a pit. Dogs that succeeded in the pits were crossed with ancestors of the Manchester Terrier; aiming for a strong, fast, and more exciting pit-fighter. Finally, after fights were banned in the mid-1800s, a few owners sought to build on the dog's personality and to refine its appearance as a show dog. The Staffordshire is very intelligent, strong, agile and courageous. It usually responds well to training, which must begin while it is very young.

GENERAL APPEARANCE

A smooth-coated terrier, of medium size, and of great strength for its size. Though muscular, it is active and agile.

CHARACTERISTICS

Its very muscular head, with pronounced stop and strong muzzle, is distinctive.

TEMPERAMENT

From its past history, the modern dog draws its indomitable courage, high intelligence, and tenacity. It is affectionate with friends, and children in particular.

GAIT/MOVEMENT

Gait is free, powerful, and agile, with economy of movement. There is a discernible drive from the hindlegs.

COAT

The coat is smooth, short, and close to the skin. The dog should not be trimmed or dewhiskered.

COLOR

Colors are red, fawn, white, black, or blue, or any of these colors with white.

KC/FCI/ANKC Any shade of brindle or brindle with white.

SIZE

HEIGHT (at shoulders)
14–16 in (35–40cm)

WEIGHT

males	females
28–38 lb (12.7–17.3kg)	24–34 lb (10.9–15.5kg)

In proportion, distance from withers to tail set is equal to that from withers to ground.

DISQUALIFICATIONS

- Black-and-tan or liver color

EYES AND EARS

EYES Medium sized, set to look straight ahead
COLOR Preferably dark, but may be similar to coat color.
SHAPE Round.

EARS Rose or half-pricked, and not large.

HEAD AND SKULL

Skull short, deep, and broad, with very pronounced cheek muscles and distinct stop.

BODY AND TOPLINE

Body is close-coupled, with a level topline; wide front; deep brisket; well sprung ribs; rather light in the loin.

TAIL

Undocked, of medium length. Low set, tapering to a point, and carried rather low.

MOUTH AND JAWS

Short foreface.
NOSE. Black.
LIPS Tight and clean.
BITE Tight scissor.

NECK

Muscular, rather short, and clean.

HINDQUARTERS

Well muscled.
HINDLEGS Hocks let-down. Stifles well bent.
DEWCLAWS Generally removed.

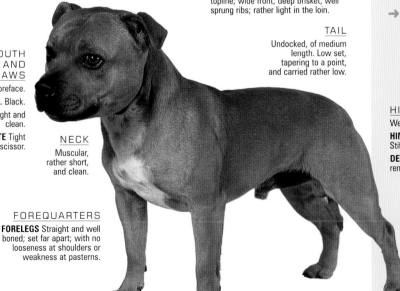

FOREQUARTERS

FORELEGS Straight and well boned; set far apart; with no looseness at shoulders or weakness at pasterns.

FEET

Well padded, strong, and of medium size, turning out a little from pasterns.

↓ WELSH TERRIER

The Welsh Terrier closely resembles the larger Airedale or the Lakeland Terrier. In shape it resembles the Wire Fox Terrier, but not as refined. Since the 1700s, it has been very popular in its native Wales as a hunter of vermin (foxes, badgers, otters, rats). By 1886 the KC had recognized the Welsh Terrier as a distinct breed. Its likely ancestor is the Old English Wirehaired Black-and-Tan Terrier, which it closely resembles and has done for over a hundred years. The first Welsh Terriers were brought to the U.S. in 1888, but the breed did not catch on with the public until after the early 1900s, and they have never achieved the level of popularity that their character deserves. The Welsh Terrier is very playful and many like water play. Generally well mannered, it is very responsive to training and wants to please its owner.

GENERAL APPEARANCE
This sturdy, compact, rugged dog is of medium size, with a coarse wire coat. The tail is docked.

CHARACTERISTICS
The Welsh Terrier resembles a smaller version of the Airedale.

TEMPERAMENT
A game dog, the Welsh Terrier is alert and spirited, but friendly. It is intelligent and eager to please. Dogs that are overly aggressive or shy should be penalized.

GAIT/MOVEMENT
Movement is straight, free, and effortless, with a good front reach and a strong rear drive.

COAT
The coat is hard, wiry, and dense, with a close-fitting jacket and a short, soft undercoat. Furnishings on the muzzle, legs, and quarters are dense and wiry.

COLOR
The jacket is black (grizzle is acceptable), spreading to the neck, down to the tail and into the upper thighs. The legs, quarters and head are clear tan (a deep reddish color, with slightly lighter shades acceptable).

SIZE
HEIGHT
Males 15–15½ in (37.5–38.75cm)
Females proportionately smaller.
WEIGHT (average)
20 lb (9.1kg).

EYES AND EARS
EYES Small, placed fairly far apart. COLOR Dark brown. SHAPE Almond.

EARS Small, V-shaped, but not too thin. Fold just above topline of skull. Carried forward close to cheek with tips falling toward outside corners of eye.

HEAD AND SKULL
Head rectangular. Foreface strong, with punishing jaws; only slightly narrower than backskull and on parallel planes. Backskull smooth and flat between ears. No wrinkles. Cheeks flat and clean. Slight stop.

TAIL
Docked to approximate level of occiput. Tail root set well up on back. Carried upright. **KC/ANKC** Customarily docked. Undocked: must be in balance with rest of dog.

BODY AND TOPLINE
Topline level. Body shows good substance; well ribbed; good depth of brisket and moderate width of chest. Loin strong and moderately short.

NECK
Of moderate length and thickness, and slightly arched. Throat clean.

MOUTH AND JAWS
MUZZLE Half the length of entire head from tip of nose to occiput. Foreface furnishings are trimmed to complete, without exaggerating, the rectangular outline.

LIPS Black and tight.

TEETH Large and strong. Complete dentition.

BITE Scissor preferred, but level acceptable. **KC/FCI/ANKC** Scissor only.

FOREQUARTERS
SHOULDERS Long, sloping and well laid-back.
FORELEGS Straight and muscular,
PASTERNS Upright and powerful.
DEWCLAWS Should be removed.

HINDQUARTERS
Strong and muscular.

HINDLEGS Well-developed second thighs. Stifles well bent. Hocks moderately straight, short from joint to ground.

FEET
Small, round and catlike.

PADS Thick and black.

NAILS Strong and black.

WEST HIGHLAND WHITE TERRIER

The first specialty club for this breed was formed in 1905, when these all-white terriers were first separated from the other short-legged terriers that had been hunting vermin in the Scottish Highlands for over three hundred years. Credit for development of the "Westie", as it is now known, goes to Colonel E. D. Malcom of Paltalloch, Scotland. Similar specialty clubs were formed in the U.S. in 1909, in Canada in 1911, and in Australia in 1963. The popularity of these perky little dogs has continued to grow throughout the last century. Like its cousins (the Skye, Dandie Dinmont, Cairn and Scottie), the Westie was a willing hunter, especially of foxes and badgers. Surprisingly, it has also shown talent at herding cows and sheep. Nevertheless, the vast majority of Westies are pets or show dogs.

→ **GENERAL APPEARANCE**

A small, game, well balanced terrier, The West Highland exhibits strength and activity.

→ **CHARACTERISTICS**

The Westie is a wholly white, hard-coated terrier. Its hair should be trimmed around the head to present the typical roundish frame.

→ **TEMPERAMENT**

This dog is alert, gay, courageous, and self-reliant, but friendly.

→ **GAIT/MOVEMENT**

Movement is free, straight, and easy all around. The gait is distinctive, not stilted, but powerful, with reach and drive. Freely flexing hocks push the body forward with some force. The topline remains level.

→ **COAT**

The ideal coat is hard, double, straight, and white. The outercoat consists of straight, hard white hair, about 2 in (5cm) long, shorter on the neck and shoulders, and longer on the stomach and legs. Furnishings may be somewhat softer and longer, but never fluffy. The head is shaped by plucking the hair to present the round appearance.

→ **COLOR**

White is the only color permitted.

→ **SIZE**

HEIGHT

males	females
11 in	10 in
(27.5cm)	(25cm)

Slight deviations acceptable. Body between withers and root of tail slightly shorter than height at withers.

EYES AND EARS

EYES Set wide apart and deep set. COLOR Dark brown. SHAPE Almond

EARS Small; carried tightly erect, and set wide apart on top outer edge of skull. Terminate in sharp point and must never be cropped. Hair on ears trimmed short, smooth and velvety. Black skin pigmentation preferred.

FOREQUARTERS

SHOULDERS Shoulderblades well laid-back; blade should attach to upper arm of moderate length and sufficient angle to allow for body overhang.

FORELEGS Muscular and well boned, reasonably straight, and thickly covered with short, hard hair. Height from elbow to withers and elbow to ground approximately equal.

DEWCLAWS May be removed.

TAIL

Relatively short, with good substance. Shaped like a carrot. Covered with hard hair, as straight as possible. Carried gaily but not curled over back. set-on high. Never docked.

BODY AND TOPLINE

Topline flat. Body compact, of good substance. Ribs deep and well arched, extending at least to elbows, with a flattish side appearance. Back ribs of considerable depth. Loin short, broad and strong.

NECK
Muscular.

HEAD AND SKULL

Trimmed to present a round appearance from the front. Skull broad, slightly domed between ears, and gradually tapering to eyes. Defined stop. Eyebrows heavy.

NOSE Large and black.

MOUTH AND JAWS

MUZZLE Blunt, slightly shorter than skull, powerful and gradually tapering to nose.

JAWS Level and powerful.

LIPS Black.

TEETH Large.

BITE Tight scissor.

HINDQUARTERS

HINDLEGS Muscular and relatively short and sinewy. Thighs very muscular, well angulated, not set wide apart. Hocks well bent and short.

DEWCLAWS May be removed.

FEET

Forefeet larger than hindfeet. Round, strong, and turned out slightly.

PADS Thick.

NAILS Black pigmentation desirable.

BRUSSELS GRIFFON

The Brussels Griffon (called the Griffon Bruxellois by the KC, FCI, and ANKC) is a Belgian breed. Early in its history, it was a street or common dog, well known by all and used to control rat populations in stables and homes. This utilitarian dog is believed to have been crossed with the German Affenpinscher, and thus began the Brussels Griffon. Later the Pug was added to the mix, imparting a smoother body outline and the brachycephalic head that enhanced its charm and appeal but ended its career as a rat-catcher. The Pug infusion also resulted in the two different coats found in the breed today. Later still it is alleged that Yorkshire Terriers and Ruby Spaniels were added.

The Brussels Griffon is a toy breed only in size. As a puppy, it is as fragile as any small dog but as an adult it is quite sturdy. While generally very easy to train, some resist leash training. Training, especially to leash, is best started while the dog is very young.

EYES AND EARS

EYES Set well apart, large, prominent. COLOR Black. Eyelashes long and black. Eyelids edged with black.

EARS Small and set rather high. Cropped or natural. Semi-erect if natural. **KC** Not cropped. **FCI** Always cropped.

HEAD AND SKULL

Head is very important to the dog's appearance. Skull large and round, with a domed forehead.

NOSE Very black, extremely short, its tip being set back deeply between the eyes so as to form a lay-back.

ABOVE Uncropped ears.
LEFT Cropped ears.

NECK

Of medium length, arched.

BODY AND TOPLINE

Back level and short. Body thickset. Brisket broad and deep, ribs well sprung. Short-coupled.

MOUTH AND JAWS

LIPS Black, not pendulous.

JAWS Must be undershot. Lower jaw prominent, rather broad with an upward sweep. Neither teeth nor tongue should show when mouth is closed.

BITE Undershot. **KC/ANKC** Not showing tongue or teeth.

FEET

Round, small and compact, facing straight ahead.

TOES Well-arched.

PADS Black.

NAILS Black preferred.

FOREQUARTERS

FORELEGS Straight, well muscled, moderately wide apart.

PASTERNS Short and strong.

GENERAL APPEARANCE

Alert and sturdy, with a thickset, short body, and an almost human expression.

CHARACTERISTICS

The fringe of hair on the face imparts a monkeylike look.

TEMPERAMENT

The Brussels is intelligent, alert, sensitive, and full of self-importance.

GAIT/MOVEMENT

The purposeful trot shows moderate reach and drive, with a steady topline.

COAT

There are two types of coat.

ROUGH—wiry and dense, never wooly or silky. Not shaggy, but distinct from the smooth coat. Head is covered with wiry hair, slightly longer around the eyes, nose, cheeks, and chin, forming a fringe. Coat is hand-stripped, never scissored or clipped.

SMOOTH—straight, short, tight, and glossy. The smooth-coated variety is known as "Brabant Griffon" in Europe.

COLOR

Colors are red (reddish brown with a little black on whiskers and chin), belge (black and reddish brown mixed, usually with black mask and whiskers), black-and-tan, or black. Any white hairs are a serious fault, except for "frost" on the muzzle of a mature dog.

SIZE

WEIGHT

8–10 lb (3.6–4.5kg)

Weight should not exceed 12 lb (5.5kg). Square in proportion.

KC/ANKC Prefer 6–10 lb (2.7–4.5kg).

FCI Small size maximum 6.6 lb (3kg); large size maximum 11 lb (5kg).

DISQUALIFICATIONS

- Dudley or butterfly nose
- Overshot
- Hanging tongue
- White spot or blaze anywhere on coat

TAIL

Set and held high. Docked to about a third. **KC/ANKC** Customarily docked. Undocked: of moderate length, curved gently over back.

HINDQUARTERS

HINDLEGS Thighs strong and well muscled. Stifles bent. Hocks well let down, turning neither in nor out.

CAVALIER KING CHARLES SPANIEL

The Cavalier is, in its loving heart, a spaniel, but it needs far less space than its larger cousins. Its history is closely aligned with that of English royalty. It was a favorite pet among ladies of the Tudor court in the time of Elizabeth I. According to the diaries of Samuel Pepys (1660-69), King Charles II (Stuart) was accused of paying so much attention to his dogs (and his mistresses) that he ignored government matters. When William of Orange came to the throne in 1689, bringing with him his Pugs from Holland, the Pug claimed the pinnacle of courtly fashion. By the time of Queen Victoria and the first dog shows, spaniels with a shorter face were more popular. It took an American, Roswell Eldridge, to persuade some British breeders to return to the older style Cavalier King Charles. A breed club was formed for devotees of the Cavaliers in 1928, and a standard was approved. In 1945, the KC began to register the Cavalier, which became one of the most popular dogs in the U.K. Easy to train because of its devotion, care must be taken not to betray the trust it places in its owner.

HEAD AND SKULL

Skull slightly rounded, but no dome or peak. Appears flat because of high placement of ears. Stop moderate. **NOSE** Black, with nostrils well developed.

EYES AND EARS

EYES Large, not prominent, set well apart. COLOR Very dark brown, with dark rims. SHAPE Round.

EARS Set high, but not close. Leather long with ample feathering when dog is alert, ears fan slightly forward to frame face.

MOUTH AND JAWS

MUZZLE Full and slightly tapering. Length from base of stop to tip of nose about 1½ in (3.75cm). **LIPS** Well developed but not pendulous. **BITE** Scissor.

NECK

Fairly long, dry, and slightly arched at crest.

BODY AND TOPLINE

Topline level when moving or standing. Body short-coupled. Ribs well sprung but not barreled. Chest moderately deep, extending to elbows. No appreciable tuck-up.

FOREQUARTERS

SHOULDERS Well laid-back.

FORELEGS Straight and well under body. Elbows close.

PASTERNS Strong.

DEWCLAWS May be removed.

FEET

Compact. **PADS** Well-cushioned.

GENERAL APPEARANCE

An active, graceful, well balanced toy spaniel. Should be natural in appearance, with no trimming, sculpting, or artificial alteration.

CHARACTERISTICS

True elegance and an untrimmed coat, a sweet, melting expression, and feathering on the feet are characteristics of this breed.

TEMPERAMENT

The Cavalier is gay, friendly, and nonaggressive, with no tendency toward nervousness or shyness.

GAIT/MOVEMENT

Free moving and elegant, with good reach in front and a sound, driving rear.

COAT

The coat is of moderate length, silky, and free from curl. A slight wave is permissible. Feathering on the ears, chest, legs, and tail should be long; feathering on the feet is a characteristic of the breed. No trimming is permitted, except for hair growing between pads on underside of feet.

COLOR

There are four colors.

BLENHEIM—rich chestnut markings on a clear, white ground.

TRICOLOR—jet black markings, well broken up on a clear, white ground. White blaze between the eyes. Rich tan markings over eyes, on cheeks, inside ears, and on underside of tail.

RUBY—self-colored rich red.

BLACK AND TAN—jet black with rich tan markings.

SIZE

HEIGHT

12–13 in (30–32.5cm)

WEIGHT

13–18 lb (5.9–8.2kg)

Weight proportionate. Body slightly longer than tall.

TAIL

Carried happily but never much above level of back. Docking optional. If docked, no more than a third to be removed.

HINDQUARTERS

Broad pelvis, moderately muscled. **HINDLEGS** Stifles well turned. Hocks well let down.

CHIHUAHUA

The Chihuahua is the smallest breed of dog in the world, and probably did not originate in Mexico. It is more likely that this little dog came to North America from Malta, where it was known for centuries as Kelb Ta But (pocket dog), although the FCI still cites Mexico as this breed's country of origin. The Maltese dogs seem to have been transported there from North Africa in about 600 B.C. It appears that they were also transported to Central America, probably by the conquistadores, and it was there, in the Villa D'Allende, in Chihuahua Province, that they were found by American tourists. American dog breeders subsequently refined the breed, seeing it to a high toy position. There are two varieties, the long coat and the smooth coat, but with the same standard. Exceptionally smart, the Chihuahua is quite agile and courageous. Obedience training is beneficial because it helps the dog to establish a sense of security.

HEAD AND SKULL
Well-rounded "apple dome" skull, with or without molera (incomplete, imperfect or abnormal closure of skull).
KC Does not include the molera.

NOSE Self-colored in moles, blues, and chocolates. Pink nose permissible in blond types.

EYES AND EARS
EYES Full, but not protruding, set well apart. COLOR Dark or ruby (light eyes are permitted in blond or white dogs).

EARS Large, erect, held more upright when alert, but flared to side at 45 degrees when in repose.

BODY AND TOPLINE
Topline level. Ribs rounded and well sprung (but not barrel).

MOUTH AND JAWS
MUZZLE Moderately short and slightly pointed. Cheeks and jaws lean.

BITE Level or scissor.

KC Scissor only.

NECK
Slightly arched.

FOREQUARTERS
SHOULDERS Lean, sloping into a level back, allowing for chestiness.
FORELEGS Straight, set well under.
PASTERNS Fine.

ABOVE smooth coat
LEFT long coat

GENERAL APPEARANCE

The Chihuahua is a graceful, swift-moving little dog, found in both smooth and long coat varieties.

CHARACTERISTICS

This diminutive dog has a domed skull and is very fine boned.

TEMPERAMENT

Alert and terrier-like. Saucy and bold.

GAIT/MOVEMENT

Movement is swift, with head held high, and a sturdy action. Good reach in front equals strong drive from the rear. Topline remains firm and level.

COAT

There are two types of coat.

SMOOTH—of soft texture, close. Heavier coats with undercoats are permitted. A ruff on the neck is preferred, and the hair is more scanty on head and ears. The hair on the tail is furry.

LONG—coat of soft texture, either flat or slightly curly, with undercoat preferred. Ears fringed, tail is full and long (a plume). Feathering on feet and legs, pants on the hindlegs, and a large ruff on the neck.

COLOR

Any color: solid, marked, or splashed.

SIZE

WEIGHT (maximum)
6 lb (2.7kg)

Body off-square, slightly longer than tall (females longer in body than males).
KC/ANKC Up to 6 lb (2.7kg) but 2–4 lb (0.9–1.8kg) preferred.
FCI 1–6½ lb (0.5–3kg); 2–4½ lb (1–2kg) preferred.

DISQUALIFICATIONS

- Any dog exceeding the stated weight
- Broken down or cropped ears
- Cropped tail, bobtail
- In long coats, too thin a coat that resembles bareness

TAIL
Moderately long, carried sickle either up or out, or in loop over back, with tip just touching back.

HINDQUARTERS
Muscular.
HINDLEGS Hocks well apart, turning neither in nor out, well let down, firm and sturdy.

FEET
Small and dainty.
TOES Well split but not spread.
PADS Cushioned.

CHINESE CRESTED

Now extinct in China, the Chinese Crested is relatively rare in all but a few areas of the world. Pockets of these dogs can still be found in ports around the Mediterranean. It probably originated from an African hairless dog that was sold or traded into China, where it was bred to reduce size. It was favored by the aristocracy, and kept as pets by the mandarins, who lavished special care on them. Dogs of this type were in the West Indies by the sixteenth century and the Americas not long after.

Cresteds are found in two varieties—the Hairless (with a crest of long hair on the head, a plume on the tail-end, and "socks" on each leg) and the Powderpuff, which is fully haired. The Crested is affectionate and intelligent, making it a delightful companion and good watch dog.

GENERAL APPEARANCE
The Chinese Crested is a toy dog, fine-boned, elegant, and graceful.

CHARACTERISTICS
There are two varieties of Chinese Crested, and both can appear in the same litter.

HAIRLESS—with hair only on head, tail, and feet.

POWDERPUFF—completely covered with hair.

TEMPERAMENT
A loving companion; playful and entertaining; gay and alert.

GAIT/MOVEMENT
Movement is lively, agile and smooth, not stilted or Hackneyed.

COAT
There are two types of coat.

HAIRLESS—hair on the head (crest), tail (plume), and feet from toes to front pasterns and rear hock joints (socks). The hair texture is soft and silky, flowing to any length. Where the body is hairless, it is soft and smooth.

POWDERPUFF—is completely covered with a double, soft, silky coat. There are long, thin guard hairs over a short, silky undercoat. Hair is straight, of medium density and length.

COLOR
Any color or combination of colors is allowed.

SIZE
HEIGHT (ideal)

11–13 in (27.5–32.5cm)

Rectangular in proportion; body length longer than height. Fine-boned and slender.

KC/FCI/ANKC Males 11–13 in (28–33cm); females 9–12 in (23–30cm). Weight not over 12 lb (5.4kg).

EYES AND EARS
EYES Set wide apart. COLOR Dark in dark-colored dogs; lighter in lighter-colored dogs. Rims match color of dog. SHAPE Almond.

EARS Uncropped, large and erect; base level with outside corner of eye.

HEAD AND SKULL
Skull arched gently over occiput from ear to ear. Distances from occiput to stop and from stop to nose tip equal. Head wedge-shaped. Cheeks taper cleanly into muzzle.

NOSE Dark in dark-colored dogs, may be lighter in lighter-colored dogs. Pigment solid.

TAIL
Slender, reaches to hock. Carried gaily, when dog is in motion, and down, when at rest. In hairless variety, two-thirds of end of tail is covered with long, flowing feathering. Powderpuff variety completely covered with hair.

BODY AND TOPLINE
Topline level to slightly sloping croup. Brisket extends to elbow. Breastbone not prominent. Ribs well developed. Depth of chest tapers to moderate tuck-up.

NECK
Lean and clean, slightly arched. Carried high.

MOUTH AND JAWS
LIPS Clean and tight.

TEETH Missing teeth in Powderpuff will be faulted.

BITE Scissor or level.

HINDQUARTERS
HINDLEGS Stifles moderately angulated. Hock joint perpendicular to ground

FEET
Narrow harefoot.

TOES Elongated.

NAILS Trimmed to moderate length.

FOREQUARTERS
SHOULDERS Clean and narrow. Layback is 45 degrees to point of shoulder.

FORELEGS Long, slender, and straight. Elbows close to body.

PASTERNS Upright, fine, and strong.

DEWCLAWS May be removed.

ENGLISH TOY SPANIEL

Toy spaniels have long been treasured as pets in Europe. Deriving its name from a dog which was a great favorite of King Charles II (c. 1630–85) and known by the KC, FCI, and ANKC as the King Charles Spaniel, the English Toy Spaniel shares its early history with that of the Cavalier King Charles Spaniel. The most likely early progenitors of both breeds were small spaniel types, crossed with toy dogs imported from the Orient. The dog that King Charles II so doted on was the Black-and-Tan English Toy. The Cavalier King Charles Spaniel was a later creation.

Both spaniel breeds have the same four colorations and the same general shape. The English Toy is rather smaller and has a more extreme head shape—brachycephalic, Puglike (muzzle foreshortened), and with a rounded skull. The English Toy Spaniel has a strong affinity for its own family and may be rather standoffish with strangers. It needs a moderate daily walk, but enjoys free play in a safe area.

→ GENERAL APPEARANCE
A compact, cobby toy dog, with a silky, flowing coat.

→ CHARACTERISTICS
The distinctive, Puglike head has a domed skull, with a short nose, and luxuriant fringing on ears.

→ TEMPERAMENT
A bright, merry little dog, this spaniel is affectionate and willing to please.

→ GAIT/MOVEMENT
Movement is elegant, with good reach in front and a driving rear action. Gait is free and lively, straight and true.

→ COAT
Coat is profuse, with heavy fringing on ears, body, and chest, and feathering on both legs and feet. It is straight or slightly wavy, and silken. Though the Blenheim and Ruby rarely attain the same length of coat and ear fringes as the Prince Charles and King Charles, good coats and long ear fringes are prized.

→ COLOR
There are four colors.

BLENHEIM (red-and-white)—There is often the "Blenheim Spot" on top center of skull.

PRINCE CHARLES (tri-color).

KING CHARLES (black-and-tan).

RUBY (self-colored rich mahogany red).

→ SIZE
WEIGHT (adult, desirable)

8–14 lb (3.6–6.4kg)

All things equal, the smaller size is preferred. Cobby and essentially square. Sturdy and solid.

EYES AND EARS
EYES Large, set on line with nose, with little or no white showing COLOR Very dark brown or black, with black rims.

EARS Very long, set low and close to head. Fringed with heavy feathering.

MOUTH AND JAWS
MUZZLE Very short, with nose well laid-back and cushioning under eyes.

LIPS Meet for a finished appearance.

JAW Square, broad, and deep. Well turned up. Slightly undershot. Teeth should not show.

HEAD AND SKULL
Large in comparison to size, with a chubby look but with refinement. Skull high and well domed, curving as far out over eyes as possible. Stop deep and well defined.

NOSE Large and jet black, with large, wide-open nostrils.

TAIL
Docked to 2–4in (5–10cm) and carried at or just above level of back. Many are born with a shorter or screw tail, which is acceptable. Feather silky and 3–4in (7.5–10cm) long, making a "flag."

BODY AND TOPLINE
Topline level. Body short, compact, square and deep, on cobby lines with broad back. Sturdy frame. Good rib and deep brisket.

NECK
Moderate in length and nicely arched.

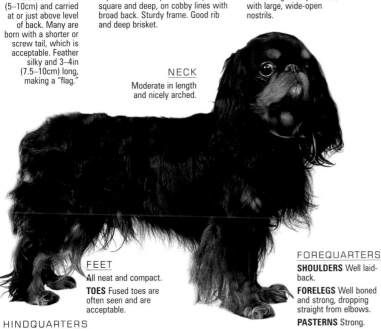

FEET
All neat and compact.

TOES Fused toes are often seen and are acceptable.

FOREQUARTERS
SHOULDERS Well laid-back.

FORELEGS Well boned and strong, dropping straight from elbows.

PASTERNS Strong.

HINDQUARTERS
HINDLEGS Well muscled and nicely angulated for strength.

ITALIAN GREYHOUND

The Italian Greyhound is a real Greyhound, but in miniaturized form. The Romans took these little Greyhounds from Egypt to the Mediterranean in the sixth and seventh centuries B.C., from where they spread throughout southern Europe, finding great acceptance in Italy. In England, by the time of the Stuart kings, the breed was as popular as the toy spaniels and both appear in many paintings of the period.

By the mid-1800s, the breed had declined in quality and numbers, until in 1890 in the U.K. a Miss Mackenzie, and later a Mrs Scarlett, undertook to revive it. Since the end of World War II, the Italian Greyhound has become one of the most popular breeds in the U.K. It also has loyal fans in the U.S., being first recognized by the AKC in 1886, but numbers remained very low until the second half of the twentieth century.

As a puppy, the Italian Greyhound can be quite fragile, and even an adult may suffer from a broken leg or tail. Otherwise it is a sturdy little dog. Periodontal disease is a concern, so it is especially important that its teeth receive daily care. Barbiturates and anesthesia pose a possible risk to the Italian Greyhound, as to other sight hounds. This dog is very affectionate with its family and needs to have its love returned. It can be aloof, even timid, with strangers, but gets along well with other dogs and household pets.

Grooming requires only a wipe-down with a soft cloth, weekly nail trimming, and daily tooth care. The dog is odorless and sheds very little hair.

BODY AND TOPLINE
Chest deep and narrow. Body of medium length, short-coupled, and high at withers. Back curved, drooping at hindquarters. Highest point of curve at start of loin, creating a definite tuck-up at flanks.

TAIL
Slender, tapering to curved end. Reaches to hock. Set and carried low.

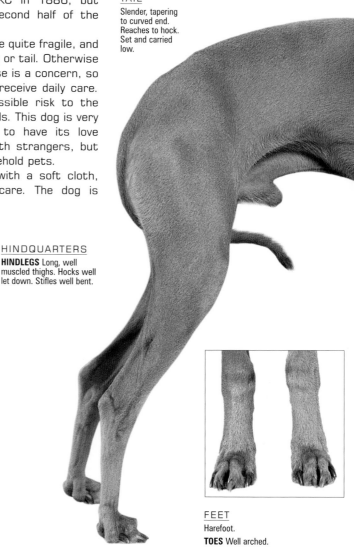

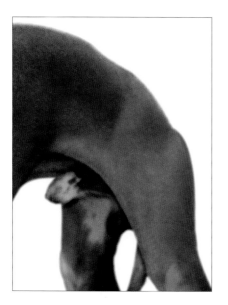

HINDQUARTERS
HINDLEGS Long, well muscled thighs. Hocks well let down. Stifles well bent.

FEET
Harefoot.
TOES Well arched.

HEAD AND SKULL

Narrow and long, tapering to nose. Slight suggestion of stop. Skull long, almost flat.

NOSE Black or brown in keeping with color of dog.

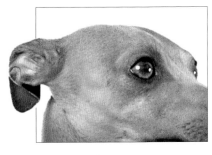

EYES AND EARS

EYES Medium-sized. COLOR Dark.

EARS Small and fine textured. Thrown back and folded or, when alert, carried folded at right angles to head.

MOUTH AND JAWS

Long and fine.
BITE Scissor.

NECK

Long, slender, and gracefully arched.

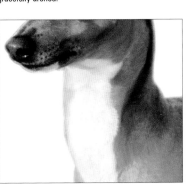

FOREQUARTERS

SHOULDERS Long and sloping.
FORELEGS Long, straight, set well under shoulder.
PASTERNS Strong, of fine bone.
DEWCLAWS Removal optional.

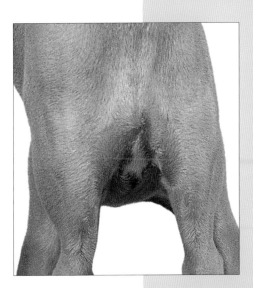

→ GENERAL APPEARANCE

The Italian Greyhound is very similar to the Greyhound, but much smaller and more slender in all proportions.

→ CHARACTERISTICS

This very refined, small, elegant dog has a short silky coat and is built along Greyhound lines.

→ TEMPERAMENT

Affectionate with family. Aloof with strangers.

→ GAIT/MOVEMENT

Gait is high-stepping and free.

→ COAT

The hair is short, glossy, and soft. The skin is fine and supple.

→ COLOR

Any color or markings are acceptable.

→ SIZE

HEIGHT (ideal, at shoulder)
13–15 in (32.5–37.5cm)
KC/FCI/ANKC Prefer slightly smaller size.

→ DISQUALIFICATIONS

- Brindle markings
- Tan markings normally found on black-and-tan dogs of other breeds

MALTESE

The Maltese has lived with people since they settled on the island of Malta, probably somewhere around 3000 B.C. It probably descends from a local spaniel-type dog on Malta. In earlier times, the Maltese could be any self-color. Size also varied; some were described as being as small as ferrets. In the last century or so, type and size have been stabilized and the color is now limited to white. The Maltese came to the U.K. somewhere around 1800. Along with some other small dogs of that time, it was often described as a comforter or sleeve dog, because it was commonly carried around in a lady's huge sleeves, or used as a foot warmer.

A very refined, clean dog, the Maltese is a delightful companion. It accommodates well to most households and to any amount of exercise that its owner is prepared to offer. It will happily adapt to a five-mile hike or a stroll around the block. The Maltese is a very intelligent dog, and needs a regimen that sets safe limits for its behavior.

GENERAL APPEARANCE
A small toy dog which, despite its size, has sufficient vigor to be a great little companion.

CHARACTERISTICS
The body is covered with long, flat, white hair that hangs almost to the ground.

TEMPERAMENT
Despite its diminutive size, the Maltese seems to be without fear. Its trust and affectionate responsiveness are very appealing. Among the gentlest of dogs, it is also lively and playful.

GAIT/MOVEMENT
The Maltese moves with a jaunty, smooth, flowing gait. The forelegs reach straight and free from shoulders with elbows close.

COAT
The single coat is long and silky, and hangs flat over the sides of the body, reaching almost to the ground. Long head hair may be tied up in a topknot or left hanging.

COLOR
Color is white. Light tan or lemon on the ears is permissible but not desirable.

SIZE
WEIGHT (preferred)

4–6 lb (1.8–2.7kg)

Weight must be under 7 lb (3.2kg).

KC/ANKC No weight limit, but maximum height is 10 in (25.5cm).

HEAD AND SKULL
Medium length and in proportion to size of dog. Skull slightly rounded on top. Moderate stop.
NOSE Black.

EYES AND EARS
EYES Set not too far apart. COLOR Very dark, with black rims. SHAPE Round.

EARS Drop ears, rather low set and heavily feathered with long hair.

BODY AND TOPLINE
Body compact. Height from withers to ground equal to length from withers to tail root. Back level. Ribs well sprung. Chest fairly deep. Loin taut, strong, and just slightly tucked-up.

NECK
Sufficiently long for high head carriage.

MOUTH AND JAWS
MUZZLE Medium length, fine and tapered, but not snipy.
BITE Even or scissor.

TAIL
A longhaired plume carried over the back, tip lying to the side.

HINDQUARTERS
HINDLEGS Strong. Moderately angulated at stifles and hocks.

FOREQUARTERS
SHOULDERS Shoulder blades sloping. Elbows held close to body.
FORELEGS Fine-boned, straight, and nicely feathered.
PASTERNS Joints free of appreciable bend.

FEET
Small and round, with toe pads black. Scraggly hairs may be trimmed.

↓ MINIATURE PINSCHER

The Miniature Pinscher is not a miniature version of the Doberman Pinscher, but has been a pure breed far longer than the Doberman. Both breeds were developed in Germany, where Pinscher means "terrier." The Miniature Pinscher is likely to be descended from the old German Smooth-haired Pinscher, a slightly larger terrier with a very similar appearance. It is impossible to be sad when near this dog. It can light up a room with its energetic, brash, fearless, and proud personality. Its sparkling personality and clean good looks have led to some being called the "king of toys" at dog shows. Its excellent hearing makes it a superior watch dog, though it considers itself a guard. It needs more exercise than some toy breeds, including needs regular walks, and loves to run and romp in a safe area.

→ GENERAL APPEARANCE
Structurally a well balanced, sturdy, compact, short-coupled, smooth-coated dog.

→ CHARACTERISTICS
A hackneylike action is typical of the breed.

→ TEMPERAMENT
Fearless animation, complete self-possession, and a spirited presence.

→ GAIT/MOVEMENT
All legs move parallel, feet turning neither in nor out. The hackneylike action is a high-stepping, reaching, free and easy gait. Smooth and strong drive from rear. The head and tail are carried high.

→ COAT
The coat is smooth, hard, short, and straight, uniformly covering the body.

→ COLOR
Colors are solid clear red, stag red (red with black hairs), black with rust-red markings, and chocolate with rust-red markings.

→ SIZE
HEIGHT (allowed)
10–12½ in (25–31.25cm)

HEIGHT (desired)
11–11½ in (27.5–28.75cm)

Length of dogs equals height at withers. Females may be slightly longer.

→ DISQUALIFICATIONS
- Deviation above or below the stated height limits
- Any color other than listed
- Thumb marks (patch of black hair surrounded by rust) on front of foreleg between foot and wrist; on chocolates the patch is chocolate
- White on any part of dog which exceeds one-half inch at its longest dimension

EYES AND EARS
EYES Full. COLOR Dark, even to true black, including rims, except chocolates, whose rims may be self-colored. SHAPE Slightly oval.

EARS Set high, standing erect. Cropped or uncropped.

HEAD AND SKULL
No indication of coarseness. Skull appears flat, tapering toward muzzle.

NOSE Black. May be self-colored in chocolates.

MOUTH AND JAWS
MUZZLE Strong rather than fine, parallel to top of skull.

LIPS Small, taut, and close to cheeks.

BITE Scissor. FCI "42 pure white teeth."

BODY AND TOPLINE
Back level or slightly sloping toward rear. Body compact, slightly wedge-shaped, and muscular. Forechest well developed. Ribs well sprung. Brisket level with elbows. Belly moderately tucked-up. Short, strong loin. Croup level with topline.

ABOVE Uncropped ears
LEFT Cropped ears

NECK
Slightly arched, gracefully curved. No dewlap or throatiness.

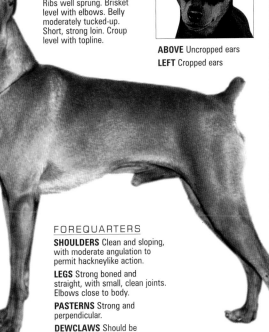

FEET
Small, catlike.

TOES Strong, well arched, and closely knit.

PADS Deep.

NAILS Thick and blunt.

FOREQUARTERS
SHOULDERS Clean and sloping, with moderate angulation to permit hackneylike action.

LEGS Strong boned and straight, with small, clean joints. Elbows close to body.

PASTERNS Strong and perpendicular.

DEWCLAWS Should be removed.

TAIL
Set high and held erect. Docked in proportion to size of dog. **KC/ANKC** Customarily docked. Undocked: Length to give overall balanced appearance

HINDQUARTERS
Well-muscled quarters set wide.

HINDLEGS Thighs well muscled. Stifles well defined. Hocks short, set well apart.

DEWCLAWS Should be removed.

PAPILLON

The Papillon's story may go back to the second century A.D., but it has certainly bred true to type for over seven hundred years. By the sixteenth century, this dwarf spaniel had spread virtually throughout Europe from Italy and Spain, where it seems to have begun. Like the toy spaniels and the Maltese, the Papillon became a favorite of the aristocracy wherever it went.

The breed occurs in two types—the Papillon (with upright ears), and the Phalene, or Continental Toy Spaniel (with drop ears). Both can, and often do, appear in the same litter. While the breed was gaining favor in France, a mutation occurred that caused some dogs to have the upright ears now thought so typical of the breed. It was these upright ears, with their flowing fringe, that so resemble the wings of a butterfly and led to their name— Papillon, which is French for "butterfly." The early Papillons were mostly self-colored, but they are now solid white, with patches of other colors.

HEAD AND SKULL
Head small. Skull of medium width, slightly rounded between ears. Well-defined stop.
NOSE Black, small, rounded, and slightly flat on top.

MOUTH AND JAWS

MUZZLE Fine, abruptly thinner than head, and tapering to nose. Length from nose tip to stop is approximately a third that of head from nose tip to occiput.
LIPS Thin, tight, and black. Tongue must not be visible when jaws are closed.
BITE Scissor.

EYES AND EARS
EYES Medium-sized, not bulging. Inner corners are on line with the stop COLOR Dark, with black rims. SHAPE Round.

EARS Erect or drop type, both large with rounded tips. Set on sides and back of head. Erect—carried obliquely and move like wings of a butterfly. When alert, each ear forms an angle of about 45 degrees to head. Leather of sufficient strength to maintain erect position. Drop— similar to erect, but carried drooping, and must be completely down.

LEFT Drop ears
RIGHT Erect ears

NECK
Of medium length.

FOREQUARTERS
SHOULDERS Well developed and laid-back to allow freedom of movement.
FORELEGS Slender, fine-boned, straight.
DEWCLAWS Removal optional.

One feature of the Papillon that should be appreciated is that it is natural, with no exaggeration of structure or behavior. As such, it is hardier than its elegant appearance implies. An active dog, it seems really to enjoy exercise, even going along on country hikes. It will equally thrive on active play in a fenced yard. It is extremely devoted to its owners, and will sound a loud alarm at the approach of strangers. The dog is very intelligent and a willing pupil—many acquit themselves with distinction in obedience competitions. It is friendly with everyone, gets along well with other dogs and household pets, and is good with gentle children.

The coat requires combing every two or three days, and an occasional bath is required. Otherwise, it is a very easy dog to maintain in good condition and health.

BODY AND TOPLINE
Backline straight and level. Chest of medium depth with ribs well sprung. Belly tucked-up.

TAIL
Long, set high, and carried well arched over body.

HINDQUARTERS
Well developed and well angulated.
HINDLEGS Slender, fine-boned. Hocks inclined neither in nor out.
DEWCLAWS Must be removed.

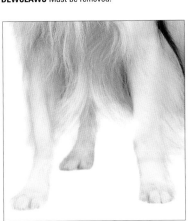

FEET
Thin, elongated (harefoot), pointing neither in nor out.

→ **GENERAL APPEARANCE**
A small, friendly, elegant toy dog of fine-boned structure. Light, dainty, and lively.

→ **CHARACTERISTICS**
The butterfly-like ears are typical of the Papillon.

→ **TEMPERAMENT**
Happy, alert and friendly, this dog is neither shy nor aggressive.

→ **GAIT/MOVEMENT**
Movement is free, quick, easy, and graceful.

→ **COAT**
The coat consists of abundant, long, fine, silky, straight hair, flat on the back and sides. Profuse frill on the chest. No undercoat. The hair is short on the skull, muzzle, front of forelegs and from the hindfeet to the hocks. Ears are well fringed. There is feathering on the back of the forelegs. The hindlegs are covered to the hocks with abundant breeches. Tail is covered with a long, flowing plume of hair. Hair on the feet is short, but fine tufts may appear over the toes and grow between them.

→ **COLOR**
These dogs are always parti-colored, or white with patches of any color(s). On the head, color other than white must cover both ears, back and front, and extend without interruption from the ears over both eyes. A clearly defined white blaze and nose band are preferred to a solidly marked head. There is no preference among colors, provided that the nose, eye rims and lips are well pigmented black.

→ **SIZE**
HEIGHT
8–11 in (20–27.5cm)
Body slightly longer than height at withers.
WEIGHT
In proportion to height. Fine boned.

→ **DISQUALIFICATIONS**
- Height over 12 in (30cm)
- All-white dog or dog with no white

↓ PEKINGESE

The Pekingese is thought to resemble the lion, an animal symbolic of Buddha. These dogs were treasured and kept exclusively for the Chinese royal families; removal of a Pekingese from the palace precincts was punishable by death. A dog very like the modern Pekingese features in Chinese art dating back to A.D. 900. Those Pekingese were extensively bred and tended by palace eunuchs, and pampered as if they were members of royalty, many having their own servants. The smallest were called "sleeve dogs" because they were often carried about within the voluminous sleeves of their master's court gown.

It is safe to assume that most of the Eastern breeds share common origins. Short-faced dogs, some having long coats like the Shih Tzu, are evident in early Eastern art. This art also featured a spaniel-type dog, higher on the leg and finer boned, not unlike later toy spaniel breeds.

When some Western countries, including the U.K. and the U.S., attacked China in 1860, the imperial summer palace in Peking was a prime target. As the armies approached, the palace inhabitants fled, taking some of the palace dogs with them, and killing others to prevent them falling into the hands of the enemy. Five favorite Pekingese of the Emperor's aunt, who had committed suicide, were found alive behind a drapery in her apartments and taken back to the U.K.. One was given

BODY AND TOPLINE
Body pear-shaped and compact. Heavy in front. Well-sprung ribs slung between forelegs. Broad chest, with little or no protruding breastbone, tapering to lighter loin and a distinct waist. Topline level.

HINDQUARTERS
Lighter in bone than forequarters.
HINDLEGS Moderate angulation and definition of stifles and hocks. Soundness is essential in both fore- and hindquarters.

TAIL
Base set high; remainder carried well over center of back. Long, profuse, straight feathering falls to either side.

FEET
Forefeet large, flat, and turned slightly out. Hindfeet point straight ahead.

→ GENERAL APPEARANCE

A well balanced, compact dog, with a heavy front and lighter hindquarters.

→ CHARACTERISTICS

The long, profuse coat, fully feathered ears and tail, and distinctive rolling movement are typical features.

→ TEMPERAMENT

Regal dignity, self-importance, self-confidence, and exasperating stubbornness especially suit the Pekingese to the right owner.

→ GAIT/MOVEMENT

Gait is unhurried and dignified, with a slight roll over the shoulders. The rolling gait is caused by the bowed forelegs and heavier, wider front pivoting on the lighter hindquarters and waist. Rolling should be free from bouncing or jarring.

→ COAT

The body coat is long, coarse, straight, stand-off, with a thick, softer under-coat. Noticeable mane on the neck and shoulders, the body coat being somewhat shorter. Long feathering on the back of the thighs and forelegs, ears, tail, and toes.

→ COLOR

All colors and markings, including parti-colors, are allowed and are of equal merit.

→ SIZE

WEIGHT (maximum)

14 lb (6.4kg)

Surprisingly heavy for its appearance. Stocky, muscular body. Length of body slightly greater than height at withers.

→ DISQUALIFICATIONS

■ Weight over 14 lb (6.4kg)

to Queen Victoria. Given her stamp of approval, the breed quickly became very popular among dog lovers everywhere. Now extinct in China, the Pekingese is very popular wherever dogs are admired.

The Pekingese is independent and stubborn, and as courageous as a lion dog should be. Not given to fawning, it needs an owner who can appreciate its distinctive, self-assured personality. It is very faithful and intelligent, and benefits greatly from at least basic obedience training, without which it will rule its owner's home and life.

HEAD AND SKULL

Topskull massive, broad, flat. Skull wider than deep, contributing to rectangular appearance of head. Flat in profile. Chin, nose leather, and brow on one plane. Wrinkle effectively separates upper and lower face, but never so prominent or heavy as to crowd facial features or obscure large part of eyes or nose. Stop deep.

NOSE Black, broad, very short. Nostrils open. Nose between eyes so that a line drawn horizontally across top of nose intersects center of eyes.

EYES AND EARS

EYES Large, set wide apart. COLOR Very dark, with black rims. SHAPE Round.

EARS Heart shaped and set-on front corners of skull, framing face.

MOUTH AND JAWS

MUZZLE Very short, broad, and high, with wide cheekbones. Skin color black.

LIPS Black. Meeting on level plane. Neither tongue nor teeth to show when mouth closed.

JAWS Lower jaw strong, firm, straight across at chin, and slightly undershot.

NECK

Very short, thick, and set back into shoulder.

FOREQUARTERS

Short, thick and heavy-boned.
SHOULDERS Gently laid-back.
FORELEGS Slightly bowed between pasterns and elbows. Elbows close to body.

↓ POMERANIAN

A miniaturized Arctic sled dog, the Pomeranian is the smallest member of the Spitz family, but thinks itself the equal of any. The modern Pomeranian was probably developed in Germany. The earliest dogs brought to the U.K. came from the Prussian region of Pomerania, hence their name. These dogs averaged 30 pounds (13.6kg) in weight and were often used in Germany to herd sheep. The size was reduced in the U.K. and, by 1896, classes for Pomeranians at Crufts were divided into those up to 20 pounds (9kg) and those under 7 lb (3.2kg).

The Pomeranian arrived in the U.S. in the 1890s. The American Pomeranian Club held its first specialty show in 1911, and the breed's popularity has grown steadily since. As with any very popular breed, some breeders have been less than careful about breeding healthy dogs with sound minds, and some buyers have paid the price for being less than careful when selecting the source of their Pomeranian.

HEAD AND SKULL
Pronounced stop. Skull closed, with top slightly rounded, but not domed. Expression foxlike. Pronounced stop.

NECK
Short. Head carried high.

EYES AND EARS
EYES Medium sized and set well into skull on either side of stop. Pigmentation black on nose and eye rims but self-colored in brown, beaver, and blue dogs. COLOR Dark. SHAPE Almond.

EARS Small, mounted high, and carried erect.

MOUTH AND JAWS
MUZZLE Rather short, straight, fine, never snipy.

TEETH One tooth out of alignment is acceptable.

BITE Scissor.

FOREQUARTERS
SHOULDER Moderate layback. Shoulders and legs moderately muscled. Shoulder and upper arm equal in length.

FORELEGS Straight. Height from elbows to withers approximately equal to height from ground to elbow.

PASTERNS Straight and strong.

DEWCLAWS May be removed.

Generally docile, the Pomeranian will not back down from other dogs, even if they are many times larger. Occasionally, its self-image is more grand than safe, and care must be taken to discourage it from challenging other dogs. Exercise needs can be met by active play in a fenced yard, but most dogs enjoy daily walks. Health benefits are gained by regular outdoor exercise. This breed has a reputation for being prone to bark, but if an owner begins training when the dog is young, and consistently enforces household expectations, it is possible to teach it to be less vocal.

BODY AND TOPLINE
Back short and level. Body compact and well ribbed with brisket reaching to elbow.

TAIL
Plumed, lying flat and straight on back.

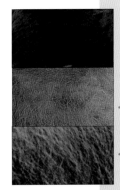

HINDQUARTERS
Angulation balances that of forequarters. Buttocks well behind set of tail.
HINDLEGS Thighs moderately muscled. Stifles moderately bent. Hocks perpendicular. Legs straight.
DEWCLAWS May be removed.

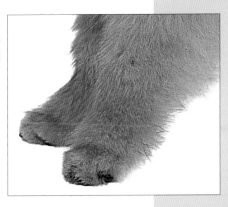

FEET
Well arched, compact, and straight ahead.

→ GENERAL APPEARANCE
The Pomeranian is a compact, short-backed, active toy dog.

→ CHARACTERISTICS
Very small toy dog with a soft, dense undercoat and a profuse, harsh outercoat. The tail is heavily plumed.

→ TEMPERAMENT
Extrovert, exhibiting intelligence and vivacity; can be excitable.

→ GAIT/MOVEMENT
Movement is smooth, free, balanced, and vigorous, with a good reach and strong drive. The topline remains level when the dog is moving.

→ COAT
The double coat consists of a soft, dense undercoat and a long, straight, harsh outercoat, held off from the body by the undercoat. The coat is abundant on the neck, the forepart of the shoulders, and the chest, forming a frill that extends over the shoulders and chest. It is shorter on the head and legs. The forequarters are well feathered, as are the thighs and the hindlegs to the hocks. The tail is profusely covered with long, harsh, spreading straight hair.

→ COLOR
All colors are allowed. Patterns include black-and-tan, brindle, and parti-color.

→ SIZE
WEIGHT (average)
3–7 lb (1.4–3.2kg)
WEIGHT (ideal show)
4–6 lb (1.8–2.7kg)
KC/ANKC Specifies weight only; males 4–4½ lb (1.8–2kg) and females 4½–5½ lb (2–2.5kg).
FCI Specifies height only at 8 in (20cm)±⅞ in (2cm).
In Germany, all German Spitz dogs of four sizes have the same breed standard with variations for size and color only.

PUG

The Pug originated in China and is one of the oldest purebred dogs, going back farther than almost any other breed. It is thought to have descended from far larger Mastiff type. Most early Pug breeding was carried out centuries ago, in Buddhist monasteries in Tibet and China.

The Pug probably came to Holland on ships of the Dutch East India Trading Company, which had established regular trade with the Far East in the 1500s. From Holland, it was introduced by William of Orange to the U.K. in the latter half of the seventeenth century, where it temporarily supplanted the English Toy Spaniel (King Charles Spaniel) as the favorite breed of the aristocracy. By 1790, it reached France, where "Fortune," the favorite of Empress Josephine, is alleged to have bitten Napoleon on their wedding night. Several Pugs were brought to the U.K., along with the Pekingese, between 1860 and 1886, after the Opium Wars, and by 1900, the Pug was established as a stylish pet and show dog.

A tough and sturdy dog, its endearing face wins many a heart. It has a delightful sense of humor and is friendly to all. While very playful, it can also be stubborn. The Pug is not usually a barker, though it does make an interesting variety of grunts, mumbles, and other snuffly sounds while awake. It also snores, sometimes loudly, when asleep. Like the Pekingese, the Bulldog and other short-faced dogs, it must be protected from both hot and humid weather, which can prove deadly.

The Pug needs a daily walk, plus the opportunity to play and run in a safe area, in order to maintain its health and condition. In hot weather, playtime should be indoors.

BODY AND TOPLINE
Short back, level from withers to tail set. Body short and cobby. Chest wide and well ribbed up.

TAIL
Curled as tightly as possible over hip. Double curl is desired.

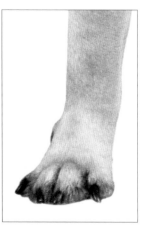

FEET
Less long than the harefoot, less round than the catfoot.
TOES Well split-up.
NAILS Black.

HINDQUARTERS
Strong and powerful. Thighs and buttocks full and muscular.
HINDLEGS Moderate bend of stifles. Short hocks.

HEAD AND SKULL

Head large, massive, round, not apple-headed, with no indentation of skull. Wrinkles large and deep.

EYES AND EARS

EYES Very large and prominent. COLOR Dark. SHAPE Globular.

EARS Thin, small, soft, like black velvet. There are two kinds—the "rose" and the "button." Preference is given to the latter.

GENERAL APPEARANCE

The symmetry of the Pug is decidedly square and cobby.

CHARACTERISTICS

This sturdy dog has a short, wrinkled face and a tightly curled tail.

TEMPERAMENT

Even-tempered, the Pug exhibits stability, playfulness, great charm, dignity, and an outgoing, loving disposition.

GAIT/MOVEMENT

The forelegs are carried well forward, and the rear action is strong and free through hocks and stifles. A slight roll of the hindquarters is typical.

COAT

The coat consists of fine, smooth, soft, short hair, neither hard nor wooly.

COLOR

Colors are silver, apricot-fawn, and black, with clearly defined markings—muzzle or mask, ears, moles on cheeks, thumb mark or diamond on forehead, and a back trace (black line extending from occiput to tail) should be as black as possible. The mask is black.

MOUTH AND JAWS

MUZZLE Short, blunt, square, but not upfaced.

JAWS Very slightly undershot.

SIZE

WEIGHT

14–18 lb (6.4–8.2kg)

Square. The Pug should be *multum in parvo* (loosely "a large dog in a small package").

NECK

Slightly arched, strong, and thick.

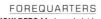

FOREQUARTERS

SHOULDERS Moderately laid-back.

FORELEGS Very strong, straight, of moderate length. Elbows directly under withers.

PASTERNS Strong, neither steep nor down.

DEWCLAWS Generally removed.

SHIH TZU

The Shih Tzu is closely related to the Pekingese, with which it shares much early breed history. Dogs like the Shih Tzu appear in Chinese art dating back to the seventh century A.D. One theory places its origins in Tibet, where it was bred and cosseted in Buddhist monasteries as a symbolic link to Buddha, along with the dog that was eventually called the Lhasa Apso. Eventually it came to the Chinese royal court as a gift from the Dalai Lama. Another theory describes how the Shih Tzu came directly to China in the seventeenth century, as a gift from the ruler of the Byzantine Empire.

By whatever means the Shih Tzu arrived in China, it became valued as a "lion dog" once there, along with the Pekingese. Both were guarded and bred by palace eunuchs and treated as royalty. Sadly, at the time of the succession by the Manchus to the Ming Dynasty in 1644, almost all the royal dogs were killed by looters, who vented their anger at the rulers on the dogs that they had left behind.

HEAD AND SKULL
Round, broad, wide between ears. Skull domed. Definite stop.

NOSE Black on all colors but liver- or blue-pigmented dogs. Liver on liver dogs and blue on blue dogs. Nostrils broad, wide, and open.

EYES AND EARS
EYES Large, not prominent, and placed well apart. COLOR Very dark with black rims. Lighter eyes and eye rims allowed in liver or blue-pigmented dogs.

EARS Large, set slightly below crown of skull. Heavily coated.

MOUTH AND JAWS
MUZZLE Square, short, unwrinkled, with good cushioning, set no lower than bottom of eye rim. Never downturned and ideally no longer than 1 in (2.5cm) from tip of nose to stop. Front of muzzle flat, with lower lip and chin not protruding and definitely never receding.

LIPS Black on all but liver- or blue-pigmented dogs.

JAWS Broad, wide, and undershot. Teeth and tongue should not show when mouth is closed.

TEETH A missing tooth or misaligned teeth not severely penalized.

NECK
Sufficiently long to permit high head carriage.

FOREQUARTERS
SHOULDERS Well angulated, well laid-back, and well laid-in.

FORELEGS Straight, well boned, muscular, set wide apart and under chest. Elbows close to body.

PASTERNS Strong, perpendicular.

DEWCLAWS May be removed.

Two pairs of Shih Tzu were brought from China to the U.K. in 1930, by two breeders who set about breeding them and attempting to gain recognition for the breed. Originally confusion reigned, because the Shih Tzu and Lhasa Apso were lumped together as one breed. They were eventually separated into two distinct breeds and the Shih Tzu Club of England was formed in 1935. After World War II, some Shih Tzu were brought to the U.S. from the U.K., and this is now one of the most popular of AKC toy breeds

Though small, this dog is a lion at heart, yet with an amusing and adaptable character, full of fun and very affectionate. It craves human attention and is quite good with gentle children. It needs a long walk daily plus play in a safe area. As with the Pekingese and the Pug, hot and/or humid weather can be lethal to this short-faced dog.

→ GENERAL APPEARANCE

The Shih Tzu is a sturdy, lively, alert toy dog.

→ CHARACTERISTICS

Typical of the breed are the long, flowing coat, with high head carriage, a tail curved over the back, and a distinct arrogant bearing.

→ TEMPERAMENT

As its sole purpose is as a companion and house pet, it is essential that the Shih Tzu is outgoing, happy, affectionate, friendly, and trusting toward all.

→ GAIT/MOVEMENT

Movement should be flowing and effortless, with good front reach and an equally strong rear drive. The topline should be level, the head carried high and the tail carried over the back.

→ COAT

The luxurious, double coat is dense, long, and flowing. A slight wave is permitted. The hair on top of head is tied up. Hair on the feet, bottom of the coat, and around the anus may be trimmed for neatness and to facilitate movement.

→ COLOR

All colors are permissible and considered equal.

→ SIZE

HEIGHT (ideal)
9–10½ in (22.5–26.25cm)
HEIGHT (range)
8–11 in (20–27.5cm)
WEIGHT (ideal, mature dogs)
9–16 lb (4.1–7.3kg)

Never so high-stationed as to appear leggy, nor so low as to appear dumpy. Slightly longer than tall.

KC/FCI/ANKC Allows weight up to 18 lb (8kg).

BODY AND TOPLINE
Topline level. Body short-coupled and sturdy with no waist or tuck-up. Chest broad and deep with good spring of rib, not barrel-chested. Ribs extend to below elbow. Croup flat. The dog must be well balanced overall, with no exaggerated features.

TAIL
Set on high, heavily plumed, and carried in curve well over back.

HINDQUARTERS
Angulation should match that of front.
HINDLEGS Well-bent stifles. Hocks well let down.
DEWCLAWS May be removed.

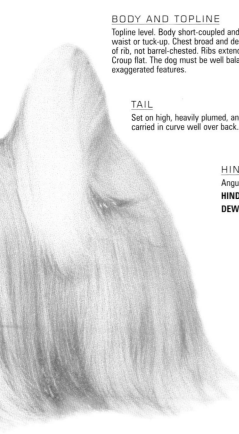

FEET
Firm, well padded, pointing straight ahead.

YORKSHIRE TERRIER

The history of the Yorkshire Terrier is somewhat obscure, even though this is not a very old breed. It was developed in the West Riding of Yorkshire, England, probably in the late 1700s and early 1800s. Originally it was bred by the Scottish weavers who immigrated to Yorkshire to work in the new textile mills. The dogs were intended to be ratters in the mills. Today's elegant Yorkshire Terrier is really a feisty rat terrier in fancy dress.

The early Yorkie was not uniform in size, weighing an average of 13–15 pounds (5.9–6.8kg), more than double their current limit. Even in its early years it had the color and coat texture so valued now, but its hair was a great deal shorter.

One likely ancestor of the Yorkie was the Waterside Terrier, once common in Yorkshire. This dog, weighing about 30 pounds (13.6kg) and having longish bluish-gray hair, was crossed with the rough-coated old Black and Tan English Terrier, and with the Paisley Terrier and Clydesdale Terrier brought from Scotland in the mid-1800s. Although each of these breeds is now extinct, the result of their blending is the modern Yorkshire Terrier.

Similar to some other toy breeds, the Yorkie does not see itself as a small dog. It is hardy, and quite game. It is alert and courageous, and thus a good watchdog, though some seem to lack an "off-button" for barking. However, it can be

BODY AND TOPLINE
Back rather short. Backline level. Height at shoulder same as at rump.

TAIL
Docked to medium length and carried slightly higher than level of back when in motion.

KC/ANKC Customarily docked. Undocked: length to give well balanced appearance.

HINDQUARTERS
HINDLEGS Straight. Stifles moderately bent.
DEWCLAWS Generally removed.

GENERAL APPEARANCE

A small toy terrier, the Yorkshire is neat, compact, and well proportioned. Its high head carriage and confident manner give the appearance of vigor and self-importance.

CHARACTERISTICS

The luxurious, floor-length, steel-blue and tan coat is typical of the breed.

TEMPERAMENT

Bold, intelligent, can be noisy.

COAT

Quality, texture and quantity of hair are of prime importance. The hair is fine and silky, the coat on the body moderately long and perfectly straight. The fall on the head is long, and should be tied with one bow in the center or parted in middle and tied with two bows. The hair on the muzzle is very long. Hair should be trimmed short on tips of ears and feet may be trimmed for neatness.

COLOR

Puppies are born black-and-tan and gradually adopt adult coloration.

BLUE (dark steel-blue)—on body from back of neck to root of tail; hair on tail is a darker blue.

TAN (darker red tan at roots, shading to lighter tan at tips)—on the headfall, at ear roots, and on muzzle and ears.

SIZE
WEIGHT (maximum)
7 lb (3.2kg).

taught to be quieter. Because of its adventurous spirit and independence, it is wise to begin training while the dog is still quite young. Though tiny, it needs supervision outdoors. It enjoys outdoor exercise and indoor play and most love to run in a fenced yard.

The long coat that is its fortune needs daily combing to prevent painful mats. Grooming, as with all coated breeds, should be started when the pup is quite young, in short, pleasant sessions.

HEAD AND SKULL
Small and rather flat on top. Skull not too prominent or round.
NOSE Black.

MOUTH AND JAWS
MUZZLE Not too long.
BITE Scissor or level.

NECK
Well proportioned and very compact.

EYES AND EARS
EYES Medium sized and not too prominent COLOR Dark, with dark rims.
EARS Small, V-shaped, carried erect and not too far apart.

FOREQUARTERS
FORELEGS Straight, elbows turning neither in nor out.
DEWCLAWS May be removed.

FEET
Round.
NAILS Black.

BICHON FRISE

The Bichon Frise originated in the Mediterranean region and is descended from the old Barbet (or Water Spaniel). From this predecessor comes the name "Barbichon," later shortened to "Bichon." Its charming personality drew fans wherever it went, and it traveled far.

The earliest record of the Bichon is in Spain, and it was probably Spanish sailors who brought these dogs to the Canary Island of Tenerife. In the fourteenth century, it was seen on Tenerife by Italian sailors, who took some dogs back to the Continent, where they were sold to, and became great favorites of, Italian aristocrats and merchants. A popular grooming style for small dogs of that era was the "lion clip" (hair cut very short from the loin back, with a full "mane," and the Bichon joined the ranks of pampered pets with that cut. By 1515 the Bichon Tenerife was established in France, but it was almost decimated during the Revolution in 1789. It was its personality, plus an ability to learn tricks, that saved

HEAD AND SKULL

Skull slightly rounded. Slight stop. Properly balanced head is three parts muzzle to five parts skull, measured from nose to stop and from stop to occiput. Slight chiseling under eyes, but never a weak or snipey foreface.

NOSE Prominent and black.

EYES AND EARS

EYES COLOR Black or dark brown. Halos (black or very dark brown skin surrounding eye) are necessary to accentuate the eye. **SHAPE** Round.

EARS Drop ears covered with long, flowing hair. Set-on slightly higher than eye level and rather forward on skull.

MOUTH AND JAWS

LIPS Black, fine, never drooping.
JAWS Lower jaw strong.
BITE Scissor.

NECK

Arched and long.

FOREQUARTERS

SHOULDERS Shoulder blade, upper arm and forearm are approximately equal in length. Layback approximately 45 degrees.

FORELEGS Of medium bone and straight. Elbows close to body.

PASTERNS Slope slightly.

DEWCLAWS May be removed.

FEET

Tight and round (cat foot), pointing straight ahead.

PADS Black.

NAILS Short.

the breed. By the late 1800s, it no longer lived in palaces, but earned its keep as an attraction with organ-grinders or by doing tricks in circuses and fairs.

In 1933, four breeders in France decided to attempt to save the breed from extinction. A standard was written and the breed's name was changed to Bichon à Poil Frisé (Bichon of the curly coat). Even so, the two world wars dramatically affected the breed, as they did most other dogs in Europe and the U.K. After the wars, a few dogs were taken to England, and later to the U.S., where the breed finally seems to have found a safe and permanent home.

The Bichon is a happy-go-lucky, snowy powderpuff, very quick to learn and curious about everything. A very active dog, it needs more exercise than its elegant appearance might suggest.

→ GENERAL APPEARANCE
The Bichon Frise is a small, sturdy dog, with no gross or incapacitating exaggerations.

→ CHARACTERISTICS
The white coat, trimmed and groomed to give the appearance of a powderpuff, is accentuated by jet-black eyes and a plume tail carried over the back.

→ TEMPERAMENT
The Bichon Frise is gentle, sensitive, playful, and affectionate. A cheerful attitude is a hallmark of the breed.

→ GAIT/MOVEMENT
At the trot, the dog moves freely, with precision. Forelegs and hindlegs extend equally and the topline holds level.

→ COAT
Coat texture is very important, the undercoat soft and dense, and the outercoat coarse and curly. This combination gives a soft, substantial feel to the coat, like plush or velvet. The coat is trimmed to reveal the natural outline of the body. The furnishings of the head, beard, mustache, ears, and tail are left longer. Head hair is trimmed for a rounded shape.

KC/FCI/ANKC Suggest only feet and muzzle tidied up. In practice, the dogs are trimmed all over Europe. In Australia the coat is usually trimmed to reveal the natural outline of the body.

→ COLOR
The color is white, although shadings of buff, cream, or apricot around the ears and on the body are permissible.

→ SIZE
HEIGHT (preferred)
9½–11½ in (23.75–28.75cm)
Body a quarter longer than high.

BODY AND TOPLINE
Topline level but for slight arch over loin. Chest well developed and wide, extending at least to elbow. Ribs moderately sprung, extending to a short loin. Moderate tuck-up.

TAIL
Well plumed, set-on level with topline, and curved over back so that hair of tail rests on back.

HINDQUARTERS
HINDLEGS Medium bone, well angulated with muscular thighs. Upper and lower thigh nearly equal in length. Stifles well bent. Hocks perpendicular.
DEWCLAWS May be removed.

BOSTON TERRIER

Much canine breed history is based on conjecture and oral history, but this is not so with the Boston Terrier. In about 1870, coachmen who worked for wealthy residents of Boston's Beacon Hill district decided to breed some of their employers' imported dogs. While these dogs were not owned by the coachmen, they were generally under their care and control. In 1893 a mix of bull and terrier types produced the first pair of dogs that was to become the foundation of the Boston Terrier. By the 1890s, a specialty club was formed in Boston. In 1891 the name was settled on, and the Boston Terrier Club of America was formed. In 1893, the breed was recognized by the AKC, yet progress to set type continued for many years.

The Boston's character has led to it being called "the American gentleman" of dogs. It is clean, trainable, and affectionate. It has no real doggy odor and coat care is minimal, but its eyes need special care because of their size and position.

ABOVE Uncropped ears.
RIGHT Cropped ears.

EYES AND EARS
EYES Set wide apart, and so outside corners are on line with cheeks. COLOR Dark. SHAPE Round.

EARS Small, erect, either natural or cropped. Set as near corners of skull as possible.

HEAD AND SKULL
Head square, flat on top, and free from wrinkles. Brow abrupt and stop well defined.
NOSE Wide and black.

BODY AND TOPLINE
Back short enough to square the body. Rump curves slightly to set-on of tail. Chest deep with good width, ribs well sprung and carried back to loin. Body should appear short.

MOUTH AND JAWS
MUZZLE Free from wrinkles; approximately a third of length of skull.

JAW Broad and square, even or sufficiently undershot to square the muzzle. Chops of good depth but not pendulous, completely covering teeth when mouth is closed.

NECK
Slightly arched.

FOREQUARTERS
SHOULDERS Sloping and well laid-back, allowing for typical stylish movement.
FORELEGS Set moderately wide. Straight in bone. Elbows turning neither in nor out.
PASTERNS Short and strong.
DEWCLAWS May be removed.

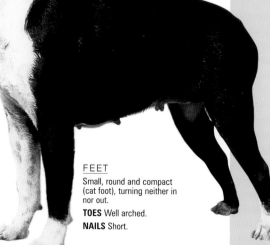

FEET
Small, round and compact (cat foot), turning neither in nor out.
TOES Well arched.
NAILS Short.

→ GENERAL APPEARANCE
This is a lively, highly intelligent, smooth-coated, short-tailed (straight or screw), and well balanced dog.

→ CHARACTERISTICS
This square-headed, cobby dog has distinctive white markings on a body of black, seal, or brindle. The combination of solid color and markings should be proportionate.

→ TEMPERAMENT
A friendly, lively dog, the Boston Terrier has an excellent disposition and a high degree of intelligence.

→ GAIT/MOVEMENT
Sure-footed, straight-gaited; moves straight ahead in perfect rhythm.

→ COAT
The coat is short, smooth, bright, and fine in texture.

→ COLOR
Color and markings include brindle, seal, and black with white markings. Brindle is preferred only if all other qualities are equal. Markings must include a white muzzle band, a white blaze between the eyes, and a white forechest.

→ SIZE
WEIGHT (classes)
Under 15 lb (6.8kg)
15–20 lb (6.8–9.1kg)
20–25 lb (9.1–11.4kg)

Leg length balances that of body for a square appearance. A sturdy dog.

→ DISQUALIFICATIONS
- Eyes blue or any trace of blue
- Dudley nose
- Docked tail
- Solid black, solid brindle, or solid seal without required white markings
- Gray or liver colors

TAIL
Short, fine, and tapering. Straight or screw. Set-on low. Not carried above horizontal.

HINDQUARTERS
Thighs, well muscled; stifles bent; hocks short.
FEET Small.

↓
BULLDOG

The Bulldog is a member of the Mastiff family, but the breed's precise background is unknown. Bred to fight bulls and other animals, it did this very well for over three hundred years. This "sport" was not only cruel to the bull, but also to the dog, and many dogs died providing entertainment for human spectators. When bull-baiting was outlawed in 1835, most Bulldogs were owned by working-class people who had no more use for the breed as a result. A few breeders decided to refine the dogs for the newly introduced dog shows. Within a few generations, the Bulldog had become far more attractive, though changed in appearance from its gladiatorial days, and without the savage tendencies that had served the breed well. The modern Bulldog is a kind and dignified companion. Not surprisingly, given its background, it can be very stubborn. Its saving grace is a strong desire to please its owner, which should be capitalized on by gentle training, begun when the puppy is very young.

HEAD AND SKULL

Head should be large, measuring, in front of ears, at least height of dog at shoulders. Forehead flat. Cheeks well rounded. Stop very broad and deep. Face from front of cheekbone to tip of nose very short. **KC/FCI** Head size "should not make the dog appear deformed or interfere with its powers of motion."

NOSE Large, broad and black, tipped back deeply between eyes.

EYES AND EARS

EYES Low down in skull, as far from ears and as wide apart as possible. Moderately sized, neither sunken nor bulging. No haw showing. COLOR Very dark. SHAPE Round.

EARS Set high, as wide apart and as high as possible. Small and thin (rose ear preferred).

MOUTH AND JAWS

MUZZLE Very short, broad, turned upward, and very deep.

JAWS Massive, broad, square, and undershot. Chops (flews) thick, broad, pendant, completely covering the teeth when the mouth is closed.

TEETH Large and strong. Canines wide apart. Six small teeth between canines in an even, level row.

FOREQUARTERS

SHOULDERS Muscular, very heavy, widespread, and slanting outward.

FORELEGS Short, very stout, straight, and muscular. Set well apart, presenting a bowed outline, but bones should not be curved or bandy, nor feet too close together. Elbows low, standing well out from body.

BODY AND TOPLINE

Slight fall in back, close behind shoulders, whence the spine rises to the loin, curving again to the tail, forming an arch that is distinctive to the breed ("wheel backed"). Ribs well rounded and very deep from shoulders to where they join chest. Well let-down between shoulders and forelegs, giving a broad, low, short-legged appearance. Chest very broad and deep. Well tucked-up. Back short and strong, very broad at shoulders, and narrower at loin.

GENERAL APPEARANCE

The perfect Bulldog is of medium size, with a smooth coat. It has a heavy, thick-set, low-slung body, a massive short-faced head, wide shoulders and sturdy limbs, all suggesting great stability, vigor, and strength.

CHARACTERISTICS

The short, front-loaded body, the massive wrinkled head, and the distinctive rolling gait are typical of this breed.

TEMPERAMENT

The Bulldog is equable, kind, resolute, and courageous (never vicious or aggressive).

GAIT/MOVEMENT

A loose-jointed, shuffling, sideways motion gives the characteristic roll. Action must be unrestrained, free, and vigorous.

COAT

The coat is straight, short, flat, and fine. The skin is soft and loose, especially at the head, neck, and shoulders. The head and face are covered with heavy wrinkles, and there are two loose pendulous folds (dewlaps) on the throat from head to chest.

COLOR

Colors are uniform and brilliant. In order of preference, they are red brindle, all other brindles, solid white, solid red, fawn or fallow, and piebald.

SIZE

WEIGHT (mature)

males	females
50lb (22.7kg)	40lb (18.2kg)

KC/FCI/ANKC Prefers males 5 lb (2 kg) and females 10 lb (4.5kg) heavier.

DISQUALIFICATIONS

- Brown or liver-colored nose

NECK

Short, very thick, deep, and strong. Well arched at nape.

TAIL

Short, hung low, with a decided downward carriage. Thick root and fine tip. Either straight or "screwed." No portion of tail should rise above its base.

HINDQUARTERS

HINDLEGS Strong, muscular, and longer than forelegs. Lower legs short, straight, and strong. Hocks slightly bent and well let-down. Stifles slightly outward, away from body.

FEET

Moderate in size and compact. Forefeet may be slightly turned out. Hindfeet turn outward.

TOES Compact, well split up, with high knuckles.

NAILS Very short.

CHINESE SHAR-PEI

This dog is believed to have existed since about 200 B.C. When the Communist party took over the government of China, early dog breeding records were lost and almost all dogs were eliminated. Until that time, the Shar-Pei had been an all-purpose farm dog, used to guard property, to herd, to hunt boar, and as a fighting dog. A few Chinese Shar-Pei remained in Taiwan and in Hong Kong. However, a major push to importation occurred in 1973, in response to an article directed to the U.S. dog fancy, entitled "Save the Shar-Pei," by a Hong Kong breeder. The response was enthusiastic, more dogs were imported into the States, and a population boom began. The Shar-Pei's independence does not make it the easiest dog to train, and lessons should begin while it is still very young. Consistency and persistence should yield a very satisfactory companion.

GENERAL APPEARANCE

The Chinese Shar-Pei is a compact dog of medium size and substance, square in profile and close-coupled. The excess skin forms into wrinkles.

CHARACTERISTICS

The short, harsh coat, loose skin on the head and body, small ears, "hippopotamus" muzzle, and high tail-set impart a unique look.

TEMPERAMENT

The Shar-Pei is regal, alert, intelligent, dignified, independent, scowling, and sober. Somewhat standoffish with strangers, it is extremely devoted to its family.

GAIT/MOVEMENT

At a trot, the gait is free and balanced, with good forward reach and a strong rear drive.

COAT

The coat is absolutely straight, off-standing on the body but somewhat flatter on the limbs. Acceptable lengths range from the extremely short "horse coat" up to the "brush coat", and should not exceed 1 in (2.5cm) in length at the withers.

COLOR

Only solid colors and sable are accepted. A solid color dog may have darker shading (a variation of the same body color) down the back and on the ears.

SIZE

HEIGHT

18–20 in
(45–50cm)

WEIGHT

45- 60 lb
(20.5–27.3kg)

Males usually larger and more square than females. Height from ground to withers equal to length from point of breastbone to point of rump.

DISQUALIFICATIONS

- Pricked ears
- Solid pink tongue
- Absence of complete tail
- Albino, not a solid color
- Brindle, parti-colored, spotted, patterned in any combination of colors

BODY AND TOPLINE
Topline dips slightly behind withers; slightly rising over the short, broad loin. Chest broad, deep, brisket extending to elbow. Back short, close-coupled. Croup flat.

EYES AND EARS
EYES Small and sunken. COLOR Dark. Dilute dogs may have lighter eyes. SHAPE Almond.

EARS Extremely small, thick, slightly rounded. Edges may curl. Set high, wide apart and forward on skull, lying flat against head.

HEAD AND SKULL
Head large, covered with profuse wrinkles on forehead and side wrinkles framing face. Skull flat, broad. Stop moderately defined.
NOSE Large, wide, darkly pigmented ("hippopotamus" nose).

TAIL
Set high. Thick, round at base, tapering to fine point. Curls over to either side of back. Base of tail extremely high, clearly exposing an up-tilted anus.

NECK
Of medium length and full. Moderate to heavy folds of loose skin and abundant dewlap about neck and throat.

MOUTH AND JAWS
MUZZLE A distinctive feature, being broad and full. Length from nose to stop is approximately equal to that from stop to occiput. Top of muzzle well padded and may slightly bulge above nose.

LIPS Well padded. Tongue, roof of mouth, gums and flews should be solid bluish-black in all colors but dilute, which has solid lavender pigmentation.

BITE Scissor.

HINDQUARTERS
Muscular, strong, moderately angulated.

HINDLEGS Hocks short, perpendicular to ground.

DEWCLAWS Must be removed.

FOREQUARTERS
SHOULDERS Muscular, well laid-back, and sloping.
FORELEGS Straight, elbows close to body.
PASTERNS Strong, flexible. Bone substantial but never heavy.
DEWCLAWS Removal optional.

FEET
Moderate in size, compact, not splayed.

CHOW CHOW

Due to a lack of early written history of dogs, the age of this Chinese breed can only be estimated. The Tartars who invaded China in the tenth century B.C. are known to have brought with them great packs of large, lionlike dogs with black tongues. Some theories suggest that the Chow Chow is a descendant of the Tibetan Mastiff and the Samoyed. Others claim that it was the first of the Spitz breeds, and therefore probably a predecessor of the Samoyed. Whatever its source, the Chow served as a herder, home guard, and sporting dog in its early years. As both a pointer and a retriever of birds and other game, it often lived in vast kennel compounds, being cared for by royal servants. When the tradition of imperial hunts ceased, so did these kennels. Importation of the Chow Chow into the U.K. did not begin in any numbers until about 1880.

The Chow is adorable as a puppy, but will grow into a very strong-willed dog. It is said that it will die for you, but not obey you.

HEAD AND SKULL

Large in proportion to size of dog. Typical scowl caused by face wrinkles and shape and placement of ears and eyes. Excessive loose skin not desired. Topskull broad and flat. Toplines of muzzle and skull approximately parallel. Moderate stop.

NOSE Broad and black.

EYES AND EARS

EYES Moderately sized, deep and wide apart, set obliquely. COLOR Dark brown, with black rims. SHAPE Almond.

EARS Small, moderately thick, triangular; slightly rounded tips. Carried stiffly erect with slight forward tilt. Placed wide apart.

BODY AND TOPLINE

Topline straight, strong and level. Body strongly muscled, deep. Body, back and croup must all be short. Chest broad, deep and muscular.

NECK

Strong, full, and nicely arched.

TAIL

Set high and carried close to back.

MOUTH AND JAWS

MUZZLE Short compared to topskull, but never less than a third of head length. Broad, width and depth being equal.

LIPS Edges black. A solid black mouth is ideal.

BITE Scissor.

FOREQUARTERS

SHOULDERS Strong, tips of blades moderately close together.

FORELEGS Length of upper arm never less than shoulder blade. Elbows well back, close to chest. Heavily boned. Widely spaced around broad chest.

PASTERNS Short and upright. Wrists should not knuckle-over.

DEWCLAWS May be removed.

FEET

Round and catlike.

PADS Thick.

GENERAL APPEARANCE

The Chow Chow is a powerful, sturdy, square, Arctic-type dog, medium in size, with strong muscles, heavy bone, high tail-set and a heavy, square head.

CHARACTERISTICS

The profuse double coat, heavy head with wrinkles, and stilted rear gait are typical.

TEMPERAMENT

The Chow Chow is keenly intelligent, independent, and reserved with strangers. Displays of aggression or timidity are unacceptable. The deep-set eyes reduce its peripheral vision, so the dog should be approached from within its visual range.

GAIT/MOVEMENT

Movement is sound, agile, quick, and powerful. The rear gait is short and stilted because of the straight rear assembly. There is no roll through the midsection, and the front and rear must be in equilibrium.

COAT

There are two types of coat; rough and smooth. Both are double coated.

ROUGH—outercoat abundant, straight, offstanding, and rather coarse. Undercoat soft and wooly. Profuse ruff around the head and neck, generally more so in males than females.

SMOOTH—hard, dense, smooth outercoat. Definite undercoat. No ruff or feathering on legs or tail.

COLOR

Allowed colors are red, black, blue, cinnamon, and cream.

SIZE

HEIGHT (average adult)

17–20in (42.5–50cm)

Square in profile.

KC/FCI/ANKC Males 19–22in (47.5–55cm); Females 18–20in (45–50cm).

DISQUALIFICATIONS

- Drop ear or ears
- Nose spotted or distinctly other than black, except in blue Chows
- Top surface or edges of tongue pink or red, or with one or more spots of red or pink

HINDQUARTERS

Broad, powerful, well muscled in hips and thighs, heavy boned. Widely spaced from a broad pelvis.

HINDLEGS Stifles have little angulation. Hocks well let-down, almost straight.

DEWCLAWS May be removed..

DALMATIAN

Spotted dogs that resemble the Dalmatian show up in sixteenth- and seventeenth-century paintings from Holland and Italy, yet this breed's early history is not known with certainty. While its name refers to Dalmatia in Yugoslavia, there is no evidence linking it to this location. However, this dog, possibly resulting from crosses of spotted pointers or harlequin Great Danes, has been known in Europe for almost five hundred years. It has been suggested that our lack of knowledge about the Dalmatian stems from the fact that it frequently lived with and was bred by the Romany peoples.

The Dalmatian is known as a coaching dog but it has also served as a hunter of rats, other vermin, and even larger game, as a draft and bird dog, for trailing, and as the well known companion and guard of fire-wagon horses. Even after firefighting became motorized, the Dalmatian remained a mascot to many fire companies. It was also a fashionable companion and guard for horse-drawn carriages. In fact, there is hardly a task meant for a canine that the Dalmatian has not performed, including that of circus trickster.

The Dalmatian is an active dog and, true to its history of long-distance travel and running under coaches, needs plenty of exercise to avoid behavior problems. It is an

BODY AND TOPLINE
Topline smooth. Chest deep, of moderate width; good spring of ribs; not barrel shaped. Brisket reaches to elbow. Moderate tuck-up. Back level and strong. Loin short, muscular, slightly arched. Croup nearly level with back.

TAIL
Natural extension of topline. Inserted not too low. Strong at insertion, tapering to tip, and reaching to hock. Never docked. Carried with slight upward curve but never over back.

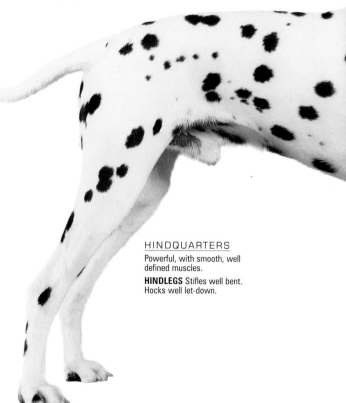

FEET
Round and compact.
TOES Well arched.
PADS Thick and elastic.

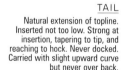

HINDQUARTERS
Powerful, with smooth, well defined muscles.
HINDLEGS Stifles well bent. Hocks well let-down.

GENERAL APPEARANCE

The Dalmatian is a square, medium-sized dog, symmetrical in outline, with no exaggeration or coarseness.

CHARACTERISTICS

Black or liver spots on a solid white ground are distinctive.

TEMPERAMENT

Stable and outgoing, yet dignified, the Dalmatian is poised and alert, intelligent and active.

GAIT/MOVEMENT

Gait and endurance are of great importance. Movement is steady and effortless, with balanced angulation fore and aft. Powerful muscles and good condition combine to produce a smooth, efficient gait.

COAT

Short, dense, and fine, neither wooly nor silky.

COLOR

Ground color is pure white. Black-spotted dogs have dense black spots; liver-spotted dogs have liver-brown spots. Spots are round, well defined, quite distinct, and vary in size from a dime to a half-dollar. They are evenly distributed, and the spots on the head, legs, and tail are smaller than those on the on body. Ears are preferably spotted.

SIZE

HEIGHT(desirable)

19–23 in (47.5–57.5cm)

Length from forechest to buttocks approximately equal to height at withers.

DISQUALIFICATIONS

- Any color markings other than black or liver
- Deviation of more than 1 in (2.5cm) above stated maximum height
- Overshot or undershot
- Tri-color
- Patches of color

excellent jogging companion and will run for miles with its owner, protecting him or her along the way. It is very intelligent and rather stubborn, so training should start early and continue consistently. Very loving to its own family, it is a good watch dog. The coat needs daily brushing because it sheds all year long. Pups are born white and develop markings by six weeks. Some Dalmatians are born deaf in one or both ears.

HEAD AND SKULL

Head of fair length and free of loose skin. Topskull flat with slight vertical furrow, approximately as wide as it is long. Stop well defined.
NOSE Completely pigmented. Black in black-spotted dogs, brown in liver-spotted dogs.

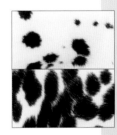

NECK

Nicely arched, fairly long, and free from throatiness.

EYES AND EARS

EYES Medium sized, set moderately wide apart and well into skull. COLOR Brown or blue, or a combination thereof; the darker the better. SHAPE Somewhat round.

EARS Moderately sized, proportionately wider at base and tapering to rounded tip. Set rather high, and carried close to head. Thin and fine.

FOREQUARTERS

SHOULDERS Smoothly muscled and well laid-back. Upper arm approximately equal in length.
FORELEGS Elbows close to body. Straight; sturdy.
PASTERN At slight angle.
DEWCLAWS May be removed.

MOUTH AND JAWS

MUZZLE Top level and parallel to top of skull. Muzzle and top of skull are about equal in length.
LIPS Clean and close-fitting.
BITE Scissor.

NON-SPORTING

↓ FRENCH BULLDOG

The merry French Bulldog began life as a small English Bulldog. In the mid-1800s, lace-workers from Nottingham in England moved to France to work in the new lace mills, taking with them Bulldogs that were of a new, smaller variety, with erect ears. This stock is thought to have mixed with short-faced bull-baiting dogs from other European countries and the resulting breed was brought to England in around 1900. In the U.S. the breed became as popular with the New York demi-monde as it had been in Paris. American breeders worked hard to perfect the breed and, after 1913, many good ones were sent back to the U.K. Currently, the French Bulldog is more popular in the U.K. and Sweden than in the U.S. The breed's sole purpose is that of companion, a role that it fulfills with great style. It is a very intelligent dog, being alert, responsive, playful, and gentle.

HEAD AND SKULL

Head large and square. Skull flat between ears. Forehead slightly rounded. Stop well defined. Heavy wrinkles form a soft roll over the nose.
NOSE Black; extremely short.

EYES AND EARS

EYES Moderately sized, wide apart, set low down in skull, and neither sunken nor bulging. COLOR Dark. Lighter colored eyes are acceptable in lighter colored dogs. SHAPE Round.

EARS "Bat ear." Broad at base, elongated, with round top. Set high on head but not too close together. Carried erect. Leather fine and soft.

BODY AND TOPLINE

Back roached with slight fall close behind shoulders, broad at shoulders, and narrowing at loin. Body short and well rounded. Chest broad, deep, and well ribbed with belly tucked-up.

TAIL

Either straight or screw (but not curly). Short, hung low, with thick root and fine tip. Carried low in repose.

MOUTH AND JAWS

LIPS Flews black, thick and broad, hanging over lower jaw at sides and covering teeth.

JAWS Undershot. Underjaw deep, square, broad, and turned up.

NECK

Thick and well arched, with loose skin at throat.

FOREQUARTERS

FORELEGS Short, stout, straight, muscular, and set wide apart.

DEWCLAWS May be removed.

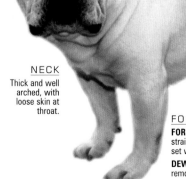

GENERAL APPEARANCE

The French Bulldog is a muscular, heavy-boned dog with a smooth coat. Compactly built, it is of medium or small structure.

CHARACTERISTICS

This charming dog resembles a small version of a Bulldog, but with a lighter head and erect "bat" ears.

TEMPERAMENT

Well behaved and adaptable, the French Bulldog makes a comfortable companion, with an affectionate nature and an even disposition. Though active, alert, and playful, it is not boisterous.

GAIT/MOVEMENT

The correct gait is double-tracking with reach and drive. The action is unrestrained, free, and vigorous.

COAT

The coat is moderately fine, short, and smooth. The skin is soft and loose, especially at the head and shoulders, forming wrinkles.

COLOR

Acceptable colors include brindle, fawn, white, brindle-and-white, and any other color not listed as a disqualification.
KC/ANKC Tan, mouse, and gray/blue highly undesirable.

SIZE

WEIGHT (maximum)
28 lb (12.7kg)

DISQUALIFICATIONS

- Any alteration other than removal of dewclaws
- Weight exceeding 28 lb (12.7kg)
- Other than bat ears
- Nose other than black, except in case of lighter colored dogs, where a lighter nose is acceptable
- Coat colors which include solid black, mouse, liver, black-and-tan, black-and-white, and white with black (black means black without a trace of brindle)

HINDQUARTERS

HINDLEGS Strong and muscular, longer than forelegs, so loin is elevated above shoulders. Hocks well let-down.

FEET

Of moderate size and compact. Hindfeet slightly longer than forefeet.
TOES Compact, well split-up, high knuckles.
NAILS Short and stubby.

KEESHOND

Now the national dog of The Netherlands, the Keeshond began as a ubiquitous farm dog, watch dog, and companion. It is best known as a guard dog on the barges that plied the Rhine between Germany and Holland. Prior to the French Revolution, social unrest spread throughout much of Europe, and Holland was no exception. The Dutch patriot Cornelius de Gysalaer owned a barge dog named "Kees," which became emblematic of the party that sought to overthrow the House of Orange. When the party fell, the breed went into decline. In 1920, through the work of Baroness von Hardenbroek, good specimens were found and the Keeshond restored. By 1925, there were Keeshonden in the U.K. and, by 1930, they had been accepted for registration by the AKC.

The Keeshond limits its affection to one person, or a select few, yet is friendly with all and still manages to be an excellent watch dog. It is a sensitive, intelligent dog and fairly easy to train.

GENERAL APPEARANCE
The Keeshond is a natural, well balanced, short-coupled dog, with a stand-off coat and plumed tail.

CHARACTERISTICS
The gray-black-cream coat, profuse with feathering and plumed tail, coupled with a foxlike expression and small pointed ears, are typical of the breed.

TEMPERAMENT
The Keeshond is neither timid nor aggressive. It is outgoing, friendly with people and other dogs, lively, intelligent, alert, and affectionate.

GAIT/MOVEMENT
The distinctive gait is unique to the breed. Movement is bold, straight, and sharp, with slight to moderate reach and drive, and the tail is kept curled over the back.

COAT
The coat is abundant, long, straight, and harsh, standing well out from the thick, downy undercoat. The head has smooth, soft, short hair. The neck is covered with a mane, more pronounced in males. Trimming allowed only on feet, pasterns, hocks, and whiskers. Hair on the legs is short, except for the feathering on the front, and the "trousers" on the hindlegs down to hocks. The hair on the tail forms a plume.

COLOR
Color is a mixture of gray, black, and cream, and varies from light to dark. The hair of the outercoat is black tipped. The undercoat is very pale gray or cream.

SIZE
HEIGHT (adult)

males	females
18 in (45cm)	17 in (42.5cm)

MOUTH AND JAWS
MUZZLE Medium length, neither coarse nor snipy.

LIPS Black and tight, with no wrinkle at mouth corner.

BITE Scissor.

FOREQUARTERS
SHOULDER To upper arm angulation slight to moderate.

FORELEGS Straight, of good bone.

PASTERNS Strong with slight slope.

EYES AND EARS
EYES Medium sized, set obliquely. COLOR Dark brown, with black rims. SHAPE Almond.

EARS Small and triangular. Mounted high on head and carried erect.

HEAD AND SKULL
Expression largely dependent on distinctive lines called "spectacles" (markings and shadings) around the eyes. Head wedge-shaped. Definite stop.

BODY AND TOPLINE
Body compact, with a short, straight back, sloping slightly down toward the hindquarters; short loin with moderate tuck-up. Chest deep and strong, well ribbed, and barrel-shaped.

NECK
Moderately long.

TAIL
Moderately long, well feathered, set-on high, and tightly curled over back. Should lie flat and close to body.

FEET
Compact, well rounded, catlike.

TOES Nicely arched.

NAILS Black.

HINDQUARTERS
Angulation in rear should complement that in front,

HINDLEGS Well muscled. Hocks perpendicular to ground.

LHASA APSO

Thought by many to resemble the Shih Tzu, the Lhasa Apso is really quite different. Whereas the Shih Tzu lived as a pampered pet of Chinese royalty in temperate southern China, the Lhasa Apso worked as a guard dog inside homes and lamaseries in the brutal climate of high Tibet. Its glamorous coat, though not so long as it is now, was necessary to protect it from the harsh mountain weather. One reason why Buddhists valued the Lhasa so highly is their belief that, when a lama dies, his soul takes up residence in the body of one of these sacred dogs.

No one can state with certainty what dogs made up the Lhasa but, like the Tibetan Terrier, it is probably descended from a longhaired Asian herding dog. The name "Lhasa" refers to the area where most of these dogs were bred. "Apso" is thought to be a corruption of the Tibetan rapso, meaning "goatlike", because of the resemblance of an ungroomed Lhasa to a small local goat.

As a puppy, the Lhasa is very appealing, but this sweet fluff-ball will quickly become an independent, stubborn, tough-minded character. Once its trust is earned, it will respond well to patient, positive, and repetitive training. A wise

HEAD AND SKULL

Heavy head furnishings, with good fall over eyes, whiskers, and beard. Skull narrow, falling away behind eyes to a marked degree, and not quite flat. Straight foreface of fair length.

NOSE Black. Length from tip of nose to eye about a third that from nose to back of skull.

EYES AND EARS

EYES Neither very large and full nor very small and sunken. COLOR Dark brown.

EARS Pendant and heavily feathered.

MOUTH AND JAWS

MUZZLE Medium length.

JAWS Level or slightly undershot.

FOREQUARTERS

FORELEGS Straight, heavily furnished with hair.

→ GENERAL APPEARANCE

The Lhasa Apso is a short-legged, long-bodied dog of elegance and endurance.

→ CHARACTERISTICS

Heavy, straight hair covers the body and droops to the ground. It is parted in the middle from head to tail.

→ TEMPERAMENT

Gay and assertive, the Lhasa Apso is chary of strangers and can be dominant.

→ GAIT/MOVEMENT

Not specified.

→ COAT

The coat consists of heavy, straight, hard hair of good length. Not wooly, nor silky, it is very dense.

→ COLOR

All colors are equally acceptable, with or without dark tips to the ears and beard.

→ SIZE

HEIGHT (at shoulder)

males

10–11 in (25–27.5cm)

Height variable. Females slightly smaller.

owner will begin training very early and plan short refresher sessions at least twice a week throughout the dog's life, in order to prevent behavior problems. Most Lhasas get on well with other dogs, but some are aggressive and dominant with people. It is a hardy dog and needs some, though not a lot, of exercise to stay healthy. A moderate daily walk, plus a safe place to run and explore will be appreciated.

Its coat must be brushed and combed at least every two or three days. Many pet Lhasas are clipped every six to seven weeks, but even then they need to be groomed every two or three days to prevent painful-to-remove mats. Short, pleasant grooming sessions should begin when a puppy is quite young to prevent any resistance to grooming later.

BODY AND TOPLINE

Length from point of shoulder to point of buttocks longer than height at withers. Well ribbed up. Strong loin.

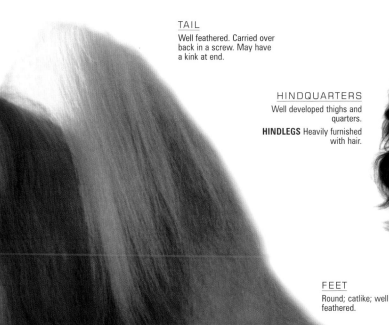

TAIL

Well feathered. Carried over back in a screw. May have a kink at end.

HINDQUARTERS

Well developed thighs and quarters.
HINDLEGS Heavily furnished with hair.

FEET

Round; catlike; well feathered.

↓ POODLE

The word "Poodle" comes from the German "Pudel," which means "to splash." It gained fame in Germany because of its ability as a water retriever, and its intelligence. It was in Germany that the Poodle coat was first trimmed to facilitate water work and to provide extra protection for its chest area. All three Poodle varieties share the same history, and each size has an individual appeal. Contrary to its image as a fluffed-up, silly dog, the Poodle has long been very useful, foremost as a water retriever in Germany and France, but also as a circus trick dog, a herder and guard, a guide dog, and it has always been an excellent watch dog and companion. The original Poodle was the Standard. The Miniature and Toy are the same dog, but bred down in size. The Standard, reputed to be one of the most intelligent of breeds, is an excellent pet for anyone with space for an active dog, and who enjoys training a dog that loves to learn. The Miniature fits well into smaller quarters, but is just as quick and active. The Toy is an excellent apartment dog, with all the qualities of the larger dogs in a small package.

ABOVE Toy Poodle

BODY AND TOPLINE
Topline level to tail, with exception of slight hollow just behind shoulder. Chest deep and moderately wide, with well sprung ribs. Loin short, broad, and muscular.

TAIL
Straight, set-on high, and carried up. Docked at sufficient length to insure balanced outline.

HINDQUARTERS
Angulation matches that of front.
HINDLEGS Muscular with width in region of stifles. Femur and tibia about equal in length. Stifles well bent. Hock to heel perpendicular to ground and short.

ABOVE Miniature Poodle

FEET
Rather small and oval, turning neither in nor out.
TOES Well arched.
PADS Firm and thick.

HEAD AND SKULL
Skull moderately rounded. Slight but definite stop. Cheekbones and muscles flat. Length from occiput to stop about equal to length of muzzle.

EYES AND EARS
EYES Set far apart to create alert expression. COLOR Dark amber in brown dogs; very dark brown in black, blue, gray, silver, cream, and white dogs; amber permitted in apricot-colored dogs. SHAPE Oval.

EARS Hanging close to head, set at or slightly below eyes. Leather long, wide, and thickly feathered, but fringe not excessively long.

MOUTH AND JAWS
MUZZLE Long, straight and fine, with slight chiseling under eyes. Strong but not lippy. Chin definite enough to preclude snipiness.

BITE Scissor.

NECK
Strong and moderately long. Skin tight at throat.

FOREQUARTERS
SHOULDERS Strong, smoothly muscled. Blade well laid-back. Approximately same length as upper foreleg.

FORELEGS Straight. Elbow directly behind highest point of shoulder.

PASTERNS Strong.

DEWCLAWS May be removed.

LEFT Standard Poodle

GENERAL APPEARANCE
A very active, intelligent and elegant dog, the Poodle is squarely built and well proportioned. Properly clipped in the traditional fashion and carefully groomed, it exudes an air of distinction and dignity peculiar to itself.

CHARACTERISTICS
A groomed Poodle is a striking dog. Its coat, in various clips, distinguishes it, as does its sparkling personality and intelligence.

TEMPERAMENT
The Poodle carries itself proudly and is very active. It is never sharp or shy.

GAIT/MOVEMENT
A straightforward trot, with a light, springy action and strong hind drive. Head and tail are carried up.

COAT
The coat is naturally harsh, and can be curly or corded.

CURLY—naturally harsh texture and dense throughout.

CORDED—hanging in tight cords of varying lengths. Longer on the mane or body, head, and ears, but shorter on puffs, bracelets, and pompons.

There are also several clips. A Poodle under 12 months may be shown in the "Puppy" clip. Over 12 months, it must be shown in the "English Saddle" or "Continental" clip. In noncompetitive classes Poodles may be shown in the "Sporting" clip.

KC/ANKC Standard recommends "lion trim" only.

COLOR
Black, blue, gray, silver, brown, cafe-au-lait, apricot, cream, and white. Clear colors preferred, shading allowed. Brown and cafe-au-lait have liver noses, eye rims, and lips. All others have black noses, eye rims, and lips.

SIZE
HEIGHT
STANDARD—over 15 in (37.5cm) at highest point of shoulder.

MINIATURE—maximum 15 in (37.5cm), minimum in excess of 10 in (25cm).

KC/ANKC Minimum in excess of 11 in (28cm).

TOY—maximum 10 in (25cm).

KC/ANKC Maximum 11 in (28cm).

Length of body from breastbone to point of rump approximates height from highest point of shoulder to ground.

DISQUALIFICATIONS
- Deviation above or below the stated height limits
- Dog shown in any clip other than those listed
- Parti-colored dogs

↓ SCHIPPERKE

The Schipperke comes from the Flemish provinces, but it is not known with any certainty when, nor from what other dogs it sprang. Among the theories about its ancestry are that the Schipperke is a small member of the Spitz family, that it came from a cross between the Pomeranian and a terrier, or even that it is a miniaturized version of the Leauvenaar, a medium-sized Belgian sheepdog variety.

Schipperke means Little Captain and many of these pert little dogs worked as watch dogs on barges traveling between Brussels and Antwerp, much like the Keeshond. In this respect, they share another similarity—just as the Keeshond is the National Dog of Holland, so the Schipperke is the National Dog of Belgium.

The modern Schipperke is independent, stubborn, and very inquisitive. Obedience training when young helps to prevent behavior problems resulting from boredom, as do regular exercise and frequent games.

GENERAL APPEARANCE
The Schipperke is a small, cobby, black, tailless dog, with a foxlike face. It is square in profile.

CHARACTERISTICS
The distinctive coat, with prescribed length patterns, is typical of the breed.

TEMPERAMENT
Very curious, the Schipperke is an excellent watchdog. Reserved with strangers, it is ready to protect its family and property if necessary. It is confident and independent.

GAIT/MOVEMENT
Gait is smooth and well coordinated. Front and rear are in perfect balance, with good reach and drive. The topline remains level when in motion.

COAT
The adult coat grows naturally in a specific pattern. The coat is short on the face, ears, front of forelegs and on hocks; of medium length on the body; and longer in the ruff, cape, jabot and culottes.

COLOR
The outercoat must be black, but the undercoat may be slightly lighter.
KC/ANKC Other colors permissible.

SIZE
HEIGHT

males	females
11–13in (27.5–32.5cm)	10–11in (25–27.5cm)

KC Weight 12–16lb (5.4–7.3 kg)

DISQUALIFICATIONS
- Drop ear or ears
- Any color other than a natural black

BODY AND TOPLINE
Topline level or sloping slightly from withers to croup. Stand-out ruff adds to the slope. Chest broad and deep, reaching to elbows. Well- sprung ribs (modified oval) are wide behind shoulders and taper to sternum. Forechest extends in front of shoulders. Loin short, muscular and moderately drawn up. Croup broad, well rounded.

HEAD AND SKULL
Skull medium wide, narrowing toward muzzle, and slightly rounded. Head forms a wedge, tapering smoothly from back of skull to tip of nose. Stop definite but not prominent.
NOSE Small and black.

EYES AND EARS
EYES Small, placed forward on head. COLOR Dark brown. SHAPE Oval.
EARS Small, triangular, placed high on head and, when at attention, very erect.

TAIL
Docked short. **KC/ANKC** Customarily docked short. Undocked: tightly curled, carried over back. **FCI** No tail.

NECK
Of moderate length and slightly arched.

MOUTH AND JAWS
MUZZLE Slightly shorter than skull.
BITE Scissor or level.

HINDQUARTERS
Appear slightly lighter than forequarters, but well muscled and in balance with front.
HINDLEGS Hocks well let-down. Stifles well bent.
DEWCLAWS May be removed.

FEET
Small, round and tight.
NAILS Short, strong and black.

FOREQUARTERS
SHOULDERS Well laid-back
FORELEGS Straight and well under body.
PASTERNS Short, thick, and strong, but flexible, with a slight angle.
DEWCLAWS Generally removed.

SHIBA INU

The Shiba Inu is the smallest and oldest of the Spitz breeds native to Japan. Historically, it was used to hunt birds and small game in the mountainous interior of Japan, where the steep, rough terrain and dense undergrowth tested its hunting ability daily. The fact that it overcame the terrain and climate to be a very successful hunter speaks volumes about its innate abilities. Today, it is among the most popular dogs in Japan and was recognized in 1936 as a "precious natural product" of the Japanese nation. The Shiba has a highly developed sense of cunning, which can make training challenging and living with one very interesting. Fortunately, it is also very friendly and can be a very good companion, especially for an experienced owner/trainer with a good sense of humor.

EYES AND EARS

EYES Deep set and upward slanting. COLOR Iris dark brown. Eye rims black. SHAPE Somewhat triangular.

EARS Triangular, firmly pricked, and small, but in proportion to head and body size. Set well apart and tilt directly forward.

HEAD AND SKULL

Skull size moderate, in proportion to the body. Forehead broad and flat with slight furrow. Stop moderate.

NOSE Black.

BODY AND TOPLINE

Topline straight, level to base of tail. Body dry, well muscled. Forechest well developed. Chest depth is one-half or less than total height from withers to ground. Ribs moderately sprung. Abdomen firm and well tucked up. Back firm. Loin strong.

TAIL

Thick and powerful. Carried over back in a sickle or curled position.

NECK

Thick, sturdy, and of moderate length.

MOUTH AND JAWS

MUZZLE Firm, full, round, with a strong lower jaw. Bridge straight, tapering slightly from stop to nose tip. Length is 40 percent of total head length from occiput to nose tip. Full cheeks.

LIPS Tight and black.

TEETH Full complement of evenly aligned teeth.

BITE Scissor.

HINDQUARTERS

Angulation moderate. Balanced with front.

HINDLEGS Strong, wide. Hock joint strong. Upper thighs long. Second thigh short but well developed.

DEWCLAWS None.

FOREQUARTERS

SHOULDERS Shoulder blade and upper arm moderately angulated and approximately equal in length.

FORELEGS Straight, and moderately spaced, like feet. Elbows close to body.

PASTERNS Slightly inclined.

DEWCLAWS Removal optional.

FEET

Catlike.

TOES Well arched and close together.

PADS Thick.

GENERAL APPEARANCE

A compact frame, with well developed muscles. Males are masculine but not coarse, while females are feminine without weakness.

CHARACTERISTICS

This is a smallish dog, longer in the back than it is tall, with a distinctively colored, stand-off double coat.

TEMPERAMENT

Spirited boldness, good nature, unaffected forthrightness, and independence. Reserved with strangers but loyal and affectionate to those who earn its respect.

GAIT/MOVEMENT

Nimble, light, and elastic. Reach and drive are moderate and efficient.

COAT

The double coat consists of a stiff, straight outercoat and a soft thick undercoat. It is short and even on the face, ears, and legs. Guard hairs stand off the body, about 1½–2 in (3.75–5cm) at the withers. Tail hair is slightly longer and stands open as a bush.

COLOR

Three allowed colors:

RED—bright orange-red with cream points (urajiro).

BLACK AND SESAME—black with tan points and cream; undercoat buff or gray.

SESAME—black-tipped hairs on a rich red background.

On all coat colors, urajiro (cream to white ventral color) is required on the side of the muzzle and on the cheeks, inside the ears, on the underjaw and upper throat, inside legs, on the abdomen, around the vent and on the ventral side of the tail. Clear white markings are permitted on tail tip, as socks on the forelegs, and hindlegs. A patch of blaze is permitted on the throat, forechest, or chest in addition to urajiro.

SIZE

HEIGHT

males	females
14½–16½ in (36.25–41.25cm)	13½–15½ in (33.75–38.75cm)

Preferred size in mid range.

WEIGHT (average)

males	females
23 lb (10.5kg)	17 lb (7.7kg)

Bone moderate.

DISQUALIFICATIONS

- Deviation above or below the stated height limits
- Overshot or undershot

↓
TIBETAN SPANIEL

Two factors greatly influenced the development of Tibetan dogs. One was the geographic and social isolation of the country. The other was the growing prevalence of the Lamaist form of Buddhism, with its veneration for all living things, ban on the killing of animals, and belief in reincarnation. Many families bred their dogs, but the best and smallest were bred in the monasteries. The first Tibetan Spaniel was brought to the U.K. in the late 1800s, but no breeding took place until just before World War II. After the war, breeding recommenced on a small scale. Finally the Tibetan Spaniel Association of England was formed and the breed was accepted for registration by the KC in 1958. The Tibetan Spaniel is described as being "catlike." Certainly it enjoys observing the world from a high level, as it did in the monasteries where it spent the days patrolling the high walls. It is sensitive, very intelligent, and readily trainable, yet can be stubborn.

GENERAL APPEARANCE
The Tibetan Spaniel is small, active, slightly longer in the body than tall, and has a protective double coat.

CHARACTERISTICS
Typical are the apelike expression, the mane, or "shawl," on the neck (heavier on males than females), and the plumed tail carried over the back.

TEMPERAMENT
Gay and assertive; highly intelligent; aloof with strangers.

GAIT/MOVEMENT
Movement is quick, free, and positive.

COAT
The double coat is silky in texture. Smooth on the face and legs, it is of moderate length on the body, but flat-lying. The ears and back of legs are feathered; there is longer hair on the tail and buttocks. Mane, or "shawl" on the neck, especially on dogs, and feathering between the toes.

COLOR
All colors and mixtures of colors are allowed. White markings are allowed on the feet.

SIZE
HEIGHT (approximate)
10 in (25cm)
Body slightly longer from point of shoulder to root of tail than the height at withers.
KC/FCI/ANKC 9–15 lb (4.1–6.8 kg)

EYES AND EARS
EYES Medium-sized, set fairly well apart but forward looking, giving an apelike expression. COLOR Dark brown. SHAPE Oval.

EARS Medium sized, pendant, and well feathered. Set fairly high and may have a slight lift from the skull but should not fly.

HEAD AND SKULL
Small in proportion to body. Moderate in dogs but never coarse. Skull slightly domed and of moderate width and length. Stop slight but defined.
NOSE Black.

BODY AND TOPLINE
Level back. Well ribbed with good depth.

NECK
Moderately short and strong.

TAIL
Richly plumed. Set high and carried in gay curl over back when moving.

MOUTH AND JAWS
MUZZLE Medium length, blunt with cushioning. No wrinkle. Chin shows depth and width.
JAWS Slightly undershot.
TEETH Full dentition, evenly placed. Lower jaw wide between canines.
BITE Level permitted, but undershot preferred.

HINDQUARTERS
Well made and strong.
HINDLEGS Stifles show moderate angulation. Hocks well let-down.
DEWCLAWS May be removed.

FOREQUARTERS
SHOULDER Well placed.
FORELEGS Bones slightly bowed but firm at shoulder. Moderate bone.
DEWCLAWS May be removed.

FEET
Harefooted.

TIBETAN TERRIER

Believed to be the original Holy Dog of Tibet, the Tibetan Terrier is not a terrier. It was given this name when it was imported into the United Kingdom because it resembled many terriers in general size and shape. It has a similar history to the Tibetan Spaniel and its build is similar to the Lhasa Apso, but taller and with a slightly shorter back. The Tibetan Terrier was bred in Lamaist monasteries two thousand years ago—like the Tibetan Spaniel—and both breeds were primarily companions. The Tibetan Terrier is gentle, very affectionate, and a delightful companion. In Tibet it was treated like one of the family's children, and it is happiest now when at the center of family life. Because it wants so much to please, it is an easy dog to train and live with.

GENERAL APPEARANCE
A medium-sized dog, profusely coated; of powerful build and square proportion. Well balanced, capable of both strong and efficient movement.

CHARACTERISTICS
Protective double coat, with a fall of hair covering the eyes and foreface. The well feathered tail curls up and falls over back. Feet are large, flat, and round ("snowshoe").

TEMPERAMENT
Highly intelligent, sensitive, loyal, devoted and affectionate, the Tibetan Terrier may be cautious or reserved, but never shy.

GAIT/MOVEMENT
Free, effortless stride, with good reach and flexibility in the rear allowing full extension.

COAT
Double coat consists of a soft, wooly undercoat and a profuse, fine outercoat (neither silky nor wooly). It may be wavy or straight. The coat is long but does not reach the ground. A natural parting is often present on the neck and back.

COLOR
Any color or combination of colors, including white, are acceptable.

SIZE
HEIGHT (average)
15–16 in (37.5–40cm)
WEIGHT (average)
20–24 lb (9.1–10.9kg)
WEIGHT (range)
18–30 lb (8.2–13.6kg)
Females slightly smaller. A well balanced, square dog.
KC/FCI/ANKC Does not specify weight.

HEAD AND SKULL
Medium-length skull, neither broad nor coarse. Lengths from eye to tip of nose and from eye to occiput equal. Head narrows slightly from ear to eye, and is well furnished with long hair, falling forward over eyes and foreface. Cheekbones curved but not bulging. Stop marked but not exaggerated.
NOSE Black.

EYES AND EARS
EYES Large, set fairly wide apart. COLOR Dark brown (may appear black) with dark rims.
EARS Pendant, falling not too close to head. Heavily feathered, with a V-shaped leather.

MOUTH AND JAWS
JAWS Lower jaw has small amount of beard. Distinct curve in jaw between canines.
BITE Tight scissor, tight reverse scissor, slightly undershot, or level all acceptable.

NECK
Length proportionate to body and head.

HINDQUARTERS
HINDLEGS Well furnished and slightly longer than forelegs. Thighs relatively broad and well muscled. Stifles well bent. Hocks low set.
DEWCLAWS May be removed.

BODY AND TOPLINE
Body compact, square, strong, capable of speed and endurance. Back level in motion. Brisket extends to elbow. Well ribbed up and never cloddy or coarse. Ribcage not too wide. Loin slightly arched.

TAIL
Medium length and heavily furnished. Set-on fairly high. Falls forward over back and may curl to either side. May have a kink near tip.

FOREQUARTERS
SHOULDERS Sloping, well muscled and laid back.
FORELEGS Straight, strong, and heavily furnished. Distance from withers to elbow equals distance form elbows to ground.
DEWCLAWS May be removed.

FEET
Unique in form, being large, flat, and round in shape ("snowshoe").
PADS Thick and strong, heavily furnished with hair between toes and pads.
DEWCLAWS May be removed.

AUSTRALIAN CATTLE DOG

The Australian Cattle Dog was bred to be a hard-working cattle-herder. It was developed in Australia from crosses between the native Dingo and some smooth-coated, blue merle Highland Collies. The goal was a dog able to withstand the climate and work silently to avoid stampeding the herds. By the late 1800s and early 1900s, after years of careful selection for working ability, color, and type, and of ruthlessly culling any dogs not up to the standard, the dogs began to breed true to type. A standard was approved by the KC of New South Wales and by the Cattle and Sheep Dog Club, both of Australia, in 1903. The Cattle Dog is very smart and active. It is not a dog for a novice or casual owner. It is first and foremost a dog with the brains, strength, and determination to handle large wild cattle and to work all day. This dog must have an experienced and involved owner. Training requires persistence, intelligence, and creativity.

HEAD AND SKULL

Head, strong. Skull broad, slightly curved between ears with slight but definite stop. Cheeks muscular. Foreface broad, well filled below eyes, and tapering to muzzle.
NOSE Black.

EYES AND EARS

EYES Medium-sized. COLOR Dark brown. SHAPE Oval.

EARS Moderately-sized (preferably smaller than large), broad at base, moderately pointed. Set wide on skull. Leather thick.

BODY AND TOPLINE

Topline level. Back strong. Ribs well sprung, not barrel shaped. Chest deep, muscular. Loin broad, strong.

TAIL

Set on moderately low, reaching approximately to hock. Hangs in slight curve at rest, but raised in movement. Never carried past vertical line drawn through root.

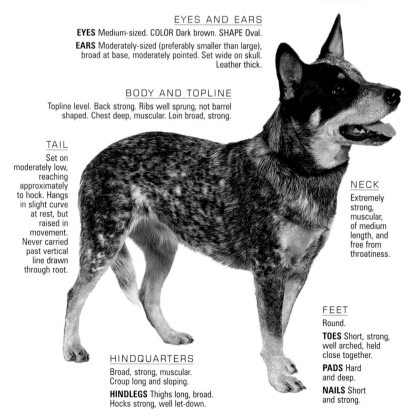

NECK

Extremely strong, muscular, of medium length, and free from throatiness.

FEET

Round.

TOES Short, strong, well arched, held close together.

PADS Hard and deep.

NAILS Short and strong.

HINDQUARTERS

Broad, strong, muscular. Croup long and sloping.

HINDLEGS Thighs long, broad. Hocks strong, well let-down.

→ GENERAL APPEARANCE

Strong, compact, symmetrically built working dog, capable of performing arduous work with great strength, agility, and endurance.

→ CHARACTERISTICS

The flat, mottled (speckled) coat and prick ears are typical of the breed.

→ TEMPERAMENT

Loyal, protective, intelligent, and determined.

→ GAIT/MOVEMENT

Action is free, supple, and tireless. Hindquarters powerful. The dog is capable of quick, sudden movement and great endurance.

→ COAT

Dense double coat, with a short, dense undercoat. Outercoat is close; hair is straight, hard, and lying flat. Under the body, to behind the legs, coat is longer, forming breeching near the thigh. The hair is thicker and longer on the neck.

→ COLOR

There are two colors.

BLUE—blue, blue-mottled, or blue speckled, with or without black, blue, or tan markings.

RED SPECKLE—good, even red speckle all over, including the undercoat, with or without darker red markings.

→ SIZE

HEIGHT

males	females
18–20 in (45–50cm)	17–19 in (42.5–47.5cm)

MOUTH AND JAWS

MUZZLE Medium length, deep, and powerful. Skull and muzzle on parallel planes.

LIPS Clean and tight.

BITE Scissor.

FOREQUARTERS

SHOULDERS Strong, sloping, muscular, well angulated to upper arm.

FORELEGS Strong, round bone, and straight.

PASTERNS Flexible, with slight angle.

AUSTRALIAN SHEPHERD

The Australian Shepherd most probably came from the great sheep farms of the Basque region in the Pyrenees Mountains between France and Spain. When sheep-farming began in Australia, herders with their dogs accompanied the sheep, and later, when the herders came to the western parts of the U.S., the dogs were called Australian Shepherds as an indication of their former home. Though the breed was greatly improved by breeders in the U.S., it was relatively unknown except on sheep farms until the early 1950s when public interest increased in most things Western, including rodeos, where the Australian Shepherd was seen working cattle and performing tricks. This dog will herd whatever is available—cattle, sheep, horses, other dogs, even groups of children. It is smart, very trainable, very alert, and very active.

GENERAL APPEARANCE

A well balanced dog, slightly longer than tall and of medium size and bone.

CHARACTERISTICS

This dog is lithe and agile, solid and muscular without cloddiness; attentive and animated. Tail is docked or naturally bobbed.

TEMPERAMENT

An intelligent, active dog, the Australian Shepherd has an even disposition, being good natured and seldom quarrelsome.

GAIT/MOVEMENT

The gait is smooth, free, and easy, displaying great agility and with a ground-covering stride. The dog must be able to change direction or alter gait instantly.

COAT

The coat is of medium texture, straight to wavy, weather resistant, and of medium length. The hair is short, and smooth on the head, ears, front of forelegs and below the hocks. The backs of the forelegs and breeches are moderately feathered, and there is a moderate mane and frill, more so in males than females.

COLOR

Colors are blue merle, black, red merle, or red, with or without white markings and/or tan points. White is acceptable on the neck, chest, legs, the muzzle underparts, and as a blaze on head. White on the head should not predominate. Eyes must be fully surrounded by color and pigment.

SIZE

HEIGHT (preferred)

males	females
20–23 in (50–57.5cm)	18–21 in (45–52.5cm)

Slightly longer than tall

DISQUALIFICATIONS

- Undershot, overshot more than ⅛ in (0.3cm)
- White body splashes (white on body between withers and tail, on sides between elbows and back of hindquarters in all colors)

EYES AND EARS

EYES COLOR Brown, blue, or amber, in any variation or combination, including flecks and marbling. Eye rims match coat and lip color. SHAPE Almond.

EARS Triangular, of moderate size and leather, set high. At full attention, they break forward and over, or to the side as a rose ear.

MOUTH AND JAWS

MUZZLE Tapers little from base to nose. Rounded at tip.

LIPS Black on blue merles and blacks. Liver (brown) on red merles and reds.

TEETH Full complement.

BITE Scissor or level.

HEAD AND SKULL

Clean cut, strong, dry. Topline of back skull and muzzle parallel; moderate, well defined stop. Topskull flat to slightly domed, with a slight occipital protuberance. Length and width equal.

NOSE Black on blue merles and blacks. Liver (brown) on red merles and reds. Adult merles may have up to 25 percent of small pink spots.

NECK

Strong, moderate length, and slightly arched at crest.

FOREQUARTERS

SHOULDERS Shoulder blades long, flat, fairly close set at withers, well laid-back. Upper arm, approximately same length as, and at right angles to, shoulder blade.

FORELEGS Straight and strong. Bone oval, not round.

PASTERNS Medium length and very slightly sloped.

DEWCLAWS May be removed.

BODY AND TOPLINE

Back straight, strong, level. Croup moderately sloped. Chest not broad but deep, reaching to elbows. Ribs well sprung and long, neither barrel nor slab-sided. Moderate tuck-up.

TAIL

Straight, docked, or naturally bobbed. Not to exceed 4 in (10cm). **KC/ANKC** When undocked, set low following line of rump. Never curled or carried over back.

HINDQUARTERS

Width equal to that of forequarters at shoulders. Angulation of pelvis and upper thigh corresponds to that of shoulder blade and upper arm.

HINDLEGS Stifles clearly defined. Hocks short, perpendicular.

DEWCLAWS Must be removed. **KC** Removal not necessary.

FEET

Oval, compact, and close knit.

TOES Well arched.

PADS Thick and resilient.

BEARDED COLLIE

The Bearded Collie may descend from the Komondor of central Europe. Alternatively, it may come from three Polish Lowland Sheepdogs—two bitches and a dog—that arrived in Scotland from Gdansk, Poland in about 1514, with a grain shipment, and in exchange for Scottish sheep.

As with many old breeds, it will probably never be known for certain which theory is correct, or whether the truth lies in a combination of the two. The Bearded Collie is among the most ancient breeds in the U.K., but little is known of the breed's history, or about any early pedigrees, because these dogs lived and worked with hill farmers, guarding and herding sheep. Originally there were two strains of Bearded Collie— the Border dogs, which were gray and white; and the Highland dogs, which were brown and white, and whose coat tended to curl. Interbreeding over hundreds of years has mixed the strains and eliminated the curl.

HEAD AND SKULL
Skull broad and flat. Stop moderate. Cheeks well filled beneath eyes. Foreface equal in length to distance between stop and occiput.
NOSE Large and squarish.

EYES AND EARS
EYES Large, not round nor protruding, set wide apart. Eyebrows arched to sides, blending into coat on sides of head. COLOR Generally tones with coat color. In dogs born blue or fawn, distinctively lighter eyes are correct and must not be penalized.
EARS Medium-sized, hanging, and covered with long hair. Set level with eyes. When alert, ears have a slight lift at base.

MOUTH AND JAWS
MUZZLE Strong and full.
TEETH Full dentition.
BITE Scissor.

FOREQUARTERS
SHOULDERS Well laid-back. Tops of shoulder blades lie in against withers.
FORELEGS Straight with substantial, but not heavy bone. Covered with shaggy hair all around.
PASTERNS Flexible without weakness.

FEET
Oval, with well padded soles. Well covered with hair including between pads.
TOES Arched and close together.

The Beardie has unflagging energy and can work sheep every day, during rain and cold and in rough country. A dog bred to work at this level needs a long daily walk, plus a large fenced yard in which to run and romp, in all weather. Though it gives every evidence of enjoying the company of youngsters, it may be too active for smaller children and will probably attempt to herd them. As a puppy, it will play for hours with its toys, and some adults never outgrow this trait, nor their typical humorous outlook. It is quite intelligent, but its innate independence makes training a slow process. To be successful, the trainer must have a sense of humor, as well as being persistent and energetic.

The coat adds to the Bearded Collie's appeal, but greatly increases upkeep requirements. It will need an occasional bath, and the long coat will form tangles unless brushed completely every day.

BODY AND TOPLINE
Body longer than high in ratio of 5:4. Back level, blending smoothly into curve of rump. Ribs well sprung from spine, but flat at sides. Chest deep, reaching to elbows. Loin strong.

NECK
Strong, slightly arched.

TAIL
Set low, but long enough for end of bone to reach at least to point of hock. Normally carried low. When in motion, tip curves upward but is never carried beyond a vertical line. Covered with abundant hair.

HINDQUARTERS
Powerful and muscular at thighs.
HINDLEGS Stifles well bent. Hocks low. Covered with shaggy hair all around.

→ GENERAL APPEARANCE
The Bearded Collie is a medium-sized dog, strongly made, with a long, lean body.

→ CHARACTERISTICS
The coat is of medium length, flat, straight, and of a muted gray or brown shade. It appears equal from nose tip to tail, with plenty of light showing under the body.

→ TEMPERAMENT
A devoted and intelligent member of the family; very active, self-confident, and independent.

→ GAIT/MOVEMENT
Movement is free, supple, and powerful, with good reach in the forequarters and strong drive from the rear. The back remains firm and level. The feet lift only enough to clear the ground. Movement is lithe and flexible, and the dog is able to make sharp turns and sudden stops like any good sheepdog.

→ COAT
Double coat, with a soft, furry, close undercoat. Outercoat is flat, harsh, strong, and shaggy; not wooly or curly; a slight wave is permissible. The coat falls naturally to either side but must never be artificially parted. The dog must be shown in a natural condition, not trimmed in any way. The nose is covered with slightly longer hair on the sides, covering the lips. From the cheeks, lower lips and under the chin, the hair increases in length toward the chest, forming the typical beard.

→ COLOR
The Bearded Collie is born black, blue, brown, or fawn, with or without white markings. Coat color may lighten with maturity and varies from light to dark. If there is any white, it appears on the foreface as a blaze, on the skull, tip of tail, chest, legs, feet, and around the neck. Tan markings may also occur. Pigmentation follows coat color. In a born black, the eye rims, nose, and lips are black. In a born blue, pigmentation is brown. Born fawns have a correspondingly lighter brown pigment.

→ SIZE
HEIGHT (ideal adult)

males	females
21–22 in (52.5–55cm)	20–21 in (50–52.5cm)

BELGIAN SHEEPDOG

There are four Belgian shepherd breeds—the Groenendael, Malinois, Tervuren, and Laekenois. All but the last are accepted by the AKC, and all are similar in type and history. For the FCI, and ANKC, all four breeds are varieties of the so-called Belgian Shepherd Dog, the only variations relating to coat and color. In the U.S., the Groenendael is known as the Belgian Sheepdog.

The Belgian Sheepdog, the only Belgian shepherd with a long black coat, was developed as a working farm dog—to guard sheep, farm, and family, and to move and gather the flocks. Since about 1900, it has also been used by the military and police as a guard or messenger dog, by the police as a patrol dog, and by the Belgian Customs to capture smugglers. It is a good choice for an experienced owner/trainer with the necessary skill and patience to train a very smart, dominant and independent dog.

EYES AND EARS

EYES Medium-sized, not protruding. COLOR Brown, preferably dark. SHAPE Slightly almond.

EARS Triangular, stiff, erect, and in proportion to size of head. Base of ear not below center of eye.

HEAD AND SKULL

Clean-cut and strong. Topskull flattened, not rounded, with width and length approximately equal, but never wider than long. Stop moderate.

NOSE Black with no spots.

BODY AND TOPLINE

Withers slightly higher and sloping to back, which is level, straight, from withers to hip joints. Chest not broad, but deep, reaching to elbows. Abdomen, neither tucked-up nor paunchy. Loin short, broad, and strong. Croup medium long, sloping gradually.

NECK

Round and rather outstretched, tapering from head to body. Well muscled, with tight skin.

TAIL

Strong at base. Bone reaches to hock. At rest, held low. In action, raised with a curl at tip.

MOUTH AND JAWS

MUZZLE Moderately pointed. Approximately equal in length to topskull.

LIPS Tight and black.

TEETH Full complement.

BITE Scissor or even.

FOREQUARTERS

SHOULDER Long and oblique, forming sharp angle with upper arm.

FORELEGS Straight and strong. Bone oval rather than round.

PASTERNS Medium length, strong, and very slightly sloped.

HINDQUARTERS

Length and substance well proportioned to size of dog. Bone oval not round.

LEGS Thighs broad and heavily muscled. Upper and lower thigh bones approximately parallel to shoulder and upper arm. Relatively sharp angles, but not extreme, at stifle and hock.

DEWCLAWS Should be removed.

GENERAL APPEARANCE

A well balanced, square dog, elegant with proud head carriage. Strong, agile, and well muscled, it is alert and full of life. Males are grand, females, feminine.

CHARACTERISTICS

The black, longish, straight double coat is typical of the breed.

TEMPERAMENT

Intelligent, courageous, alert, and devoted to its owner. Protective of the person and property of its master. Vigilant with strangers. Showing no signs of fear or shyness, nor of unprovoked aggression, it is affectionate with its family and very possessive.

GAIT/MOVEMENT

Movement is smooth, free, and easy, rather than hard driving. The back remains firm and level in motion. There is a marked tendency to move in a circle rather than a straight line.

COAT

The coat is double. The guard hairs are long, straight, and abundant, medium harsh and not silky or wiry. Undercoat is extremely dense, commensurate with climatic conditions. The hair is shorter on the head, outside of the ears, and lower parts of the legs. Ear opening protected by hair tufts. Especially long and abundant hair, like a collarette, circles the neck. There is a fringe of long hair on the back of the forearms and trimming on the hindquarters and tail.

COLOR

Only black is permitted, though there may be a small or moderate patch of white on the forechest, between the pads of the feet, on the tips of the foretoes and hindtoes, and on the chin and muzzle.

SIZE

HEIGHT

males	females
24–26 in (60–65cm)	22–24 in (55–60cm)

Length from point of breastbone to point of rump should equal height.

DISQUALIFICATIONS

- Deviation of more than 1½ in (3.75cm) above or below the stated height
- Ears hanging as a hound
- Cropped or stump tail
- Any color other than black
- Viciousness

FEET

Forefeet round. Hindfeet slightly elongated. All, well padded.

TOES Curved close together.

NAILS Strong and black, except white to match white toe tips.

BELGIAN TERVUREN

A distinct breed in the U.S. but not the U.K., the Belgian Tervuren (spelled "Tervueren" by the KC, FCI, and ANKC) owes a debt to Mr. Corbeel, of Tervuren village, who was an early breeder and proponent of the breed. Since the formation of the Belgian Shepherd Club in 1891, there have been accurate records of the breed. By the end of World War II, the breed had almost disappeared and it was re-created by breeding the longhaired Malinois to the fawn-gray Groenendael. Offspring of these crosses were bred to the few remaining Tervuren. The resulting dogs are now the most popular of Belgian shepherds, both in the U.S. and on the Continent. Though the Tervuren was first registered by the AKC in 1918, it was only recognized as a separate breed in 1959. The Tervuren has a tendency to circle any area that it is guarding; it needs daily strenuous exercise of mind and body; and it is loathe to be separated from its family.

GENERAL APPEARANCE

A strong, well balanced, medium-sized dog, elegant and square. Agile and muscular, alert and full of life, it has depth and solidarity without bulk.

CHARACTERISTICS

This dog is similar to the Belgian Sheepdog except for color.

TEMPERAMENT

Observant and vigilant with strangers, but not apprehensive, shy, nor vicious. It must be approachable, standing its ground and showing confidence.

GAIT/MOVEMENT

Covers maximum ground with minimum effort. Always in motion, seemingly never tired, it shows ease of motion rather than hard driving action. Back is level and firm in motion.

COAT

The coat is adapted to extremes of temperature or climate. Guard hairs must be long, close fitting, straight, and abundant. Texture is medium harsh. The undercoat is very dense. The hair is short on the head, outside ears, and front of the legs. Ear openings are protected by tufts of hair. There is a mane, or collarette, of long, abundant hair on the neck, and a fringe on the back of the forearm, breeches, and on the tail.

COLOR

Color is a rich fawn to russet mahogany on the body, with black overlay. Characteristically each fawn hair has a blackened tip. Chest is normally black, or mixture of black and gray. A single white patch is permitted on the chest, but should not extend to the neck or breast. The face has a black mask, and the ears are mostly black. Underparts of the body, tail, and breeches are cream, gray, or light beige. Tail typically has dark or black tip. Tips of the toes may be white.

SIZE

HEIGHT (ideal)

males	females
24–26 in (60–65cm)	22–24 in (55–60cm)

Body square. Females may be somewhat longer in body.

DISQUALIFICATIONS

- Deviations of 1 in (2.5cm) below or ½ in (1.25cm) above the stated ideal heights
- Hanging ears, as on a hound
- Undershot teeth such that contact with upper incisors is lost by two or more of lower incisors
- Cropped or stump tail
- Solid black, solid liver, or any area of white, except as specified on chest, tips of toes, chin, and muzzle

HEAD AND SKULL

Well chiseled, skin taut, long without exaggeration. Topskull flattened, not rounded, with width approximately equal to, but never wider than length. Stop moderate. Toplines of muzzle and skull parallel.

NOSE Black. Nostrils well defined.

EYES AND EARS

EYES Medium-sized, not protruding. COLOR Brown. SHAPE Slightly almond.

EARS Triangular, well cupped, stiff, and erect. Height equals width at base. Set high, with base of ear not below center of eye.

MOUTH AND JAWS

MUZZLE Moderately pointed.

LIPS Tight, black, no pink.

JAWS Strong, powerful.

TEETH Full complement.

BITE Scissor or level.

FOREQUARTERS

SHOULDERS Long, laid-back 45 degrees, forming right angle with upper arm. Top of shoulderblades roughly two thumb-widths apart. Forearms long and well muscled.

FORELEGS Straight. Bone oval not round.

PASTERNS Short, strong, slightly sloping.

DEWCLAWS May be removed.

BODY AND TOPLINE

Withers accentuated. Topline level, straight, and firm to sloping croup. Chest neither broad nor narrow, but deep, reaching to elbows. Abdomen, neither tucked-up nor paunchy. Ribs well sprung and flat on sides. Loin relatively short, strong, and broad.

NECK

Round, muscular, rather long and elegant, and slightly arched. No loose skin.

TAIL

Strong at base, bone reaching to hock. Held low at rest, with tip bent up. In action, raised level to topline in slight curve. Not carried above backline.

FEET

Forefeet rounded. Hindfeet slightly elongated. Both turn neither in nor out.

TOES Curved close together.

PADS Well padded.

HINDQUARTERS

HINDLEGS Powerful, not heavy. Bone oval, not round. Thighs broad and heavily muscled. Stifles clearly defined. Upper shank at right angle to hipbones. Hocks moderately bent.

DEWCLAWS Should be removed.

BORDER COLLIE

The Border Collie, as a distinct breed, probably dates back to the Roman invasion of Britain. This dog, as its name indicates, was developed in the Border regions between Scotland and England. By the late 1800s, every region had its own herding dog, and each was claimed to be the best. To settle the conflicting claims, the first sheep-dog trial was held in 1876, in a park near Alexandra Palace in London. Organized by Mr. R. J. Lloyd Price, who provided a hundred wild sheep for the trial, the net effect was to amaze all watchers with the ability of the Border Collie to manage, separate, and drive the sheep. Ever since, the Border Collie has been acknowledged as a superlative practitioner of the herding arts.

The Border Collie manages sheep by using its "eye"—staring intently and silently at the sheep until they are intimidated into moving in the desired direction. Its ability to force sheep to move is uncanny, and the stare can be unnerving to other animals and people when it is turned in their direction.

HEAD AND SKULL

Skull broad, with pronounced occiput. Skull and foreface approximately equal in length. Stop moderate.

NOSE Color matches primary body color. Nostrils well developed.

EYES AND EARS

EYES Moderately sized, set well apart. COLOR Full range of brown. Dogs whose primary body color is black will have dark eye color. Blue eyes allowed in merles, where one or both may be partly or wholly blue. SHAPE Oval.

EARS Medium-sized, set well apart, and carried erect and/or semi-erect. Tips may fall forward or outward to side. Sensitive and mobile.

NECK

Of good length, strong, muscular, and slightly arched.

MOUTH AND JAWS

MUZZLE Moderately short, strong and blunt, tapering to nose.

JAWS Underjaw strong and well developed.

BITE Scissor.

FOREQUARTERS

SHOULDERS Long and well angulated to upper arm. Elbows turning neither in nor out.

FORELEGS Well boned.

PASTERNS Slightly sloping.

DEWCLAWS May be removed.

Typically, a Border Collie is very intense and very fast. It must have work to do every day, plus strenuous exercise, or it can be destructive and very difficult to live with.

The first standard for this breed described only its working ability; most breeders are still more concerned with what the dog can do than what it looks like. This may change somewhat because the Border Collie is now seen at conformation shows. Nonetheless, it is far more often seen at agility and obedience trials, fly-ball competitions, and herding trials—at all of which it excels.

This Collie responds well to training by an experienced, persistent, and energetic trainer who is able to concentrate on the dog for hours each day and to keep the dog's mind occupied. Even a young puppy shares this need for work and exercise. The Border Collie tends to be reserved with strangers, saving its energy and attention for its master and its work.

BODY AND TOPLINE

Topline level with slight arch over loin. Body athletic. Chest deep, moderately broad. Brisket reaches to elbow. Ribcage well sprung. Loin moderately deep, muscular, and slightly arched, with no tuck-up. Croup gradually sloped downward.

TAIL

Set low, moderately long, with bone reaching to hock. May have upward swirl to tip. Carried low when working. In excitement, may rise level with back.

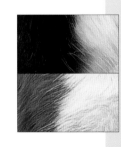

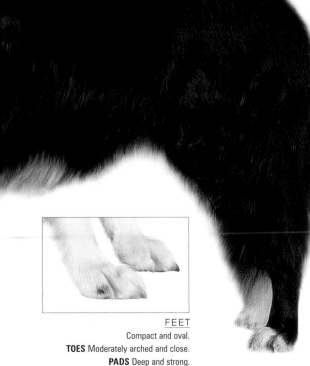

HINDQUARTERS

Broad and muscular, sloping gracefully to set of tail.
HINDLEGS Straight and parallel or very slightly cowhocked. Thighs long, broad, deep, and muscular. Stifle well turned. Hocks strong and well let-down.

FEET

Compact and oval.
TOES Moderately arched and close.
PADS Deep and strong.

➔ GENERAL APPEARANCE

A medium-sized, well balanced dog of athletic appearance. It is energetic, alert and eager, and intelligence is its hallmark.

➔ CHARACTERISTICS

An athletic appearance in a hard, muscular body, and great intensity, is typical of this breed.

➔ TEMPERAMENT

Intelligent, alert, and responsive. Affectionate with friends, the collie is reserved with strangers. An intensive worker, it is eager to learn and to please, and thrives on human companionship.

➔ GAIT/MOVEMENT

Able to suddenly change speed and direction with no loss of balance or grace. Great endurance, a free, smooth trotting gait, and minimum lift of feet. Topline remains steady in motion. Stride covers maximum ground with minimum speed.

➔ COAT

There are two varieties, both with a soft, dense, weather-resistant double coat. The puppy coat (soft, short, dense and water-resistant) becomes the undercoat in adults.

ROUGH—medium to long, texture from flat to slightly wavy. Short, smooth on face. Forelegs feathered. Rear pasterns may have coat trimmed short. With advancing age coat may become very wavy; this not a fault.

SMOOTH—short over entire body. May have feathering on forelegs and fuller coat on chest.

➔ COLOR

Many colors, and various combinations of patterns and markings, are allowed. Most common is black, with or without a white blaze, collar, stockings, and tail tip, and with or without tan points. Solid colors include bi-color, tri-color, merle, and sable, and all are judged equally.

➔ SIZE

HEIGHT

males	females
19–22 in (47.5–55cm)	18–21 in (45–52.5cm)

Body slightly longer than tall. Bone strong, not excessive. Overall balance is crucial.

BOUVIER DES FLANDRES

The Bouvier des Flandres began as a farm dog in the Flanders region of Belgium, where it was used for herding and protecting cattle, and is now known primarily as a show dog. Though it is now all spruced up, it is still the tough, fearless cowherd and draft dog of early days. Similar to the Border Collie, the early Bouvier was bred for working ability, not looks. The Bouvier almost disappeared during World War I. One of the few survivors, a dog of wonderful soundness and type, set its stamp on the breed's revival after the War. This breed has been used extensively as a police dog in Europe.

Despite this ferocious appearance, it is very responsive to an experienced trainer smart enough to use persuasion rather than force.

ABOVE Uncropped ears
BELOW Cropped ears

EYES AND EARS

EYES Neither protruding nor sunken. COLOR Dark brown, with black eye rims. Haw barely visible. SHAPE Oval.

EARS Placed high, and alert if cropped. A triangular contour, in proportion to size of head. Inner corner should be in line with outer corner of eye.

MOUTH AND JAWS

MUZZLE Broad, strong, tapering gradually toward nose. Cheeks flat and lean.

LIPS Dry and tight fitting.

JAWS Powerful and of equal length.

BITE Scissor.

FOREQUARTERS

SHOULDERS Relatively long, muscular but not loaded, with good layback. Shoulder blade and humerus approximately equal in length, forming an angle slightly greater than 90 degrees.

FORELEGS Straight, well muscled, and strong boned. Elbows close to body.

PASTERNS Quite short, slightly sloped.

DEWCLAWS May be removed.

BODY AND TOPLINE

Back short, broad, and well muscled. Topline firm, level, supple, and flexible. Body powerful, broad, and short. Chest broad. Brisket extends to elbows. Ribs deep and well sprung. Flanks and loin short, wide, and well muscled. Abdomen only slightly tucked-up. Rump wide.

HEAD AND SKULL

Head impressive in scale, accentuated by beard and mustache. Skull well developed, flat, less wide than long. Toplines of skull and muzzle parallel. Wide between ears. Frontal groove barely marked. Stop more apparent than real, due to upstanding eyebrows. Proportions of length of skull to muzzle are 3:2.

NOSE Large, black, well developed, and round at edges. Flared nostrils.

NECK

Strong, muscular, and gracefully arched. No dewlap.

FEET

Round and compact, turning neither in nor out.

TOES Close and well arched.

PADS Thick and tough.

NAILS Strong and black.

→ GENERAL APPEARANCE

The Bouvier des Flandres gives the impression of great strength without any heaviness or clumsiness. It is a square, large dog of substance.

→ CHARACTERISTICS

This is a powerfully built, short-coupled, rough-coated dog of rugged appearance, accentuated by the beard and mustache.

→ TEMPERAMENT

An equable dog, steady, resolute, and fearless.

→ GAIT/MOVEMENT

The gait is free, bold, and proud. The reach of the forequarters must be in balance with the driving power from the rear. The back remains flat and firm.

→ COAT

Tousled, double coat is capable of withstanding the hardest work in the most inclement weather. Coat may be trimmed slightly but only to accent the body line. Outercoat is rough, harsh, and dry, and may be trimmed to approximately 2½ in (6.25cm). It is not curly and is short on the skull. It is particularly close and harsh on the upper part of the back. The ears are rough coated. The undercoat is a dense mass of fine, close hair, thicker in winter. The mustache and beard are very thick, imparting a typical gruff expression. The erect hairs of the eyebrows accentuate the shape of the eyes.

→ COLOR

Colors range from fawn to black, including salt-and-pepper, gray, and brindle. A small white star on the chest is allowed.

→ SIZE

HEIGHT

males	females
24½–27½ in (61.25–68.75cm)	23½–26½ in (58.75–66.25cm)

Mid-range is the ideal. Body square. Substance powerful, strong boned.

KC/ANKC Weight—males, 77–88 lb (35–40 kg); females, 59–77 lb (27–35 kg).

TAIL

Docked, leaving two or three vertebrae. Must be set high and align normally with spinal column. Preferably carried upright in motion. Dogs born tailless not penalized. **KC/FCI** Customarily docked. When undocked, carried gaily when moving.

HINDQUARTERS

HINDLEGS Moderately long and well muscled. Thighs wide and muscular. Upper thigh neither too straight nor too sloping. Moderate angulation at stifle. Hocks strong, short, with slight angulation.

DEWCLAWS Should be removed.

COLLIE

Somewhere around 1800, the small Rough Collie, then called the "Shepherd's Dog," and the larger Smooth, called the "Ban Dog" were very different in appearance, though they are now judged by the same standard. For the KC, FCI, and ANKC, the Collie is divided into two distinct breeds, the Rough and the Smooth. In the late 1700s, the Scotch Collie, which looked much like a small Border Collie, guarded and moved herds of sheep. The Smooth Collie drove both sheep and cattle to market. In 1867, a dog called "Old Cockie" was born that dramatically altered the Rough Collie, increasing its size, refining its type and adding colors to the gene pool. By 1886, when the breed standard was written, the type was sufficiently set for both Rough and Smooth that no changes to height or weight have been made in the standard since. Long removed from its days as a sheep/cattle dog, the Collie is now primarily a gentle and affectionate pet. Its desire to please makes it readily amenable to training.

GENERAL APPEARANCE

The Collie is lithe, strong, and active. With its deep chest, sloping shoulders, and well bent hocks, it is built for speed and grace. It is balanced overall, with no parts out of proportion.

CHARACTERISTICS

The abundant coat of the Rough Collie and the shorter, but still dense coat of the Smooth Collie, and the three-quarter pricked ears are typical of the breed.

TEMPERAMENT

Highly intelligent, the Collie is never timid, sullen, or vicious.

GAIT/MOVEMENT

Gait is sound, powerful, and propelling. The reach is smooth and even, keeping the backline firm and level. The Collie moves with effortless speed and is able to change direction instantaneously.

COAT

There are two types of coat.

ROUGH— luxuriant, full. When properly textured this is the crowning glory of the Rough Collie. Outercoat, straight and harsh. Undercoat, soft, furry, and very dense. The hair is very abundant on mane and frill, but the face and hindlegs below the hocks are smooth. Forelegs are smooth but well feathered above pasterns. Hair very profuse on tail; long and bushy on hips.

SMOOTH— short, hard, dense, flat, of good texture, with an abundance of undercoat.

COLOR

There are four recognized colors—sable and white, tri-color, blue merle, and white. There is no preference.

SIZE

HEIGHT (at shoulder)

males	females
24–26in (60–65cm)	22–24in (55–60cm)

WEIGHT

males	females
60–75lb (27.3–34.1kg)	50–65lb (22.7–29.5kg)

KC/FCI/ANKC Males 45–65lb (20.5–30kg); Females 40–55lb (18–25kg).

EYES AND EARS

EYES Medium-sized, never large nor prominent. Placed obliquely and forward-looking. COLOR Must match in color, except for blue merles. In blue merles, dark brown is preferred, but one or both eyes may be merle or china in color. SHAPE Almond.

EARS In proportion to size of head. Seldom too small if carried properly and break naturally. In repose, folded lengthwise and back. Alert, carried about three-quarters erect, with a quarter "breaking" forward. **KC/FCI/ANKC** Moderately large (Smooth); Small (Rough).

HEAD AND SKULL

Head of great importance to the Collie look; never appearing massive. Resembles well blunted, lean wedge, smooth and clean in outline, tapering gradually from ears to end of nose. Not cheeky (flared in backskull) or snipy (pinched in muzzle). Top of backskull and top of muzzle approximately parallel, straight planes of equal length. Very slight but perceptible stop. Very slight prominence of eyebrows. Backskull flat. Occiput not highly peaked.

BODY AND TOPLINE

Body firm, hard, and muscular, a trifle longer than high. Ribs well rounded. Shoulders well sloped. Chest deep, extending to elbows. Back strong and level. Powerful hips and thighs. Croup sloped. Loin strong and slightly arched.

NECK

Firm, clean, muscular, heavily frilled. Fairly long and carried upright, with slight arch at nape.

MOUTH AND JAWS

MUZZLE End blunt but not square.

JAWS Underjaw strong. Depth of skull from brow to under jaw not excessive.

BITE Scissor.

FOREQUARTERS

FORELEGS Straight, muscular, with good bone, and moderately fleshy.

PASTERNS Flexible but not weak.

FEET

Oval.

TOES Well arched and close together.

PADS Soles well padded and tough.

TAIL

Bone reaching to hock or below. Carried low with upward swirl. When excited or in motion, carried gaily but not over back.

HINDQUARTERS

HINDLEGS Less fleshy. Thighs, muscular and very sinewy. Hocks and stifles well bent. Comparatively small.

GERMAN SHEPHERD DOG

Contrary to popular myth, the German Shepherd Dog is no more closely related to the wolf than the Cocker Spaniel or the Shetland Sheepdog. As a result of this popular misconception about wolflike qualities, the German Shepherd, along with the Siberian Husky or Alaskan Malamute, has sometimes suffered from less-than-wise ownership.

The German Shepherd Dog is a relatively new breed and can be traced back only to 1899 and the formation of the Verein für Deutsche Schaferhunde SV, the original parent club for the breed in Germany. Captain Max von Stephanitz founded the organization and is probably the person most responsible for the breed's development. Von Stephanitz's goal was the creation of the ultimate dog for herding and guarding flocks. Working ability remains of primary importance to the SV, and dogs must pass a test of character before being allowed to compete in open classes at SV shows.

The German Shepherd Dog is used almost worldwide by police departments, and also by customs departments and the military. It works as a guard dog, a tracker of criminals and lost people, and a guide for the blind, and is used in crowd control, search and rescue, drug and explosives detection, and cadaver search. It is also used in obedience and tracking competitions, and as a herder, show dog, and family companion. A more intelligent or versatile dog hardly exists. A well bred, well socialized, and well trained German Shepherd Dog achieves von Stephanitz's goal, and more.

EYES AND EARS

EYES Medium-sized and set a little obliquely, not protruding COLOR As dark as possible. SHAPE Almond.

EARS Moderately pointed, open toward the front, and carried erect when at attention.

BODY AND TOPLINE

Withers higher than and sloping to the back. Back straight, with no sag or roach; relatively short. Body gives impression of depth and solidity without bulkiness. Chest, from prosternum, is well filled, carried down between legs, and deep and capacious. Prosternum shows ahead of shoulders. Ribs well sprung and long, not barrel-shaped, nor flat, reaching to elbows. Moderate tuck-up. Loin broad and strong. Croup long, gradually sloping.

TAIL

Bushy. Last vertebra extends at least to hock joint. Set smoothly into croup and low. At rest, hangs in slight saber curve. In motion, curve accentuated and tail raised, but never above vertical line.

HINDQUARTERS

HINDLEGS Whole assembly of thigh broad, with both upper and lower thigh well muscled, forming close to a right angle. Upper thigh bone parallel to shoulder layback. Lower thigh parallels upper arm. Metatarsus, short, strong.

DEWCLAWS Should be removed.

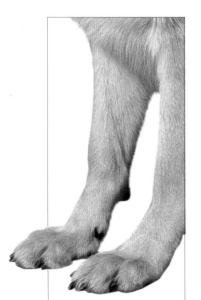

FEET

Short and compact.
TOES Well arched.
PADS Thick.
NAILS Short and dark.

The dog's independence does not interfere with its quick and retentive learning ability. It wants and needs almost constant companionship and attention from its master. It needs daily exercise for mind and body to prevent behavior problems, including destructiveness and barking that result from boredom. A German Shepherd can be quite dominant. It can also be aggressive with other dogs but is usually good with smaller pets. It is usually good with children once it has made their acquaintance.

HEAD AND SKULL

Head cleanly chiseled and strong, without coarseness or fineness. Forehead only moderately arched. Skull slopes into long, wedge-shaped muzzle, with no abrupt stop.

NOSE Black.

MOUTH AND JAWS

MUZZLE Long and strong. Topline parallel to topline of skull.

TEETH Twenty upper teeth. Twenty-two lower teeth. Complete dentition preferred.

BITE Scissor.

NECK

Strong, muscular, clean-cut, relatively long, and dry. When moving, head is typically carried forward rather than up, but little higher than top of shoulders.

FOREQUARTERS

SHOULDERS Shoulder blades long and obliquely angled. Upper arm joins blade at right angle. Both upper arm and shoulder blade well muscled.

FORELEGS Straight. Bone oval, not round.

PASTERNS Strong, springy, and angulated at approximately 25 degrees.

DEWCLAWS May be removed but normally left.

GENERAL APPEARANCE

The German Shepherd is a strong, agile, well muscled dog, alert and full of life. Of medium size, it is longer than tall and deep-bodied, and its outline presenting smooth curves rather than angles. Secondary sex characteristics are strongly marked.

CHARACTERISTICS

This dog has a distinctive posture resulting from the angles of the hindlegs, never from a deformity of the spine. It has a gradual but never extreme slope from withers to tail, and prick ears.

TEMPERAMENT

The ideal German Shepherd is a working animal with an incorruptible character. Direct, fearless, but not hostile, aloof but approachable, it should show confidence and be eager and alert.

GAIT/MOVEMENT

This is a trotting dog, and its gait is outreaching and elastic. It covers the maximum ground with the minimum effort. The feet travel close to the ground with no wasted motion. The hindfeet pass the imprint of the forefeet, power being transferred through the strong, level back.

COAT

The coat is double and of medium length. Outercoat as dense as possible, with harsh, straight hair lying close to the body. A slightly wavy outercoat, often of wiry texture, is permitted. Short hair on the head, inner ear, foreface, legs, and paws, and longer, thicker hair on the neck. The backs of the forelegs and hindlegs have somewhat longer hair, extending to pastern and hock.

COLOR

Most colors are permitted. Strong, rich colors are preferred.

SIZE

HEIGHT (at highest point of shoulder blades)

males	females
24–26 in (60–65cm)	22–24 in (55–60cm)

Longer than tall, proportion of 10:8½.

DISQUALIFICATIONS

- Cropped or hanging ears
- Nose not predominantly black
- Undershot jaw
- Docked tail
- White dogs
- Any dog that attempts to bite judge

OLD ENGLISH SHEEPDOG

Developed in the southwest of England, the Old English Sheepdog may have descended from the Bearded Collie but other breeds may also be in its background. The breed has been known since at least the 1770s and was primarily a drover's dog, taking sheep and cattle to market towns. Unlike hunting dogs, working dogs, such as those owned by drovers, were not taxed, and their tails were cut or bobbed to prove their tax-free status. Old English Sheepdogs may be born without tails, or with tails of of varying lengths; most have tails at birth and they are usually cut when the puppies are three to four days old.

Drovers' dogs were responsible for keeping the herd or flock together, steering the stock as directed by their master, finding and collecting strays, and guarding their charges from other dogs, wolves (then still found in England), or people intent on mischief. This vocation required intelligence, strength, agility, endurance, and speed—all of which the Old English Sheepdog still retains. The Old English has an antic sense of humor, is devoted to its family and home (it is not generally given to roaming),

HEAD AND SKULL
Skull capacious and square. Supra-orbital arch (bones over eyes) well arched. Head well covered with hair.
NOSE Black and large.

EYES AND EARS
EYES COLOR Brown, blue, or one of each. If brown, very dark is preferred. If blue, a pearl, china or wall-eye is considered typical.
EARS Medium-sized, carried flat to side of head.

MOUTH AND JAWS
MUZZLE Stop well defined.
JAWS Fairly long, strong, square, and truncated.
TEETH Strong and large.
BITE Scissor or level.

NECK
Fairly long and arched.

FOREQUARTERS
SHOULDERS Well laid-back and narrow at points.
FORELEGS Straight, with plenty of bone. Distances from withers to elbow and elbow to ground equal.

and good with children. It is an alert watchdog, although it tends to treat everyone as a friend. It is also equable in temperament, steady and sensible, tolerant of other dogs, and tends to herd small animals, and sometimes children. It can also be stubborn, and some bark more than necessary. The Old English's bark is surprisingly deep and low in tone. For a moderately large dog it occupies surprisingly little house room and makes a pleasant home companion— providing it receives adequate exercise (long walks twice daily plus a safe space to run). Its coat provides good protection from heat as well as cold and wet, but it must be groomed daily from a very young puppy onward, or its coat will quickly become a mass of painful tangles and mats.

BODY AND TOPLINE

Topline stands lower at withers than at loin, with no weakness. Body rather short, compact, broader at rump than at shoulders. Ribs well sprung. Brisket deep and capacious. Neither slab-sided nor barrel-chested. Loin very stout and gently arched.

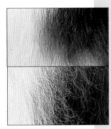

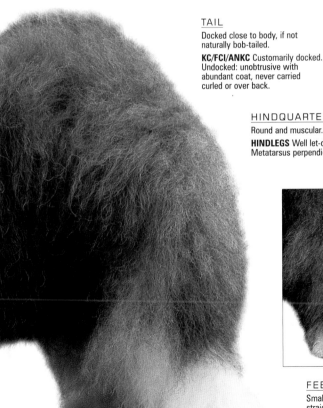

TAIL
Docked close to body, if not naturally bob-tailed.
KC/FCI/ANKC Customarily docked. Undocked: unobtrusive with abundant coat, never carried curled or over back.

HINDQUARTERS
Round and muscular.
HINDLEGS Well let-down hocks. Metatarsus perpendicular to ground.

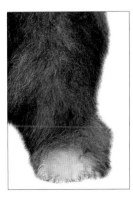

FEET
Small and round, pointing straight ahead.
TOES Well arched.
PADS Thick and hard.

⇒ GENERAL APPEARANCE
The Old Engish Sheepdog is a strong, compact, square, balanced dog. Profusely but not excessively coated, it is thickset, muscular, and agile.

⇒ CHARACTERISTICS
The unique topline, lower at the withers than at the loin, bob-tail, profuse hair coat, and bearlike amble at slow speeds are typical of the breed.

⇒ TEMPERAMENT
Adaptable and intelligent, the Old English has an even disposition, with no sign of aggression, shyness or nervousness.

⇒ GAIT/MOVEMENT
Movement is free and powerful, with good reach and drive, covering maximum ground with minimum effort. The gallop is very elastic, but the dog may amble or pace at slow speeds.

⇒ COAT
Coat is profuse, but not excessive. It is hard in texture, and though not straight, is shaggy and free from curl. The quality and texture of the coat is more important than profuseness. The undercoat is a waterproof pile. The ears are moderately coated. The whole of the skull, neck, and forelegs is well covered with hair. The hams are densely coated with a thick, long jacket, in excess of any other part. The feet and rear may be trimmed for cleanliness.

⇒ COLOR
Colors are any shade of gray, grizzle, blue, or blue merle, with or without white markings, or the reverse.

⇒ SIZE
HEIGHT

males	females
22 in (55cm)	21 in and up (52.5cm)

Length of body practically equal to height. Well muscled with plenty of bone.

KC/FCI/ANKC Males 24 in (60cm) and upward; Females 22 in (55cm) and upward.

SHETLAND SHEEPDOG

The Shetland Sheepdog, Collie and Border Collie share a common ancestry in the early sheep-herding dogs of the U.K. and were only separated into three distinct breeds during the 1800s. From that point, the Collie became larger, with added colors; the Border Collie stabilized in size and type; and the smallest dog ultimately became the Shetland Sheepdog. This breed continues to bear a striking physical resemblance to the rough Collie, not in size, but in coat, body shape, and colors. The two were interbred until about 1900.

The Shetland Islands, off the northern coast of Scotland which lay claim to this dog's ancestry, are basically treeless and have a harsh, stormy climate all year. All livestock on the islands is small in stature, as are the dogs that tended it. Food was scarce on the Shetlands, and animals with lower nutritional needs tended to survive. The small local sheepdog was an invaluable all-purpose farm dog. The islands had few fences, so the dogs had to keep stock out of cultivated fields and vegetable gardens. The little Shetland Sheepdog also gathered and protected the islands' sheep, ponies, and chickens, and even the children. Many families brought their stock, and their dogs, into the family shelter to live. It was but a short step to the dog becoming a regular family companion, as well as a highly valued co-worker. This long, close association with humans contributes to the dog's apparent deep understanding of human ways, and makes the Shetland Sheepdog a responsive companion and natural student.

BODY AND TOPLINE
Back level and strongly muscled. Chest deep. Brisket reaching to elbow. Ribs well sprung. Moderate tuck-up. Slight arch at loin. Croup slopes gradually.

TAIL
Sufficiently long for last vertebra to reach hock joint. At rest, carried straight down. When alert, normally lifted, but never curved over back.

HINDQUARTERS
HINDLEGS Thigh broad, muscular. Angle of rear leg same as shoulder. Hocks short and straight.

DEWCLAWS May be removed.

FEET
Oval and compact.

TOES Well arched and tight together.

PADS Deep and tough.

NAILS Hard and strong.

The Shetland Sheepdog has a typical sheepdog character. It is only content when at work and close to its master, and does not like to be separated from its family. It also shares the sheepdog tendency to bark a great deal unless trained otherwise. It dislikes being touched by strangers. Training is very simple. Some lessons are learned immediately, because of its quick intelligence and strong desire to please. It makes an excellent candidate for obedience or agility competition. It is a very clean dog and is easy to housetrain.

GENERAL APPEARANCE
The Shetland Sheepdog bears a marked resemblance to the rough Collie, but on a smaller scale. Males are masculine, and females feminine.

CHARACTERISTICS
Symmetrical, with no part out of balance with whole. A sturdy, workmanlike dog, it is neither diminutive nor dwarflike.

TEMPERAMENT
Intensely loyal, affectionate, and responsive, the Shetland Sheepdog is reserved with strangers but not to the extent of showing fear or cringing.

GAIT/MOVEMENT
The trotting gait should appear effortless and smooth, with no jerkiness, nor stiff, stilted, up-and-down movement. Strong drive from the rear. Feet lift only enough to clear the ground.

COAT
Double coat. The outercoat consists of long, straight, harsh hair. The undercoat is short, furry, and very dense, giving the coat a "standoff" quality. Hair on the face, ear tips, and feet is smooth. Mane and frill are abundant, especially in males. The forelegs are well feathered—the hindlegs heavily so—but are smooth below hock joint.

COLOR
Colors are black, blue merle, and sable, each with varying amounts of white and/or tan.

SIZE
HEIGHT (at shoulder)
13–16 in (32.5–40cm)

DISQUALIFICATIONS
- Deviation above or below the stated height range
- Brindle color

HEAD AND SKULL
Refined. A long, blunt wedge, tapering slightly from ears to nose. Topskull flat, showing no occipital prominence. Topline of skull parallel to topline of muzzle. Slight but definite stop. **NOSE** Black.

EYES AND EARS
EYES Medium-sized, set somewhat obliquely. COLOR Dark. Blue or merle eyes permitted in blue merles only. SHAPE Almond.

EARS Small and flexible. Placed high and carried three-quarters erect, with tips breaking forward. In repose, folded lengthwise and thrown back into frill.

NECK
Muscular, arched, and of good length.

MOUTH AND JAWS
MUZZLE Skull and muzzle of equal length. Cheeks flat, merging smoothly into well rounded muzzle.

LIPS Tight. Upper and lower lips meet tightly all the way around.

JAWS Clean and powerful. Deep, well developed underjaw, rounded at chin.

BITE Scissor.

FOREQUARTERS
SHOULDERS Shoulder blades slope at 45 degrees to juncture with upper arm, at close to a right angle. Elbow joint equidistant from ground and from withers.

FORELEGS Straight and muscular.

PASTERNS Very strong, sinewy, and flexible.

DEWCLAWS May be removed.

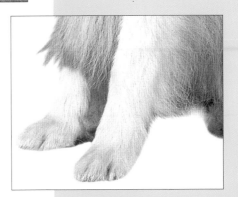

WELSH CORGI—CARDIGAN

This dog is believed to have come to the high hills of Cardiganshire in Wales, especially those around Bronant, around 1200 B.C., with the Celts when they emigrated from central Europe. The Cardigan is functionally built, being strong, agile, and tough enough to drive and herd wild cattle, dairy cows, and mountain ponies. It also helped to find and hunt game, and served as a child's guardian and companion. A versatile, hardy, tough, and affectionate dog, it was held in great esteem by the agrarian Welsh. Despite their different origins, both the Cardigan and the Pembroke are now Welsh breeds, having been interbred during the nineteenth century, and they are now more alike than dissimilar. This practice of interbreeding ceased in 1934, when the single Welsh Corgi was categorized as two distinct breeds for show purposes. The Cardigan is more easy-going than the Pembroke, and possibly less bold. It requires firmness and consistency from its owner to avoid behavior problems, and does well in obedience competition and at agility.

EYES AND EARS

EYES Medium to large, not bulging. Widely set. COLOR Clear. Dark, in harmony with coat color. Blue eyes (or partially blue), or one dark and one blue, permitted in blue merles. Dark rims.

EARS Large in proportion to size of dog. Slightly rounded at tips, with strong leather. Moderately wide at base. Carried erect.

MOUTH AND JAWS

MUZZLE Distance from tip of nose to base of stop shorter than from base of stop to high point of occiput (ratio of muzzle to skull 3:5). Rounded, not blunt. Tapered, not pointed. Plane of muzzle parallel to that of skull.

LIPS Clean.

JAWS Strong. Underjaw moderately deep.

BITE Scissor.

HEAD AND SKULL

Refined in accordance with sex and substance of dog. Skull moderately wide and flat between ears. Occiput not prominent. Cheeks flat. Some chiseling under eye and at juncture of cheek and foreface. Moderate stop.

NOSE Black. "Butterfly" noses tolerated in blue merles.

NECK

Moderately long and muscular, but not throaty.

BODY AND TOPLINE

Topline level. Body long and strong. Chest moderately broad with prominent breastbone. Brisket deep. Ribs well sprung, extending well back. Loin short, strong, and moderately tucked-up. Waist well defined. Croup sloping down slightly.

TAIL

Set fairly low, reaching well below hock. Carried low at rest, parallel to ground when running. Lifted when excited, but never curled over back.

FOREQUARTERS

Chest well let-down between forelegs. Overall bone heavy, but not coarse.

SHOULDERS Sloping from withers. Shoulder blades long and well laid-back, meeting upper arm at close to right angle.

FORELEGS Elbows fit close. Forearms curved to fit spring of ribs, making carpal joints somewhat closer than elbows.

PASTERNS Strong, flexible.

DEWCLAWS Removed.

FEET

Forefeet relatively large and rounded, pointing slightly outward. Hindfeet slightly smaller and more oval, pointing straight ahead.

HINDQUARTERS

Well muscled, strong, but slightly less wide than shoulders. Hipbone slopes down from croup, forming right angle with femur at hip.

HINDLEGS Stifle and hock moderately angulated. Hocks well let-down.

DEWCLAWS Removed.

GENERAL APPEARANCE

The Cardigan is a low-set dog, with moderately heavy bone and a deep chest. Long in proportion to its height, it is powerful, capable of speed and endurance, and sturdily built but not coarse.

CHARACTERISTICS

The erect, rounded ears, brushy tail, long body, and short legs are typical of this breed.

TEMPERAMENT

Even-tempered, loyal, affectionate, and adaptable, the Cardigan is never shy nor vicious.

GAIT/MOVEMENT

Gait is free and smooth. The forelegs have good reach, with a little lift, and a long stride. There is a strong drive from the rear, with good follow-through. The dog is agile.

COAT

The double coat is of medium length, dense, and flat-lying. The outer hair is slightly harsh. The undercoat is short, soft, and thick. There is short hair on the ears, head, and legs, and medium hair on the body. Slightly longer, thicker hair occurs in the ruff, on the backs of the thighs, forming "pants", and on the underside of the tail. Trimming is not allowed, except to tidy the feet.

COLOR

Colors include all shades of red, sable, and brindle, as well as black or blue merle, with or without tan or brindle points. White is usual on the neck, chest, legs, muzzle, underparts, tail tip, and as blaze on head. The eyes should never be surrounded by white.

SIZE

HEIGHT

10½–12½ in (26.25–31.25cm)

WEIGHT

males	females
30–38 lb (13.6–17.3kg)	25–34 lb (11.4–15.5kg)

Overall balance is more important than size.

KC/FCI/ANKC Weight in proportion to size with overall balance the prime consideration.

DISQUALIFICATIONS

- Blue eyes, or partially blue eyes, in any coat color other than blue merle
- Drop ears
- Nose other than solid black, except in blue merles
- Any color other than specified
- Body color predominantly white

CREDITS

Quarto would like to thank and acknowledge the following for permission to reproduce the pictures;

Key: b=bottom, t=top, c=center, l=left, r=right

The American Kennel Club, 22 tl, 22-23 bc (©DogPhoto.com); 27 (©Kent and Donna Dannen); 30-31 bc, 31 c, 31 br (©Kent and Donna Dannen); 32-33 bc, 33 br (©Bonnie Nance); 43 (©Kent and Donna Dannen); 46 tl, 47 bcr (©Tara Darling); 47 br, tcr (©AKC, photo by Mary Bloom); 53 tr, 53 br (©Kent and Donna Dannen); 64-65 bc (©DogPhoto.com); 67 b (©Tara Darling); 69 (©AKC, photo by Mary Bloom); 77 (©Kent and Donna Dannen); 84 l, 85 c (©Kent and Donna Dannen); 104 l, 105 rbc & rtc (©Kent and Donna Dannen); 107 b (©Kent and Donna Dannen); 108 bl (©Alice Su); 110-111 bc, 111 tc (©Alice Su); 112-113 bc, 113 bc (©Dog.Photo.com); 128 (©Kent and Donna Dannen); 130-131 bc, 131 bc (©Kent and Donna Dannen); 139 (©Kent and Donna Dannen); 141 br (©AKC, photo by Mary Bloom); 146 b (©DogPhoto.com)

Paulette Braun, 6, 11 t, 12-13 b, 14, 17, 24-25 bc, 25 tr, 30 tl, 31 cr, 35, 42, 50-51 bc, 51 cr, 52-53 bc, 53 bcr, 56 tr, 57 cr, (both pictures), 58 tr, 59 cr, 62 b, 64 l, 65 crt, 66 b, 74, 78, 79 bc, 80-81, 89, 91 b, 98 b, 100-101 bc, 101 tl, 101 cr (both pictures), 116-117 bc, 117 tr , 122 b, 130 bl, 131 tc, 132-3 bc, 133 ct, 154

The Kennel Club Picture Library, 24 tr, 25 tcr, 25 br (©Lynn Kipps); 36 tr, 36-37 bc, 37 cr (©David Dalton); 54 (©David Dalton); 92 l, 93 tr (©D Bull); 97 (©The Kennel Club); 103 (©David Dalton); 108 tr, 109 tr (©David Dalton); 111 bc, 111 br (©Colin Seddon); 112 cl, 113 tc (©David Dalton); 114 t, 115 bc, 115 br (©Colin Seddon); 118-119 bc, 119 c (©The Kennel Club); 144 bc, 145 br (©Colin Seddon); 150-151 bc, 151 tr (©David Dalton); 152 tr, 153 tr (©Lynn Kipps).

Brian Leonard, 8 l, 10-11 b,